DATE DUE

APR 0 5 2006			
DE 15 08			

"Miller nails it. He powerfully and persuasively articulates the folly, the harm, and the unconstitutionality of our government's War against Drugs."

"Drug abuse is bad. But Joel Miller demonstrates that the War on Drugs is far worse. The government is financing terrorism and underwriting corruption even as it violates the freedom of Americans. Yet drug use continues unabated. As Miller so ably proves, the government's drug war is the ultimate bad trip."

"Joel Miller's book *Bad Trip* is a must-read for anyone wishing to learn of the horrors created by the United States' drug policy. Miller's exquisitely researched work lists each of the issues and sets before the reader massive documentation of these destructive policies and their more destructive unintended consequences. More important, rather than just complaining, Miller gives his readers sound suggestions for policy solutions that could effectively replace the failed War on Drugs—solutions that would actually lower the incidence of death, disease, crime, and drug addiction."

"If you are interested in our freedoms or fearful of the government destroying human lives and wasting tax dollars on another American Prohibition, read this book and send a copy to every lawmaker and judge you know."

"It took guts to write *Bad Trip*. In clear and riveting language, and with irrefutable facts, Joel Miller explains why laws against drugs—just like laws against guns—help no one except criminals. Such laws enrich gangsters, corrupt politicians, criminalize honest citizens, and eat away at our Bill of Rights. Freedom-loving Americans should resist the War on Drugs as implacably as we defy the War on Guns."

> RICHARD POE, best-selling author of
> *The Seven Myths of Gun Control* and
> *Hillary's Secret War*

"The U.S. government is addicted to the drug war and the power and pelf it reaps from it. But anyone who cares about freedom and justice can only be horrified. Thank goodness for Joel Miller and this important book. As he shows, we have to send the feds to rehab."

> LEW ROCKWELL, editor of
> LewRockwell.com, president of the
> Ludwig von Mises Institute

"Joel Miller shows in convincing detail why the War on Drugs is a war on our liberties."

> JACOB SULLUM, *Reason* magazine
> senior editor, nationally syndicated
> columnist, and author of *Saying Yes*

BAD TRIP

How the War against Drugs
Is Destroying America

Joel Miller

WND Books
A Division of Thomas Nelson Publishers
Since 1798

www.thomasnelson.com

Published in Nashville, Tennessee, by WND Books.

Library of Congress Cataloging-in-Publication Data

Miller, Joel, 1975–
    Bad trip : how the war against drugs is destroying America / Joel Miller.
      p. cm.
    Includes bibliographical references and index.
    ISBN 0-7852-6147-8
    1. Narcotics, Control of—United States. 2. Drug abuse—Government policy—United States. I. Title.
    HV5825.M545 2004
    363.45'0973—dc22   2004004976

Printed in the United States of America

04 05 06 07 QW 5 4 3 2

for Lydia

The government offers to cure all the ills of mankind. . . . All that is needed is to create some new government agencies and to pay a few more bureaucrats. In a word, the tactic consists in initiating, in the guise of actual services, what are nothing but restrictions; thereafter, the nation pays, not for being served, but for being disserved.

—FRÉDÉRIC BASTIAT, 1845

CONTENTS

AUTHOR'S NOTE

ANY TIME SOMEONE COMES FORWARD WITH A CRITICISM OF the drug war, a chorus of nay-sayers leaps into the fray and—in so many words—declare the critic's position null because he either consumes drugs or wishes to do so without fear of going to jail.

I don't follow that logic to begin with, but in my case it is far off the mark nonetheless. I'm with Cole Porter on this one—"I get no kick from cocaine." Actually, I haven't tried it. Neither have I tried marijuana, meth, ecstasy, heroin, or any other illegal substance. Nor do I intend to rush out and do so if they ever become legal.

As far as psychoactive substances, here's a note of self-disclosure. I find myself in the vein of the American founders: a wine and beer man, who likes the occasional pipe or cigar.

My concern over the drug war is also in the vein of the founders. As I look at the effects of prohibition and arguments behind it, I cannot help but worry that vital constitutional rights and liberties are being undermined daily across the country. In my mind, it's not really about drugs. It's about freedom and the disastrous overreach of government.

TRIPPIN'

A prince must punish the wicked in
such a way that he does not step
on the dish while picking up
the spoon. . . .

—MARTIN LUTHER[1]

MAISHA HUBBARD—A TWENTY-EIGHT-YEAR-OLD BRIDE-TO-BE—
was shot while sitting in her bedroom watching a football game with her
brother-in-law. When the staccato sounds of gunfire erupted outside, he
dove for the carpet like a well-trained soldier. She didn't have a chance.
One of the bullets blasted through a window of their home in the
Brooklyn projects and struck her in the head. The moment the shooting
was over, Maisha's sister ran for the room and found the pair sprawled on
the floor. "My husband stood up," she said. "But my sister didn't."[2] Maisha
died just hours later.

Police blamed the young woman's death on a drug-related scuffle. She
wasn't the target, just collateral damage in America's war on narcotics.

"Ninety-nine times out of a hundred, it's drugs," said one investigator about the incident. "The real issue here is that we have a lot of young
men out here who have nothing to do. As long as that's the case, nothing will change."[3] Only half-true. Drug dealers don't gun people down
because they "have nothing to do," as if knocking off the neighbors were
as fulfilling a pastime as canasta and checkers. They shoot people

because that's part of their business, and "as long as that's the case, nothing will change."

The business is, of course, the manufacture, distribution, and sale of illegal drugs—the key word there being "illegal."

Dope is verboten for a variety of reasons, and this book is only peripherally concerned with any of them. Getting to the nub requires going beyond the basic arguments behind drug prohibition and looking at what it actually accomplishes. Yes, crime and the financing of terrorists are worrisome. But what if prohibiting drugs to fight crime actually made crime worse? Terrorists and their schemes must be stopped, no doubt about it. But is the continued ban on narcotics making things hard for them or merely padding their purses? That's what *Bad Trip* is about. It takes President George W. Bush seriously when he said in April 2002 that "The measure of compassion is more than good intentions, it is good results." Thus, whatever its reasons and intentions—many of which might be noble—the question about the drug war ultimately boils down to the tradeoff: We know why we want drug laws, but what are we actually getting in the bargain?

To answer that question in full, you have to start by answering it in part. One thing we're getting, the most basic thing, is government. It goes without saying that if something becomes illegal you've got to factor in the State. After all, someone has to make the laws and enforce them. Government is just as important a player in the drug business as the dopers—in some sense, more so.

By its intervention in the drug market, the State sets in motion an economic and political domino-collapse that exacerbates crime and corruption, gnaws away at privacy and property rights, endangers people's wellbeing, jails them, and sometimes takes their lives. Far from a simple attempt to rid the nation of crime and drugs, our policy against narcotics—like any public policy—comes with strings attached. And increasingly these strings are constricting around the necks of American lives and liberties. In Martin Luther's parlance, it's a case of stepping on the dish while fetching the spoon, creating a big problem while trying to solve a small one.

People usually take a drug of some sort to feel good—or, at least, better. Sometimes, however, the high is twisted and the trip goes bad. Suddenly, it's a terrible experience, not a euphoric one, after which the user seriously considers ever taking the drug again. (With psychoactivity going far off course, something safer is usually in order.) The drug war is no different. Prohibition is supposed to make America better. In reality it makes it manifestly worse—just like a drug trip gone bad.

1

CRACK VIALS AND VIOLENCE

Prohibition doesn't lessen crime; it creates it.

BECAUSE OF TRAGEDIES LIKE THE KILLING OF MAISHA HUBBARD, crime and drugs are closely linked in the minds of most Americans. The question is the nature of the link: Do drugs themselves cause crime, or are other factors at play?

Drug warriors often see dope as "criminogenic," by which they mean that it spawns lawbreaking by its very use. Prohibitionists have long exploited the perceived link to crime and social upheaval with this claim and have scare-pitched their schemes to ban drugs and other intoxicants with horrifying images and knuckle-whitening news copy. America's own history makes this clear; just look at the debate over alcohol Prohibition in the early 1900s.

When Sen. Morris Sheppard introduced a draft of the Eighteenth Amendment to ban booze, he labeled it "a narcotic poison, destructive and degenerating to the human organism," saying that it "undermin[es] the public morals" and "produces widespread crime."[1] One pamphlet published by the Anti-Saloon League claimed that bars produced "eighty percent of the criminals in this country." How it came up with that statistic is beyond me, but the threat was accessible to all: "The saloon is responsible for more vice, degradation, sorrow, misery, heartaches, and deaths than any other cause tolerated by Government."[2]

This type of rhetoric has traveled far on thick shoe leather, arriving with little wear into the modern debate on drugs.

Fingering Dope

"Let's say it's 1960, and the devil has just appointed a committee to worsen the problem of crime in America to the point of unendurability," proposed columnist William H. Rusher. "What steps might the committee take?" Aside from overturning vagrancy laws and liberating kooks from the booby hatches and asylums, "the committee would surely recommend encouraging the use of drugs—first marijuana (which could be pooh-poohed as harmless) and then a flood of harder drugs culminating in crack cocaine, whose users will kill to finance their habit and then kill again under the drug's malignant influence."[3]

Pointing to a spike in "drug-related crime," columnist Don Feder explains, "It's not just that people do bad things to get drugs; drugs make them do bad things."[4]

Echoing Feder, former president of the Family Research Council, Gary Bauer, says that "Drugs are the raw explosive for many criminal acts."[5] He once hammered a 1995 ABC news special on drugs for suggesting legalization as a solution to the problem. "The astonishing thing is how the facts are ignored," said Bauer. "ABC points to the drug policies of the Netherlands where drugs are accepted and, according to ABC, crime isn't a problem. But the research shows that the Netherlands now ranks first in Europe in assaults, and robberies are up by more than two thirds in the last four years."[6]

The problem with Bauer's argument is that he's fingering the Netherlands as both uniquely lax on dope and high in crime—both of which are wrong. Holland is not Europe's Lone Ranger. The Dutch have plenty of toking Tontos across the continent who practice a sort of de facto drug decriminalization.

According to the European Monitoring Center for Drugs and Drug Addiction (a going affair of the European Union), Denmark does not prosecute for minor marijuana possession, issues "warnings" about other drugs, and reserves jail cells only for crimes "involving supply for commercial reasons or organized trafficking."[7] In Sweden, Ireland, France, Italy, and Spain, most users are variously referred to treatment centers, fined, or get off with only a warning, instead of jail time. Austria and Luxembourg go further, staving off prosecution for use, possession, and even distribution of "insignificant quantities" of dope.[8] Portugal has basically decriminalized all drug use—hard and soft.[9] And Germany now permits heroin injection rooms, "Fixerstube centers," similar to Holland's "tolerance zones," where addicts are treated rather than imprisoned.[10]

If Bauer were on target, why isn't his "raw explosive" igniting all across Europe? The answer is that the explosive is much more firecracker than TNT.

Holland makes an easy target because, in all the world, it is the nation best known for its *laissez faire* drug-use policies. And, just like an overly talkative kid in school, it tends to get scolded the most.

Berating this wild child doesn't even require correct facts. Because so many are willing to assume the worst whenever drugs are involved, people swallow lines about drugs leading to violence with hardly a hiccup. Freed from the usual scrutiny, drug warriors can spin crime however they please. Just before visiting the Netherlands in 1998, US drug czar Gen. Barry McCaffrey said the Dutch's per capita murder rate was twice that of the US. "That's drugs," said McCaffrey.[11] "That's bunk" is closer to the truth. McCaffrey's data put the Netherlands murder rate at 17.58 per every 100,000, with the US easing under the statistical limbo bar at only 8.22. Within twenty-four hours, the Dutch fired back an important correction. Seemed the general had lumped murder *and* attempted murder together, grossly inflating the figures. According to the Dutch Central Planning Bureau, the official murder rate in 1996 was only 1.8 per 100,000, ratcheted up slightly from the 1990 figure of 1.5—significantly lower than that of the US.[12]

The Dutch treat is that, even with easy access to drugs, crimes such as murder are not gnawing away at the social fabric—certainly no more than in America, where drug enforcement is anything but lax.[13]

Scary Mary

With drugs and crime so widely accepted as born under the same black star, exciting fears of the twin evil sports a long legacy.

Railing against pot's deleterious effect on America's youth, Federal Bureau of Narcotics Commissioner Harry J. Anslinger penned his now-famous exposé, "Marihuana: Assassin of Youth," for the July 1937 edition of *The American Magazine*. "How many murders, suicides, robberies, criminal assaults, holdups, burglaries, and deeds of maniacal insanity [marijuana] causes every year, especially among the youth, can only be conjectured," he wrote. The piece is jam-packed with anecdote after anecdote of some clean-shaven, upstanding kid who after taking a toke or two of "muggles" proceeds upon inexplicable fits of criminality and mayhem. "In at least two dozen . . . recent cases of murder or degenerate sex attacks, many of them committed by youths, marihuana proved to be a contributing cause."[14]

In 1938, Anslinger's FBN agents told a *New Yorker* reporter that "an overdose of marijuana generates savage and sadistic traits likely to reach a climax in axe and ice-pick murders."[15] Too often, news reporters eagerly bought FBN propaganda. As one reporter penned in a 1936 syndicated story for the Universal News Service,

Shocking crimes of violence are increasing. Murders, slaughters, cruel mutilations, maimings, done in cold blood, as if some hideous monster was amok in the land.

Alarmed Federal and State authorities attribute much of this violence to the "killer drug." . . . Those addicted to marihuana, after an early feeling of exhilaration, soon lose all restraint, all inhibitions. They become bestial demoniacs filled with the mad lust to kill. . . .[16]

Anslinger whistled the same tune throughout his long career. In his 1961 book, *The Murderers*, he runs through a series of ghastly crimes, including gang rape, mass murder, and murder-suicide, summing up, "Every one of these crimes had been preceded by the smoking of one or two marijuana 'reefers'."[17]

Due to the work of men like Anslinger, sensationalizing newspapers, and producers of films like the 1936 *Reefer Madness* (which dubbed marijuana "public enemy No. 1"), the road was smoothed for national criminalization of pot with the 1937 Marijuana Tax Act. All but two of the forty-eight states already had laws against marijuana on the books, but Anslinger deemed them ineffectual at stemming the criminal scourge. In his mind, the feds had to be called in to put a stop to the madness.

Government officials may be a bit less sensationalistic today, but blaming pot for crime is still common. In remarks at a conference on marijuana sponsored by the National Institute on Drug Abuse, the director of National Drug Control Policy, Lee Brown, made much of the "strong link between marijuana use and violence."[18] Similarly, Clinton-era health and human services secretary Donna Shalala opined in the *Wall Street Journal* that marijuana "is clearly associated with increased truancy and crime."[19]

And it's not just pot. Any drug targeted by the law gets sent to the same publicist.

Cocaine Express

In the late 1800s, cocaine was viewed as a wonder substance, the Holy Grail of pharmacology. Sigmund Freud called it "a magical drug" and began hyping its use far and wide. A powerful analgesic and stimulant, cocaine could soon be found lacing elixirs, cordials, even cigarettes, and was in wide use throughout American society.

The wine-and-cocaine liqueur Vin Mariani was enjoyed by inventor Thomas Edison, adored by Pope Leo XIII, and apparently possessed, according to those who consumed it, the ability to fortify and refresh the body and mind and restore health and vitality. For the last months of his life, Ulysses S. Grant drank some every night before bed.[20] Other cocaine-enhanced beverages soon hit the marketplace, including the popular Coca-Cola and now lesser-knowns: Nerv-Ola, Wise-Ola, Quina-Coca, Inca Cola, Pemberton's French Wine Coca, and the aptly named Dope.

People figured cocaine could cure anything: headaches, asthma, indigestion, the blues. One medicine marketed by Lloyd Manufacturing Co., dubbed "Cocaine Toothache Drops," boasted an "Instantaneous Cure!" Price: fifteen cents. The ad would drive present-day anti–Joe Camel types into frothy-mouthed fits of apoplexy. Featuring two young children building a toy house with miniature wooden logs, the copy notes that the wonder medication is "for sale by all druggists." What? Without a prescription? Over-the-counter cocaine? For kids? Indeed. Cocaine was thought harmless in its Western salad days. Freud even considered it a sovereign remedy for morphine addiction.

But it wasn't long before Freud's magical drug was being labeled a scourge. Casual users began reporting problems such as addiction, intoxication, and occasional death. Ultimately, however, it was the media which stoked cocaine's admittedly troubling downsides into a raging inferno of public fear and dread. Ever-striving for an attention-grabbing headline, newspapers began spinning stories that not only overplayed fears of cocaine's addictiveness but, worse, inflated maniacal crimes committed by its users. Blacks who used the drug were soon labeled "cocaine fiends," and worry spread in the South that, doped out of their gourds, "cocainized Negroes" would run rampant through the countryside, looting chicken coops and making off with the white women.

"Use of cocaine by negroes in certain parts of the country is simply appalling," reported the American Pharmaceutical Association in 1901. "The police officers of questionable districts tell us that habitués are made wild by cocaine."[21]

These "wild" blacks, according to a statement by Colonel J.W. Watson in a 1903 *New York Tribune* article, were responsible for "many of the horrible crimes committed in the Southern States. . . ."[22] In 1914, Atlanta's police chief blamed drugs for a whopping "70 percent of the crimes."[23] Worse, these cocamaniacs supposedly couldn't feel pain and were thus impervious to bullets. One doctor described "a temporary immunity to shock—a resistance to the 'knock-down' effects of fatal wounds. Bullets fired into vital parts . . . fail to stop his rush or weaken his attack."[24] Cops throughout the South traded up to larger caliber handguns with more stopping power. But they had to watch out nonetheless; supposedly, cocaine transformed blacks into better pistol marksmen, too.[25]

It wasn't that the entire raft of news was bunk. Cocaine abuse did create problems, but the fact that whites had been using the stuff for well more than a decade without hell coming to town somehow failed to raise reasonable doubts about the veracity of such claims. At the very least, it should have taken the edge off the blatantly racially-charged exaggerations.

Acting Beastly

The scene would play out much the same way with the cocaine wars of the 1980s, made all the scarier by the advent of crack. The smokeable form of cocaine, peddled in little chunks called "rock," was blamed for all the same crimes cocaine was a century before—only worse—and the media's coverage was even more sensational and horrific.

CBS's Harold Dow interviewed senior DEA agent Robert Stutman during America's early flirtation with rock cocaine. "This is it!" Dow said excitedly. "This drug is so powerful that it will empty the money from your pockets, make you sell the watch off your wrist, the clothes off your back—" Stutman finished the sentence: "—or kill your mother!"[26]

It was like dropping horseflesh in a school of hammerheads. The media frenzied. The spirit of impending drug-induced doom wafted so thickly through the air that in a signed editorial *Newsweek* Editor-in-Chief Richard M. Smith actually compared crack to "the plagues of medieval times"—the Black Death, which killed a third of Europe's population.[27] Do the math, and kiss goodbye nearly a hundred million Americans.

The only other drug in recent times receiving as much frightening hype is methamphetamine, or speed, sometimes billed as the crack of the new millennium. Chemically different than cocaine, amphetamines nonetheless react similarly in users' brains, and the federal Drug Enforcement Agency is convinced this reaction is terrible. Lumping all forms of amphetamines together, the DEA Web site warns that speed can lead to "psychotic behavior. . . . Chronic use can cause violent behavior . . . confusion . . . mood disturbances, delusions, and paranoia." Sounds like terrible stuff, right? Not entirely, if you listen to the US Air Force.

After two of its pilots who had taken amphetamines (the Air Force regularly prescribes them for its pilots) accidentally killed four Canadian soldiers and injured eight others with a quarter-ton bomb in Afghanistan,[28] the Air Force surgeon general's office sent one if its physicians to do something few would ever expect from their government: Dr. Pete Demitry actually praised speed. Explaining at a press conference that flyboys have been using amphetamine stimulants safely since the 1940s, Demitry said that speed beats coffee at keeping pilots awake and also keeps them more alert. "There had been no known speed-related mishaps in the Air Force, whereas there had been many fatigue-related accidents, Demitry said," according to Reuters.[29]

Granted, some folks abuse it, but the irony is that the Air Force isn't concerned with men in F-16 fighter jets taking amphetamines and acting violently without warrant.

Even minor drugs that fly under most people's radar are hyped into colossal threats to peace and safety. When US forces were in Somalia in 1992, the press introduced America to a very helpful Scrabble word and a very frightening new substance—*qat*. "The intellectual community [of Somalia] concedes its widespread use is a culprit in Somalia's violent anarchy, as do the United Nations and the non-governmental relief agencies," wrote Jonathan Stevenson in the *New Republic*. "A drug-conjured insistence on personal supremacy turns pubescent energy into casual, cheap violence."[30] As with those who hyped pot, coke, and crack scares, Stevenson was blowing smoke. Trouble is, smoke travels.

"A chewable African shrub used by Somali gunmen fighting US troops in Mogadishu is posing concerns for US East Coast federal officials who believe it may offer the latest cheap amphetamine high." So reported Agence France-Presse in 2000 as smuggling of qat into the US increased.[31] From the battlefield to the backyard—the drug that makes Somali youths maniacal and violent was now being chewed by American college students! All that is needed is one kid to kill a friend while supposedly under the influence, and bladders across the fruited plain will drain in fright.

As with many other drugs, it turns out qat fears are unfounded. The drug's main psychoactive ingredient, cathinone, is low in concentration and potency. Swiss pharmacologist Peter Kalix notes that qat use probably predates that of coffee, and its effects have been known in part for more than seven hundred years.[32] It was even recommended as a lubricant for socializing—the same way alcohol is in the West. Despite worries, it is not likely to lead to mayhem in the streets. Kalix says going batty on the shrub is "rather exceptional," and *Reason* magazine senior editor Jacob Sullum writes, "Although millions of people consume [qat] each day, researchers have reported only a few cases of paranoia or violence allegedly precipitated by the drug."[33]

The Devil Didn't Make You Do It

Sullum's comments point to a handy measuring rod for drug scares. If drugs cause crime, then how can millions of Americans who use drugs without committing crimes be explained? Fears over qat don't pass the sniff test because most use creates little or no problems. The DEA even admits as much. Associated Press reporter Stephanie V. Siek explains that while the DEA claims that "chronic use [of qat] can cause violence . . . the agency said it was unaware of any examples."[34] This is true for most illicit drugs. An overwhelming percentage of drug users never thump old ladies, loot convenience stores, beat their children, or shoot police officers. Perhaps this is because drugs do not themselves cause crime and violence.

When Richard Nixon picked former Pennsylvania governor Ray

Shafer—a Republican and noted drug-war hawk—to spearhead a commission on marijuana, he was flabbergasted by the final report. Instead of validating the president's uncompromising antimarijuana position, in 1972 the Shafer Commission actually recommended decriminalizing pot. Having extensively studied the cannabis-crime link, the commission concluded,

> although the available evidence suggests that marihuana use may be statistically correlated with the incidence of crime and delinquency, when examined in isolation from the other variables, no valid evidence was found to support the thesis that marihuana by itself, either inevitably, generally or even frequently causes or precipitates the commission of crime, including acts of violence, or juvenile delinquency.[35]

Not surprisingly, Nixon shelved the report. But most recent data has only confirmed its conclusions. Referring particularly to charges that marijuana and opiates are to blame for criminal behavior, researcher Paul J. Goldstein says such criminogenic notions "have now been largely discredited."[36]

Even in Anslinger's day, drug warriors were swinging at these pitches with a short bat. The 1925 Canal Zone Report, commissioned to study the use of marijuana by US troops stationed in Panama, discovered "no evidence that marihuana . . . has any appreciably deleterious influence on the individual using it."[37] This finding echoed those found by the Indian Hemp Drug Commission, 1893-1894. According to the commission, "moderate use of hemp drugs is practically attended by no evil results at all" and "moderate use . . . produces no injurious effects on the mind" inflicting "no moral injury whatsoever."[38] Unsupported by the science of the day, Anslinger's bunkum was buttressed only by bureaucrats looking for more work at the Federal Bureau of Narcotics and newspapermen hot to peddle more sheets.

Heroin has also received a bum rap regarding crime. "There is no doubt that heroin use in and of itself . . . is a neutral act in terms of its potential criminogenic effect upon an individual's behavior," explains Arnold S. Trebach in *The Heroin Solution*. "There is nothing in the pharmacology or physical or psychological impact of the drug that propels a user to crime."[39] In 1976, conservative hardballer Pat Buchanan recognized this well enough to actually use his nationally syndicated column to give credence to the policy of providing heroin addicts their fixes for free.[40] Users may suffer from the drug, yes, but if jailing people who harm their own bodies were justified by that harm alone, we should likewise punish gluttons and people who don't eat their veggies.

Tougher Customers

Pot and heroin are one thing, some might say. What about crack and PCP?

With rising crime stats often labeled "drug-fueled" or "drug-related," perhaps the average person could be forgiven for fingering crack as pharmacologically responsible for the hundreds of New York City homicides that Paul Goldstein reviewed in the late 1980s. The research, however, dropped a hammer on the criminogenic explanation.

Police characterized more than half of the 414 murders in 1988 as drug-related, with crack as the principal culprit. But after looking at all the killings, Goldstein determined that less than three dozen could be attributed to psychoactive factors, and even then most of those could be blamed solely on booze. When the numbers were crunched, crack-use figured in just five murders—and in all but one case, the drug's effects could not be isolated from the effect of other factors (including alcohol). In short, out of 414 murders in New York during the heyday of crack cocaine, only one murder could be pinned squarely on the use of crack, the granddaddy of scary drugs.[41]

The same ho-hum result comes after looking at the granddaddy's nephew, PCP— "angel dust" as it's also known. In 1978 Congress labeled PCP "one of the most dangerous and insidious drugs known to mankind"; one congressman went on record saying it was "a threat to national security."[42] "It's a real terror of a drug," said Robert DuPont, director of the National Institute on Drug Abuse, the year before. "Everything people used to say about marijuana is true of angel dust."[43] (Don't miss the implicit argument in DuPont's statement: Yes, the fear-mongers were wrong about pot, but we're on the level with PCP. Unlike marijuana, angel dust is *actually* dangerous.)

But PCP fears are not relegated to the age of the Village People and discotheques. In 1990, research scholar Rachel Ehrenfeld wrote, "both crack and PCP are big and fast rush stimulants, which accounts for the penchant for violence by those under their spell."[44] The cause-and-effect link between violence and PCP (not to mention the supposed voodoo-like power of the drug itself) is so quickly assumed that when an upswing in Washington DC murders happened in 2002, PCP became the prime suspect for the higher homicide rate.[45]

While research has shown that high doses of PCP lead to "severe agitation and hyperactivity" and "cognitive disorganization, disorientation, hallucinations, and paranoia," according to psychiatrist Martin Brecher and his colleagues in a review of some 350 journal articles on human PCP use, there is much more to the story. Jacob Sullum explains that "in their search of the literature, Brecher and his co-authors found only three documented cases in which people under the influence of PCP alone had committed acts of violence. They also noted that between 1959 and 1965, when PCP was tested as a human anesthetic, it was given to hundreds of patients, but 'not a single case of violence was reported.'"[46]

"As is the case with any other drug," notes psychiatrist Norman E. Zinberg, "users learn how to use it so as to avoid the most dysphoric effects; these subjects have reported little of the violence and a few of the toxic symptoms that have been emphasized in the recent flurry of frightening reports a about PCP."[47]

Unlike love and marriage in Sinatra's song, it seems you can have PCP *without* brutal aggression. Brecher and company concluded, "PCP does not live up to its reputation as a violence-inducing drug."[48]

Justice Department numbers bear out these conclusions. In a report for the Independent Institute, David W. Rasmussen and Bruce L. Benson point to DOJ data that show recidivist drug criminals are far more likely to end up in jail on another drug charge, not a property or violent offense. The data, they write, "suggest that the set of people who are drug offenders only partially overlaps with the set of people who commit Index 1 crimes (homicide, sexual assault, robbery, burglary, aggravated assault, larceny, and auto theft)."[49] In other words, most drug offenders are not dangerous. And, remember, these numbers show people entangled in the legal system, where the sample is clearly skewed toward all sorts of unsavory characters. In the larger population, most drug consumption escapes detection precisely because users are not behaving in ways that require the neighbors to call the police in fear for their lives and property.

That does not mean that people who take this or any other drug are always tranquil, law-abiding citizens. But, as Sullum points out, neither can you assume a simple cause-and-effect relationship when they are not. Too many other things are at play: the expectations of the person using the drug, his or her personality and physiology, dosage, method of intake, and the environment in which the drug is taken—to name a few such factors. All of these play important roles in the drug user's experience.

Playing the straight criminogenic game is certainly good for justifying current drug policies, but it is also poor science and does nothing to help foster a genuine understanding of drugs and crime. And such an understanding is crucial, because an off-kilter diagnosis means off-kilter treatment and policy.

Carole Barnes, director of the Institute for Social Research at California State University, Sacramento, knows this. A study by the institute in 2002 showed that the biggest group of people booked for violent crimes in Sacramento County was clean and sober. "The results of this study call into question the link between illegal drug use and violent criminal behavior," said the analysis. "If we assume we need to treat the drug use to stem the violence," Barnes said, "we may be missing other causes and perhaps the real causes."[50]

And what *is* causing all the crime associated with the drug trade?

Finding out why Maisha Hubbard died requires what Rush Limbaugh would call a "profit-center break," an interlude about money.

Paint It Black

Rannell Rogers is just twenty-three and makes "between $1,000 and $2,000 a week," by his accounting. But much more money is in play than his two Gs. "I worked for a guy, and I counted his money one time and for a week," said Rogers, a member of the Mafia Insane Vice Lords gang in Chicago, "counted $1.2 million sitting on my table. But it was his money. I wanted to get my gym bag and run. But he knows where my house is. That was his take."[51]

Boiled down, the subject of drugs is all about cold, hard cash. There is a reason, after all, that it is referred to as the drug *trade*. Drugs are a product, just like cabbage or semiconductors; they are of no value unless people wish to buy or sell them. Realizing there is demand for chemical mindbenders is fundamental to evaluating the drug scene in America. Folks *want* to buy dope. And it is here—at the very first step—that prohibitionists begin their policy pratfall.

The idea of stamping something out by simply making it illegal ignores the role of demand in an economy. A law doesn't stop the drug buyer from buying drugs; it merely puts a fence in his way. The demand is still there, and with sufficient means and intelligence, the man will simply go around or over the fence or find a new way to slake his desire. Further, because the demand is present, suppliers, like Rogers' boss, also busy themselves figuring out ways to breach the fence and get their products to willing consumers.

The illegal meeting of the two, buyer and seller, takes place on the black market. Economist Faustino Ballvé actually calls it the "true market" because it is the only market realistically dealing with supply and demand. During any sort of prohibition, the "economic dictatorship" is "not one hundred per cent effective," he says. "The market continues to function . . . in a clandestine form."[52] Walter Dixon, an

English pharmacologist and League of Nations adviser on addiction, made note of this back in the early days of American drug prohibition: "Everything can be obtained if the price is commensurate with the risk, with the result being that smuggling is rampant from end to end in America."[53] Likewise, said Dr. Charles E. Terry in 1920, just six years after the enactment of the United States' first federal antidrug law, the Harrison Narcotics Act, "We had counted without the peddler. We had not realized the moment restrictive legislation made these drugs difficult to secure legitimately, the drugs would also be made profitable to illicit traffickers."[54]

Drug prohibition does not end drug use. It simply forces the consumer to break the law in order to get what he wants. And by pushing the trade into the dark corners and alleyways, prohibition sets off a string of nasty reactions.

Making Bank

The first thing that happens when drugs are forced onto the shelves of the black market is that sticker prices go up—way up. Prohibition limits supply as legal suppliers step out of the now-illegal market. The twofold, inevitable result: First, whenever demand outpaces supply, it becomes a "sellers' market," and, as any smart businessman would, the seller typically charges as much as he can get (just ask anyone trying to buy an electric generator after a hurricane strikes).

Second, prohibition increases the costs of getting the goods to market. Drug growers, producers, traffickers, and sellers all face legal sanctions for what they do. To balance that risk, the rewards must be great indeed. And they are. Between its heroin and crack sales, one New York-based drug organization in the 1990s took in about $100,000 weekly, and this was after a police crackdown hampered earnings by an estimated 20 percent—usually considered by such organizations to be little more than a tax on the trade. This is no fluke. Working just one intersection, New York police guessed that drug dealers raked in $6 million a year.[55] Given the source of the figure, the real number might be quite higher; downplaying the count is only natural when the estimators tend to look increasingly worse in direct proportion to the size of their estimate.

Drugs are lucrative in a way no other product is. Because of government-created shortages, a grower in South America can earn three, four, even ten times the cash for growing coca (the bush from whose leaves cocaine is produced) as he can cultivating an ordinary subsistence crop. The wholesaler can peddle the cocaine in US cities for around $15,000 a kilo (2.2 pounds)—ten times what the grower makes per hectare of coca. And an ounce dealer, the final Joe in the supply chain, is sitting even prettier depending on the quality and the cut of his product. Marijuana is similar. A Mexican grower can get about $250 a kilo; for the same weight, a US seller can fetch $3,000, $5,000, and more depending on quality. Opium/heroin is the most striking. In the early 1990s, "South American drug cartels . . . discovered that growing opium poppies and refining their gum into heroin yields 10 to 20 times more profit per unit shipped than cocaine . . . heroin brings $150,000 or more [per kilo]," explained Daniel K. Benjamin in an analysis for the Independent Institute.[56]

These high prices lure entrepreneurs into the illegal drug markets like honey draws flies. With few suppliers in the burgeoning Blow Boom of the early 1970s, profits were as mind-blowing as the drug. While in prison following a major pot bust, "narcopreneur" George Jung started calculating the money he could make smuggling cocaine instead. Any thought of a legal occupation was drowned in an ocean of profit figures. The crystalline white powder, *wholesale*, was pulling prices of $50,000 and $60,000 a kilo in 1974.

"Moving from wholesaling to retailing, the numbers climbed higher still as the quality of the product got worse," writes journalist Bruce Porter in his biography of Jung. "Cut a number of times by interim dealers, who would add inert substances to boost the weight and maintain their profit margin, the common street product in some cases would contain no more than 15 or 20 percent cocaine. . . . Selling for one hundred dollars a gram, a thousand grams to the kilo, with all the deals running smoothly . . . this meant the kilo purchased for six thousand in Colombia would generate street sales in America of between two and three hundred thousand dollars. . . ."[57]

The money rolled in so fast and furiously that Jung recalled counting it became impossible. Handing a pile over to his Colombian partners, "Sometimes it was, 'Here's two and a half million dollars, and maybe it's fifty thousand off that number. I don't know.' And nobody would care. It was just, 'When can you leave and bring back more?'"[58] The parole board thought Jung was holding down an honest job as a fisherman in Boston while all this was going on, but mackerel can't compete with that kind of mammon.

Smugglers in Jung's boat processed so much money, they often didn't count it. They weighed it. Porter explains that an even million weighs 20.4 pounds in hundred dollar bills, 40.8 in fifties.[59] Reporter Robert Sabbag tells the story of marijuana smuggler Allen Long counting eight million dollars this way:

> The smugglers, emptying one of the cardboard boxes, placed it on the scale and came up with a tare weight. They reloaded the box, weighed it and all the other boxes, and then did the arithmetic, calculating a US banknote at precisely a gram. They came up $100,000 short, which out of $8 million-plus, fell well within the margin of error. Perhaps they overestimated the weight of the rubber bands. A hundred thousand was small change at the level at which everyone was operating. Long was spending around half that much every week in expenses.[60]

This kind of instant wealth presents a big problem for drug warriors in inner cities. Where job prospects appear bad and hopes low, kids growing up surrounded by poverty see drug dealers rolling by in expensive cars, handing out money and favors to neighbors, and dressing well, sometimes extravagantly.

"From flashy SUVs such as the Cadillac Escalade to the fanciest clothes and jewelry, gang members show it off to command respect and lure new recruits," write *Chicago Sun-Times* reporters Carlos Sadovi and Frank Main. They mention the case of Elbert Mahone, headman of one of the Windy City's most notorious gangs. Before he was gunned down, Mahone "drove a Rolls-Royce, wore full-length fur coats and had built up a reputation as a Robin Hood for spreading money around his impoverished Lawndale community."[61] Some of these guys are heroes on their streets, and the incredible lucre they flash and lifestyle they live draws newbies into the underground world of crime to get a piece of the action.

Crackdown

Naturally, as people rush into the market with wads of dope and loads of hope, the government steps in to crash the party. But the efforts prove counterproductive and self-defeating. "Paradoxically, every 'victory' in the 'war against narcotics' increases the profitability of this trade and soon creates new pushers, more addicts, and bigger profits," explains Peter Drucker. "When the narcotics agents 'smash a drug ring' and confiscate 50 kilograms of heroin, the drug temporarily become scarce. . . . The price goes up—and with it the profit for the drug rings whose sources remain intact. Addicts become more desperate. Crime and violence . . . rise more sharply. More people are lured by their own need and by the high profits into becoming peddlers and pushers, producing more addicts."[62]

But this is no paradox. Shortages in supply created by crackdowns are only mating calls to suppliers. Dollar signs are fiscal pheromones. The costs may be high for suppliers, but the profits soar higher still—incentive to stay in the game (or start playing) and satisfy the demand at a price worth their while. As a result of their profit-seeking, more supply makes its way into the market, driving down prices as the shortage is slaked. Thus, what appear to be absurdly high prices are simply the way the market rations supply and encourages new supplies in response to demand.[63] And what lucrative encouragement.

When alcohol Prohibition became law in 1920, Rev. Billy Sunday gushed with high-sounding praise. "The reign of tears is over. The slums will be only a memory. It will turn our prisons into factories and our jails into storehouses and corncribs. . . . Hell will be forever for rent."[64]

Wrong. The government just gave Hell a housing subsidy.

Most of the drug crime people worry about—the kind that killed Maisha Hubbard—is a direct result, not of the pharmacological effects of dope, but of the distortion of drug markets by laws.

Users, Hookers, Dealers, and Thieves

Prohibition creates crime in a number of ways. First, anyone who continues involvement in the once-legal trade after laws are passed against it is made a criminal—a felon not because he has harmed or defrauded his neighbors but by fiat. Other forms of crime basically break down into two groups: (1) property crimes committed by addicts to get the necessary funds to score their necessary fixes and (2) violent crimes committed by those in the trade.

In 1980 New York fell prey to a rash of necklace nabbing by train-going ne'er-do-wells, acting both alone and sometimes in packs. In one instance, after an Amtrak passenger train rammed a freight train, hoodlums ran through the cars filching gold chains and purses. The police were basically useless; the public grew fearful.

Rising above the panic and anxiety, Gov. Hugh Carey tried to make some sense of the events rippling through his crime-stricken state. "The epidemic of gold-snatching in the city," he explained in a public address, preparing to prove he had learned very little in his college Econ 101 class, "is the result of a Russian design to wreck America by flooding the streets with deadly heroin. . . . Women are afraid to walk with a chain around their neck. Why? Somebody's grabbing that chain to get enough money for a fix. . . . [If the Russians] were using nerve gas on us, we'd certainly call out the troops. This is more insidious than nerve gas. Nerve gas passes off. This doesn't. It kills. I'm not overstating the case."[65] Or his ignorance.

Junkies commit property crimes like theft to get cash to buy a fix—that much Carey had right. But what he missed was why the fix costs so much in the first place. As the illegality of drugs inflates their prices, in many cases users are priced out of the market—at least in terms of legally acquired funds. Not able to procure enough money by methods that keep the angels smiling, some drug users turn to crime to generate the necessary greenbacks. As George Will breaks it down, "If you must steal $20 worth of property to raise $5 from a fence, then a $100-a-day habit requires $400 worth of stolen stuff."[66] If crime were Carey's concern, then he should have been thanking the Soviets for "flooding the streets" with smack. With surpluses instead of shortages, the price would go down, thus mitigating the need to rob and pillage for a fix. The opposite is true as well. When Nixon vowed to crack down on drugs, it was in response to rising property crimes. However, more crackdowns mean more shortages, which create higher prices, which create more property crimes.

This argument *can* be overstated, as drug users often do procure cash by means other than theft—including, as many addicts do, selling drugs or prostituting themselves. This by itself is troubling, since (sans prohibitionary inflation) the price of many drugs would be no more than a cup of coffee. But because of the law, people who fall into a drug habit who do not wish to harm others by stealing must instead harm themselves by whoring for drug money or risking their safety to enter the dangerous drug market to generate funds for their own habit. In a legal market, however deplorable their habit may be, they would neither have to harm others nor themselves in order to procure drugs.

What *cannot* be overstated is the breach in the wall this creates for the rest of society—a breach through which burglars pass daily. Property crimes are exacerbated by more than junkies jacking car stereos. Because limited police resources are focused on busting drug users and dealers, they are *not* making sure that uninvited guests are keeping sticky fingers off china cabinets and auto ignitions. In the 1980s, during the first major drug crackdown since Nixon, "At least 50 percent of property crime increase was due to a shift out of property crime control to drug control," explains economist Bruce L. Benson.[67]

The federal government actually encourages this problem. Promiscuous in its dolling out of tax dollars, Uncle Sam makes funds available to state and local law enforcement. On the state side, an agency will divvy it up as best fits that state's needs. The Wisconsin Office of Justice Assistance, for instance, disburses millions of federal dollars to the state's drug-task force units. The money then goes to reimburse local agencies for overtime costs tied to drug policing—anything from traffic stops where drugs are discovered to full-throttle SWAT raids. Here's the problem: In a world of scarce resources, while you get more of what you subsidize, you also get less of what you do not. Non-drug related enforcement sees nothing of this largesse. So while busting dopers is a budgetary boon, a stake-out to nab a burglar is just a drain on the department—no doubt an uncomforting thought when one's house is robbed.[68]

Dodging Bullets

Because of what crimes drug users actually do commit—mainly property crimes—human life is rarely endangered by them. A stolen TV set is only a material loss and a missed episode of *The Simpsons*. But the same is not true on the dealers' end, where Homer and Bart are likely to get shot in a drive-by.

Because the illegality of the drug trade removes legal protection from its participants, the business is subject to brutality. The people who thrive in the drug market are those with, as the Cato Institute's David Boaz once put it, a "comparative advantage in violence." Why? When Pfizer has a problem with a client or competitor, it calls the lawyers. But for those dealing in an illegal trade, contracts become enforceable with guns, not lawsuits. Indeed, "Much of the gunfire is connected with routine practices of the drug trade, claiming territory, punishing people who do not fulfill contracts," writes Will.[69]

Drug prohibition "encourages entry [into the market] by suppliers who are more ruthless, innovative, and have a lower regard for civility and the law," explains Walter Williams. "Pantywaist, petty, otherwise law-abiding practitioners are ousted."[70]

A 1995 study by University of Missouri criminology professor Scott Decker confirms these observations. Using Justice Department numbers, Decker found that sellers—not cash-strapped users—are the gun-packers of the drug market. To protect his property, a drug seller is forced to go armed, since he is all the protection he is going to get. "This is an important study," said criminologist Alfred Blumstein, "because it suggests we should rethink the presumption that the pharmacological effect of drugs makes people violent and do crazy things."[71] In the majority of cases, it's not the dope that makes people violent. It's the legal strictures themselves that encourage violence and violent participants.

Uncle Sam is not stupid about this reality. The government knows full well its policies produce violence. As noted by a 1989 US attorney general report, "the normal commercial concept of contracts, in which disputes are adjudicated by an impartial judiciary and restitution is almost always of a financial nature, is twisted, in the world of drug trafficking, into a system where the rule of law is replaced by the threat of violence."[72]

The story was the same during Prohibition, the seedbed years of the American Mob. It was the time of the gangster, the Mafioso, retaliatory gang warfare, and the original drive-by shooting. During Prohibition, "if I'm not exaggerating, there were about ten mobs in Chicago," one illicit liquor distributor recalled. "Of course you had to protect your territory. You couldn't call for help. If you couldn't handle it yourself, you lost it. That was the law. So when you were infringed upon, you had to retaliate immediately, or you didn't have nothing left."[73]

During the thirteen-year "Ignoble Experiment," property crimes ratcheted up 13.2 percent, homicide 16.1 percent, while robbery soared 83.3 percent. "Fluctuations in economic activity and major government programs . . . no doubt played some role in these statistics," explains Mark

Thornton in *The Economics of Prohibition*, "but Prohibition appears to be the significant explanatory variable for changes in the crime rate. . . ."[74]

In a study that echoes Thornton's conclusion, researcher Kirby R. Cundiff compared homicide rates and government control of intoxicants. He found a clear picture in the statistical peaks and valleys since Prohibition: As the long blue arm of the law puts dope or drink in a hammerlock, murders increase. When the grip loosens, homicide rates slide back down. Concludes Cundiff, "the best theory of the primary cause of violent crime in the United States is a violent black market caused by the War on Drugs today, and Prohibition in the 1920's."[75]

Patterns in Predation

When Washington DC police chief Charles H. Ramsey fingered PCP as part of the cause in the District's higher murder rate for 2002, he left people with a false assumption about the drug and neglected telling two important facts. The false assumption was that the drug itself was responsible for the increase in corpses. The first neglected fact was that the murder rate rose in many cities across the US in the same year, cities with no special increase in PCP use, which would point elsewhere for causation. The increased murder rate "is very serious cause for concern," admitted University of Pennsylvania criminology professor Lawrence W. Sherman. "But explaining it is premature."[76] One would think that caveat would hold doubly true to pinning the answer at PCP's door—especially when the second neglected fact is explained.

Ramsey failed to give his hearers some necessary context about DC's murder rate, something that sheds more credible light on the increase than a bedeviling chemical. District murders, while indeed up in 2002, were still fewer in number in the early 1990s, when the streets were turned to war zones by crack-selling hoodlums fighting over turf.[77] Goldstein's research on "drug-related" killings in New York City showed the same cause for the city's high murder rate. After reviewing the relevant data, he concluded fully three quarters of "drug-related" homicides resulted from dealers squabbling and then killing each other over trade disputes and turf battles.[78]

The same remains true today. While other types of homicide and most crime in general are on the downswing, gang killings are on the rise, spiking 50 percent between 1999 and 2002. Calling it "the emerging monster of crime in America," Los Angeles police chief William J. Bratton blamed street gangs for more than half of L.A.'s annual homicides.[79]

Even police crackdowns in these drug-selling areas can create problems. In the early 1990s, for instance, police in Tampa, Florida, worked diligently to bust up deals in the city but noticed that while drug activity dropped in one area, it mushroomed in others—dealers just migrated to different sectors of town. Sometimes the new dealing went on in previously untapped areas, but plenty of it went on in areas already controlled by other drug interests. By upsetting a market in which turf issues were already settled, the crackdowns actually helped encourage more gang warfare and violence by driving dealers into each others' territory.[80]

Blame It on the Law

While these crimes are drug-related, they are more accurately prohibition-related. If cocaine and other drugs were legal, do you think Wal-Mart and Walgreens pharmacists would be shooting each other in the streets over turf disputes? Violence and crime have little to do with dope itself and much to do with drug *laws*.

The family of young Maisha Hubbard, killed by a stray bullet in a prohibition-related gunfight, can certainly blame her death on the gang member who pulled the trigger. But it was misguided policies that empowered those gangs. As we'll see in the next chapter, those same policies also corrupt the people we rely on most to protect us from predatory criminals—the cops.

2

DIRTY BLUE

Prohibition corrupts law enforcement.

DECORATED GANGS-CRIMES INVESTIGATOR JOSEPH MIEDZIANOWSKI'S moonlighting days were over. He was busted in 1998 after a long and fruitful side career of dope-peddling, extortion, stealing money and jewelry from drug dealers, torturing suspects, lying to obtain search warrants, seizing guns and drugs from suspects and keeping them for personal use or giving them to gang members as favors, turning a blind eye to a fugitive murder suspect, and finking the identity of undercover drug cops and snitches to gang members.

Nice work if you can get it.

Miedzianowski was part of a Chicago-to-Miami drug-running conspiracy in which crack cocaine by the duffel-bagful exchanged hands in places as unlikely as a church parking lot and behind the station house where he worked. In January 2003, a judge sentenced Miedzianowski—now known infamously as the "the most corrupt cop in the history of Chicago"—to life in prison.[1]

"It is unfortunate that a Chicago police officer has chosen to tarnish the badge that so many carry with dignity and honor," said the Chicago PD when Miedzianowski's partner, John Galligan, was indicted in

2000.[2] The statement is far too tidy. More than merely unfortunate, such corruption is also *predictable* and *pervasive*.

In March 2002, a pair of Jefferson County, Kentucky, Metro Narcotics detectives were slapped with an indictment that read like a paean to unscrupulous behavior. The 472-count document included allegations of tampering with drug evidence, stealing money from informants, burglary, and forging judges' signatures on warrants. The amazing total of alleged offenses came from just twenty-four of the detectives' cases. When the dust settled in early 2003, the worst of the two agreed to fink on his partner for a mitigated sentence. Mark Watson pled guilty to 299 felony counts in exchange for testifying against Christie Richardson, who was found guilty of twenty felonies and a misdemeanor.[3]

Widespread Corruption

While the two cases just mentioned may sound especially egregious, finding stories about police drug corruption is as easy as opening the newspaper. Shady dealing, protection rackets, growing or slinging stashes on the side, collusion, and cover-ups—they may not hit the metro section on a weekly basis, but they're hardly scarce.

In 1972 the Knapp Commission found that "police corruption [was] an extensive, department wide phenomenon, indulged to some degree by a sizable majority of those on the [New York City] force." Twenty years later, the Mollen Commission struck the same chord, highlighting the ongoing corruption problem in the Big Rotten Apple. In one of the most brazen examples, the 1992 commission ran into the case of one officer who scored some eight thousand dollars a week selling drugs while snorting lines of coke right off the dashboard of his cruiser.[4] Thanks to the relentless Rudy Giuliani, Gotham is much improved today, but the problem goes far beyond New York. Examples are so plentiful around the nation that scanning corruption stories can cause one's eyes to glaze over.

One 1998 study showed that the number of federal, state, and local officials wearing orange jumpsuits and scarfing federal prison food quintupled in just four years. In 1994, the number was 107. By 1998, it had soared to 548.[5] "It's a big problem across the country, in big towns and small towns, and it's not getting any better," said Chicago police superintendent Mike Hoke.[6]

"[S]everal studies and investigations of drug-related police corruption found on-duty police officers engaged in serious criminal activities such as (1) conducting unconstitutional searches and seizures; (2) stealing money and/or drugs from drug dealers; (3) selling stolen drugs; (4) protecting drug operations; (5) providing false testimony; and (6) submitting false crime reports," according to a 1998 General Accounting Office report. The GAO additionally found that, between 1993 and 1997, drug-related charges ended in convictions for about 50 percent of officers busted by the FBI in corruption stings.[7]

As with drug-related crime, prohibition bears the brunt of blame for the problem. "Corruption is a regular effect of [market] interventionism," explained economist Ludwig von Mises in his magnum opus, *Human Action*. Why? The officers of the law, he said simply, "are not angelic."[8] Definitely not.

In August 1990, six law-enforcement officers from Eastern Kentucky, including four sheriffs, were busted in an FBI sting. "A 42-count indictment charged them with conspiracy to extort money, distribute drugs and protect dealers. Five of the six were convicted."[9]

Federal prosecutors dropped the hammer on Cleveland police officer Gregory Colon in January 2000. The charge: Operating a cocaine ring that used topless dancers to boost clientele from show bars.[10]

In a case marked more by stupidity than titillation, Deputy Teddy Willis missed his 2003 retirement ceremony from the Caswell County, North Carolina, Sheriff's Department. Just hours before the shindig, Willis was arrested for allegedly buying fifteen pounds of marijuana in a nearby county. "We were suspecting him of other things anyway," said Person County sheriff Dennis Oakley of Willis. "We had received reports of drugs and other illegal activities."[11]

When agents from the FBI and Georgia Bureau of Investigations tried to arrest Coffee County sheriff Carlton Evans in October 2000, he bolted for a nearby wood. Five hours later, the sheriff's body was found in the forest after having apparently shot himself. The reason for his evasion of arrest and subsequent suicide? If busted, Evans faced charges of conspiracy to grow more than a thousand pounds of pot. Charges were also directed at a former captain in the department and a former chief deputy.[12]

Pay Day

Observers could have seen this pervasive pattern of corruption coming at a gallop if their understanding of history went back any further than yesterday's breakfast. During Prohibition, corruption was rife, the slammer door shutting on hundreds of government agents in just the first five years. In April 1925 alone, the Prohibition director for Ohio was convicted for mob ties and a federal jury in Cincinnati lowered the boom on fifty-eight officers. "[T]wo Pullman cars were needed to haul the miscreants to the Atlanta Penitentiary," according to one account.[13]

The situation was so bad, President Hoover set up a body to probe the problem and explain what was going on. The Wickersham Commission pointed to "revelations [of] police corruption in every type of municipality, large and small throughout the decade . . . to the evidence of connection between corrupt local politics and gangs and the organized unlawful liquor traffic, and of systematic collection of tribute from that traffic, for corrupt political purposes." According to the commission's 1931 report, Prohibition itself was the key offender.

The reason? Just as it does for crime, prohibition creates incredible incentives for corruption. The illegality of a banned substance drives its price sky-high, and with big money involved, somebody—poor hoodlum, high-school dropout, white-collar exec, even police officer—is going to figure out a way to deal himself into the game.

"The illicit drug market is probably the most lucrative source of police corruption that has ever existed in the United States," confirm economists David W. Rasmussen and Bruce L. Benson.[14] As one newspaper editorialized following the sentencing of four North Carolina officers, their case (detailed later in the chapter) "showed how the huge amount of money involved in the illegal drug trade can turn heads, even the heads of those charged with enforcing the law. Corruption is not limited to big-city law enforcement agencies. Unfortunately, it can wedge its way in almost anywhere."[15]

This is especially obvious when you consider law enforcement's low pay scales. A pile of seized drug money can be awfully appealing when an officer makes only thirty to thirty-five Gs a year.

If a cop seizes five hundred dollars from a suspect, who does it hurt if he only reports four hundred? Former police sergeant Edwin Bradley of West Memphis, Tennessee, must have pondered the same question before a jury found him guilty of skimming seizure money—some twenty-five hundred dollars in just one case. Bradley's big mistake was nabbing money used in an FBI sting.[16]

After mentioning a story of a smuggler "standing knee-deep in twenty-dollar bills," one narcotics officer explained, "That's why there's so much corruption among law-enforcement people involved in the drug war. Cops will bust a place and one of them will find thousands of dollars stashed away in a back room. He'll grab a handful and stuff it into his pocket. He knows that what he grabs in that handful will be more than his salary for the entire month. He also knows that nobody will be doing any counting until he turns the money in."[17]

L.A. sheriff Sherman Block led an investigation from 1988 to 1994 that nailed twenty-six deputies on narc duty—nearly 15 percent of his narcotics officers—for skimming off the top.[18]

And once an officer starts down the path, making the trek into more dastardly behavior is just a matter of going with the flow. As economist Mark Thornton explains, "When an official commits one act of corruption, the costs of additional acts decline, in a fashion similar to the marginal cost of production in a firm."[19] Pocketing that Franklin gets easier every time—other crimes, too.

This should be both obvious and cautionary. Miedzianowski and others like him did not start out as crooks. In most cases they were good, straight-laced cops who did their best to uphold the law, bust the bad guys, and protect the community. At some point, however, they started down the wrong path and didn't stop until their rap sheets were as bad, or worse, than those of many they had arrested over the years.

Protection Racket

Crooked cops are empowered by prohibition because it gives them an incredibly valuable asset. Police are in the unique position to insulate drug dealers from arrest, something drug dealers appreciate and richly reward. If the price is right, an even sexier bargain can be arranged—one in which Johnny Flatfoot actually runs off competitors. "They can allow certain individuals or groups to operate illegally while harassing other potential market participants and discouraging them from entering the market," explains Thorton. "In effect they can sell monopoly rights to a private-sector underground market and then enforce that rights allocation."[20] This was a big part of Miedzianowski and Galligan's arrangement with the various drug gangs they protected.

If officers are both motivated and unscrupulous, they will search out the drug dealer and pitch him the offer (with the implicit or explicit threat of arrest or harassment if he does not comply). If an officer has failed to ponder the payoff or his scruples hold him back, the drug dealer may seek him out—hence Arthur Niederhoffer's verdict: "Every policeman patrolling the streets sooner or later faces the temptation of a 'payoff.'"[21] With beaucoup bucks on hand, buying off police is just a question of finding the willing officer and setting a price. Rasmussen and Benson cite figures of a hundred thousand dollars offered by traffickers to DEA agents just "for openers" and five million dollars offered to a high-ranking US Border Patrol official.[22]

Either way, it's a good arrangement for both. The cops make money, and the peddler does too.

After only three hours of deliberation, a Louisiana jury ruined the day of former Duson police chief Thomas Deville in such a case, convicting him in February 2000 of conspiracy, weapons, and drug charges. Deville was a member of the Lanier "Pops" Cherry drug organization, which distributed more than two tons of pot, according to authorities.[23] The chief's role was to provide protection for the ring; he'd let it operate free and clear, provided he got a cut.

Similarly, according to evidence in his trial, former Washington DC cop, Andrew James McGill Jr., alerted gang members to drug raids to prevent police from finding evidence. He was rewarded with cash payoffs for his trouble.[24]

Described as a physically fit, nice person with "a lot of good qualities for the job," Maui patrolman James Mateaki also had qualities favored by meth maven and close friend Polotani Latu. In February 2003, Mateaki pled guilty to conspiring with Latu, who authorities claim was responsible for *half* of Maui's crystal methamphetamine trade, possibly more. Like McGill, Mateaki tipped his man about police investigations into his business.[25]

And it's not just police who render this sort of assistance. Former district judge Gigi Sullivan was busted in 1999 and convicted of tipping a drug dealer to a police raid; when police waited for her to sign a warrant, she called the dealer and warned him of "dinner guests." How did she have his number and the secret code worked out with which to warn him? The man was *her* dealer. She admitted to dealing drugs and allegedly shot heroin and snorted coke in her chambers. Prosecutors claimed she dismissed charges against her dealer in exchange for smack and blow.[26]

It's Everywhere

This kind of thing can affect many more than the occasional officer; it's systemic. As the result of a 1998 FBI sting in Cleveland, Ohio, some fifty-one officers were busted "on charges of protecting the transfer or sale of large amounts of cocaine."[27]

In 1999, a consulting group gave Jackson, Mississippi, officials cause to fear when it reported what the *Clarion-Ledger* editorialized as "a serious perception of police corruption by the department's rank-and-file." More than 75 percent of survey participants suspected a full quarter of fellow officers were on the take.[28]

Out of twenty-eight criminal organizations studied in five counties by Eastern Kentucky University criminal justice professors Gary W. Potter and Larry K. Gaines in the late 1980s, "25 benefited from some corrupt or compromising relation with government and law-enforcement officials." Family ties between cops and scofflaws, payoffs, and "official acquiescence" (a technical term for turning the head and whistling "Me and My Shadow" while nefarious deeds are underway) were the order of the day. A 1999 report by the Appalachia High Intensity Drug Trafficking Area confirmed that little had changed in the decade following Potter and Gaines's study.[29]

Explains economist Murray Rothbard, "whether consciously or not, the government proceeds as follows: first it outlaws a certain activity—drugs, gambling, construction, or whatever—then the governmental police sell to would-be entrepreneurs in the field the privilege of entering and continuing in business."[30] It's such an alluring opportunity, only the most deluded utopian would not *expect* some officers to take advantage.

Hoover Institution scholar and former San Jose, California, police chief Joseph McNamara calls this kind of corruption the "Serpico Model . . . accepting bribes from gangsters. . . ." But, as he points out, some cops go far beyond playing hush-hush for gang members. Sometimes they become thugs themselves. "Now, thanks to the climate created by our drug laws, we have . . . small gangs of cops who are the gangsters. They've committed murders, kidnapping, and armed robberies—sometimes for, and sometimes against, drug dealers."[31]

Shakedowns

Because of their unique positions of being both close to lawbreaking and often the only witnesses to it, police are in a rare place to shake down ne'er-do-wells for money and drugs.

In July 2002, four North Carolina officers were sentenced to prison on federal drug trafficking charges—three of them worked vice for the Davidson County Sheriff's Office. One officer, David Scott Woodall, sold steroids and cocaine, planned on doing the same with pot and ecstasy, and stole a hundred and sixty thousand dollars in cash from co-defendant Wyatt Kepley, one of two civilian accomplices in the case. Another officer, Douglas Westmorland, helped Woodall filch the money from Kepley, helped fabricate a search warrant for his house, supplied a fellow officer with pot, and stole more than four pounds of coke and some sixty pounds of grass from the evidence room.[32]

Darnyl Parker and three other Buffalo, New York, narcotics detectives were indicted in 2002 for stealing thirty-six thousand dollars from an undercover FBI agent who they thought was a drug dealer. The jury nailed Parker and two others. Similarly, another Buffalo detective, Rene Gil, admitted to dealing coke while working a year-and-a-half stint on the narc squad. By his confession, "he shook down drug dealers and split the proceeds with fellow detectives."[33]

Chicago patrol officer Mario Morales was arrested in 2001 on extortion charges stemming from allegations that he and another man stole hundreds of pounds of pot and thousands of dollars after breaking into the home of a Latin Kings gang member. In a strange twist, according to an FBI affidavit, the five-year veteran of the force next turned on his accomplice, telling him that the gang member wanted to kill him and offered protection if the guy would shell over five thousand dollars.[34] How does someone go to the police with that? They may get the blue-pants extortionist, but chances are good they'll land the snitch too.

One officer nicknamed "the Abuser" not only ripped off dealers on the streets, according to the Mollen Commission, he also concocted a protection racket in which the dealers would pay him to look out for their interests. If they failed to fork over the loot, he just robbed them. In one instance, while in uniform, he gunned a dealer, pinched his drugs, and enlisted the help of fellow officers to cover up for the deed.[35] Fear of retaliation for finking on a brother officer or simply shame for turning informant will often keep officers from snitching on each other and will sometimes even move them to aid in hiding a crime. Alexandria, Virginia, police chief Ed Samarra spent five years working internal affairs in Washington DC. "I never encountered an officer willing to talk about the conduct of another officer, even if he was video-taped committing a crime," he said.[36]

Contrary to the stereotypes and TV caricatures, it's not just the mean and nasty who get involved in such criminal enterprises. As a fifteen-year veteran and many-time officer of the month, former Jackson, Mississippi, police detective Alvaline Baggett isn't the type usually fingered as a shakedown artist, but in 2000 she was convicted on charges of extorting cash from dealers to "fix" their cases. Working the city's antidrug unit, Baggett prided herself as being the "No. 1 narcotics officer in Jackson."[37]

No doubt.

Stolen Dope

As with Westmorland and company, sometimes cops will pilfer straight from their own departments.

After their biggest bust ever—five thousand pounds of weed—Chatham County, North Carolina, sheriff's deputies were unable to stuff the whole pile in the evidence room. Only able to shoe-horn two thousand pounds inside, the rest, one and a half tons of grass, they decided to store elsewhere in the department building. "I am concerned someone was goofball enough to allow it to sit around long enough to have it stolen," said one county commissioner.[38] Stolen out of the sheriff's office—any wagers on how many deputies are enjoying a slightly better standard of living (or doing a lot of off-hour giggling)? No wagers needed after $456,000 in cocaine and marijuana went missing from the Volusia County, Florida, Sheriff's Office. Sheriff Ben Johnson made no bones about who he suspected as the thief—one of his employees.[39]

Chicago cop John L. Smith retired from the force in 1999 after twenty-three years on the force. In 2003 he was arrested and charged with filching at least five kilos of coke from the evidence locker before hanging up his holster. What tipped off the authorities? Something about jewelry, furs, a Mustang convertible, a $174,000 Rolls Royce, a home in the 'burbs, an apartment building, and $580,000 of unreported income—all of which Smith supposedly owned—not being in his retirement package.[40]

Former California antinarcotics agent Richard Wayne Parker was convicted of stealing six hundred and fifty pounds of cocaine from a police evidence locker and selling the blow in a multistate drug-running network that extended from Honolulu to Detroit. In January 2000, he was sentenced to life in prison and fined a total of sixteen million dollars. Two others charged in the same case were Parker's former partner and his half brother—a former California Highway Patrol officer.[41]

As with any story in which lawmen become lawbreakers, these cases are flush with irony, but sometimes Providence looks down and—as with the case of DEA supervisor Rene de la Cova—provides a little more. De la Cova became an instant drug-war star in 1989 when the US military turned Panamanian General Manuel Noriega over to his custody. Recall that one of the stated reasons for the invasion of Panama, "Operation Just Cause," was to bring the strongman to trial in Florida, where two federal grand juries had indicted him on drug charges. This made it all the more curious when de la Cova himself later pleaded guilty to heisting $760,000 in laundered drug loot.[42]

Blaming "The lure of fortunes to be made in illegal drugs" for "thousands of police felonies: armed robbery, kidnapping, stealing drugs, selling drugs, perjury, framing people and even some murders," McNamara points out that "These police crimes were committed on duty, often while the cop gangsters were wearing their uniforms, the symbol of safety to the people they were supposed to be protecting."[43]

Liar, Liar

These very egregious offenders—sometimes called "meat eaters"—are not the only law enforcers touched by blue cancer. It's easy to focus on thuggish gangster cops; they certainly make for scintillating news copy. But far more in number and thus even more pernicious are "grass eaters," the small-fry offenders who bend the law a little here and a tad there. Beyond the basic rights of suspects and traditional protections against unjust search and seizure, their usual victim is the truth.

Officers desire to pad their résumés by hiking their bust counts, and they are certainly encouraged to do so by their superiors. Like politicians, police are sometimes willing to fib to forward their careers. Unlike pols, however, cops do not make grand and sweeping lies—about magically saving Social Security, for instance. In most cases, their lies are small, day-to-day lies, such as fudging the facts about a search to keep it "legal." Or, at least, legal on the report. Close enough for government work.

Sometimes drug smugglers and powder peddlers are caught by their own stupidity or mistakes. In March 2000, a British woman with three kilos of heroin strapped to her chest bollixed the job at Ataturk Airport in Istanbul on her way back home. According to Reuters, she was nabbed when her "intimate body piercing" gave a metal detector something to talk about. The smack, estimated to be worth nearly half a millions dollars, was discovered when she was searched. Said one Turkish paper, "Her piercing did her in."[44] Others are done in by less intimate items—their own big mouths, for instance. A suspected drug dealer in court on drug-possession charges in 2002 must have been short on places to stash his cocaine and pot because he brought it *with him*. According to the Associated Press, officers knew he would be present that day and tried to serve a warrant in a different case. When they accosted him, the guy blurted, "Man, I got the blow on me." Busted. Said the man's own attorney, "We would hope that they have enough brain cells to know not to bring illicit drugs into the court-house."[45]

As far as most drug busts go, these fumbles are rare. Because of the strict penalties for possessing or selling dope, what most folks lack in smarts they at least make up for in caution. No one wants to try explaining to a cop what those vials of crack are doing rolling around on the dashboard, so they carefully stash them, secret them away.

This creates a problem because, to make an arrest, police must be able to show that the bustee had dope in his possession. If it is adequately stashed, how are cops supposed to do that? The Fourth Amendment forbids their poking around and turning out pockets without probable cause. As a result, many officers run into problems making arrests that are constitutionally kosher.

With reference to 1.4 million annual arrests for drug possession, Joseph McNamara questions the legitimacy of the searches that helped rack up such a tally:

> Rarely does it happen that a cop pulls a guy over and says, "I'd like to look in your trunk," and the driver says, "Sure, officer, I've got a kilo of cocaine in there, but I don't want you to think that I don't cooperate with the local police." Equally unlikely is a scenario where an ounce of cocaine is sitting on the dashboard, or the suspect throws a baggie at the cop's feet, for the cop to conveniently find. Situations like these certainly don't happen 1.4 million times a year.[46]

So what's going on? Police, he says, are taking illegal shortcuts.

Since those shortcuts won't hold up in court, if the officer wants to get a conviction, he must lie to cover up his actions. And police certainly do. "There is substantial evidence," one criminologist notes, "to suggest that police often lie in order to bring their conduct within the practices sanctioned by judicial decisions."[47]

Tell It to the Judge

President Clinton's big legal sin wasn't sex in the Oval Office; it was
lying about sex in the Oval Office while under oath. Perjury's the pits.
But it's all too common in drug cases.

Some 92 percent of Chicago judges surveyed by University of
Minnesota law professor Myron Orfield admitted they thought officers
fudged facts at least "some of the time." Orfield also found that 22 percent of judges believed that officers lie in court *more than half* of the time
that they testify about the legitimacy of searches. "In fifty percent of small
drug cases," one Chicago prosecuting attorney reported, police "don't
accurately state what happens." Worse, 38 percent of judges surveyed
believed that rank-and-file officers are encouraged to lie in court by their
superiors.[48] The Mollen Commission found that such truth triflery was so
common, in fact, that officers had given it the everyday name "testilying."

Attorney Tim Lohraff points to a terrible irony here: "There's a curious thing about these drop cases. They're usually the lowest level
felony—straight possession. Yet the cop will testify in court and lie—
which is perjury. So you have a cop committing a greater felony to convict a lesser felony. It's gotta have an impact on a cop to stand up and lie
on a regular basis and think nothing of it."[49]

Worse, actually, is what they *do* think of it. Says McNamara, "[O]ften
it is an otherwise good cop who is lying—yet he still believes that he's a
good cop. He believes that in drug cases he's morally justified to illegally
search someone and perjure his testimony."[50] Because of the incredible danger that drugs supposedly present, getting the stuff off the street is such a
lofty good that petty scruples about bearing false witness must be discarded.

Framed

Beyond lying about how evidence is obtained, sometimes police will
actually lie about the *presence* of the evidence—more explicitly, they'll
plant dope on suspects.

After a call from CrimeStoppers, police went to the home of Darick Owens's sister in Davidson County, North Carolina. They were looking for a stash of drugs. Owens gave them what he had—two joints. A day later, however, police found a pound of pot and ten ecstasy tablets under the front seat of his '89 Chevy. He was at his girlfriend's home when they busted him. Trouble was, the pot and pills weren't his. But while he protested his arrest, saying that it was a setup over a domestic dispute, no one listened, not even his attorneys. "Someone planted those drugs, honest," he said. Turns out he was right. "The drugs were planted. And whoever did it had some help in nasty places. One of the three detectives in the Davidson County Sheriff's Office who pleaded . . . to drug-conspiracy charges supplied the drugs for the frame-up."[51]

Sometimes cases like this are never brought to the bar of justice because men like Owens have so little standing. Unable to prove his allegation, he languished in a jail cell for nearly two months before finally copping a deal—no contest. That meant he didn't confess to the crime but still got saddled with the sentence: two years probation, six months worth of curfews, and fifty hours of community service. What else could he do? "Every one of us has represented people who tell us they didn't do it," said an attorney not involved in the case. "Sometimes you just don't know. Sometimes the odds against them in court are just so great and the inherent credibility of law-enforcement officers is just so great that it's tough. I don't think anyone could fault the guy for taking the plea or fault his lawyer."[52] Sadly, if their innocence is not confirmed later, they are marked regardless of guilt. This case in particular should cause some worry since "the three detectives in the Davidson County Sheriff's Office who pleaded . . . to drug-conspiracy charges" were the same ones involved in the whole Woodall/Kepley debacle mentioned earlier.

A few months after his drug-corruption conviction, Woodall also admitted to planting drugs on a man who began serving a decade-long sentence in 2000. "Terrence Maurice Barriet did not have drugs on his person or property" before his arrest in May 1999, Woodall said in an affidavit. To make a charge stick against Barriet, "officers of the arrest detail

[Woodall among them] manufactured evidence and testimony/statements against Terrence Maurice Barriet; to wit, planted crack cocaine in a drain plug" in his house.[53]

Pattern liars and abusers like Woodall create a tremendous amount of damage; they become moving violations of the law and hurt unknown numbers of innocent people along the way. And Woodall is certainly not alone in this.

Five deputies in the Sarasota County, Florida, Sheriff's Department, part of an elite drug-fighting group called the Delta Task Force, framed Sarah Louise Smith by planting drugs in her home. They then lied to jurors, which resulted in her 1997 conviction and loss of custody of her baby daughter for a year and a half. Eventually the truth came out and Smith settled with the sheriff's office for two hundred and seventy-five thousand dollars. But like Woodall being able to inflict pain and punishment before his arrest, the offenders here established a pattern of abuse. "All five deputies were sentenced to prison for their role in the scheme, which involved planting drugs on suspects, stealing money from people under arrest and lying. . . . [P]rosecutors said their scheme lasted from 1995 to 1999."[54]

Like Smith, others do prevail. While the city admits no wrongdoing, Chicago paid Elizabeth Geannopulos sixty-five thousand dollars to settle a federal lawsuit alleging she was falsely arrested after an officer planted cocaine in the backseat of her car.[55]

Joining the Liar's Club

Police also lie to get search warrants. Multimillionaire Donald Scott was killed in his Malibu, California, home in a drug raid authorized with a bogus warrant. A later investigation found that Los Angeles County deputy sheriff Gary R. Spencer withheld evidence from the judge who signed the warrant and supported his case with false and misleading affidavits. Spencer was, incidentally, the same officer who shot Scott— two bullets to the chest.[56] No drugs were found.

Some of the 299 felonies to which former detective Mark Watson pleaded guilty in January 2003 included creating and serving bogus warrants. "Watson said he created fraudulent search warrants because he didn't have time to get signatures and feared suspects would flee or hide their contraband."[57] Worried crimes would go unpunished, he quickly committed more crimes to prevent bad guys from slipping through his fingers.

Judge Peter Nimkoff slammed a DEA agent who, as a last resort to nab a suspect—after he had already fruitlessly employed "outrageous" tactics—obtained a search warrant by lying in an affidavit.[58] With the warrant, the agent was able to read confidential material (protected by the Fourth Amendment) that, had he obeyed the law, he should have never seen. The issue isn't whether the confidential material had incriminating evidence, or whether the individual indeed committed any crimes. What is at issue is that, since the officer did not have sufficient evidence for a warrant, he lied and fabricated evidence. The issue moves beyond the incrimination of the suspect to include the incrimination of the officer.

The worst part about the misreporting and lying is summed up nicely by criminologist Randy E. Barnett: "The only person who can usually contradict the police version of the incident is the defendant, and the credibility of defendants does not generally compare favorably with that of police officers"[59]—especially, in a drug case, as addicts and dealers rate in popular conception right up there with child molesters and former Enron executives.

With the cult of silence that surrounds police malfeasance and the growing acceptance of lying as part of the job (L.A. cops call it "Joining the Liar's Club"), deception becomes the rule of the day. Explains philosopher J. Budziszewski, "the moment lying is accepted instead of condemned, it has to be required. If it is just another way to win, then in refusing to lie for the cause . . . you aren't doing your job."[60]

Thus, with ethical boundaries gone rubbery and self-justification running at full throttle, it's not hard to see how even well-meaning and moral cops can become twisted.

Staining the Shield

When the public perceives police as corrupt and untrustworthy, even if the actual number of law-breaking law enforcers is minute, the entire community suffers immensely. For the criminal justice system to have any trust at all, it must be *just*, and when officers deal wrongly—in ways either big or little—they chip away at their own legitimacy, eroding community trust and endangering the very people they are sworn to protect by allowing violent drug dealers to continue operating or by wearing the drug-dealer hat themselves.

"Every time you turn around, somebody's sheriff has been convicted for being involved in the drug trade," says Federal District Court Judge Joe Hood for Eastern Kentucky.[61] The result is that citizens can't even go to the police when drug deals occur right in front of them. Because of the perverse incentives that drug laws give to violent thugs, many of these dealers are dangerous people who should have the boom lowered, but with cops on the take, to whom can citizens turn?

The badge—the shield—stands for something. "[Y]our sheriff is supposed to be your symbol, your representation of the law," says University of Kentucky criminologist Graham Ousey. "When they end up dead or involved in some drug conspiracy, it really challenges the whole legitimacy of the legal order."[62]

Corruption has always existed and will continue to do so. But no other factor inflates corruption as much or as perniciously as drug prohibition. As long as it persists, the economic incentives for corruption will also persist, while public trust in law enforcement falters.

3

JUNK FOR JIHAD

Prohibition empowers terrorists and violent insurgents.

STILL STINGING FROM THE SEPTEMBER 11, 2001, TERRORIST assault on the US, the president's Office of National Drug Control Policy kicked off an ad campaign during Super Bowl XXXVI that linked drug users to terrorists.

"This is Dan," started one, following a script borrowed from a children's book. "This is the joint that Dan bought. This is the dealer who sold the joint that Dan bought," and so it goes until Dan's purchase ties him directly to terrorists.[1]

Another ad that ran later in the campaign featured a ghostly girl suddenly appearing in a dark office space: "You killed me," she says twice to a woman at her desk. "There was a bomb. I was going to school." When the woman asks the obvious question ("What does that have to do with me?"), the ghost replies, "You bought drugs. You gave them money. They can't do things like that without money. It's the money." And with that she disappears.[2] Contrived and grotesque as the ad may be, the little girl is correct—it is the money.

But it's not quite so simple.

Good as Gold

Terrorists and insurgents have often resorted to the illegal drug trade to fatten their bank accounts. For those willing to flout the law and take the risks, the economics of prohibition make narcotics absurdly lucrative. And absurd amounts of lucre are the only way backwater Mideast terrorists can afford training nearly two dozen men to commandeer four commercial airliners and fly them into choice targets on US soil. A bake sale won't cut it.[3]

"Mao's dictum, that all power flows from the barrel of a gun, presupposes the means to buy the gun and to pay the soldier who wields it," notes drug historian David T. Courtwright.[4] More than a decade ago, most terrorist groups raised funds by sticking the offering plate under the nose of sympathetic states: Iran, Syria, Libya, Iraq, Cuba, and the Soviet Union before it collapsed. After the Big Slav kicked the bucket, however, the financial springs began to dry up.[5] Nor did it help that—as terrorist organizations became more international in scope, kicking up bigger clouds of dust and garnering the attention of bigger nations better equipped to react with substantial force—the old model of state sponsorship became a liability to the very states signing the checks. "State-sponsors are increasingly difficult to find," explained Raphael Perl, terrorism expert for the Congressional Research Service just months after 9/11. "What world leader in his right mind will risk global sanctions by openly sponsoring al-Qaida or funding it?"[6] Amplify that question tenfold given the fall of both the Taliban and Hussein's regime in Iraq.

So what's a cash-strapped terrorist to do?

Thanks to inflated prices caused by global narcotics prohibition, whoring after state sponsors is no longer needed. Because of black-market profits, growing, marketing, or taxing dope opens insurgents and terrorists to astronomical amounts of loot. Guerrillas in Colombia have used coca and opium to fund their ongoing war with the government. Rebels in Peru have followed the same game plan. Islamist terrorists buy weapons and train men with proceeds from opium traffic. Before the recent rise and fall of the Taliban, Afghani warlords held their power via drug profits. The Taliban itself was no different once it dominated the country. The Northern Alliance, the Taliban's main opposition, played regional power politics with opium profits as well.

Having the muscle and moxie to back up their middle finger to established authority either at home or abroad, terrorists and insurgents naturally excel in illicit markets. Raking in the necessary funds to finance their unlawful activities with the drug trade is just smart business.

And it has been for years. While the difficulty in getting state sponsorship for terrorism has increased in the last fifteen, both the sponsoring states and the terrorists have utilized drugs to fund their schemes for decades.

"In 1958, Fidel Castro stated publicly that he was going to export his revolution beyond Cuba using 'his' methods," writes Rachel Ehrenfeld in *Narco-Terrorism*. "His methods included a twofold purpose for involvement with the narcotics trade: to damage US society by aiding drug traffickers and to finance Marxist terrorists and guerrilla activity in Latin America, including training and arms shipments for insurgency."[7] For many years the success was lackluster. But by the middle seventies, US noses had an increasing itch for cocaine, and Castro's ship—or rather *ships*, scads of them—had finally come in. Allowing coke smugglers en route from Colombia access to Cuban waters, Castro's government offered assistance and protection and garnered half a million dollars per shipment—small change for traffickers hauling blow by the boatload. The money and trade routes were then used by Cuba to shuttle cash and weapons to groups like Colombia's M-19 guerrillas and the fledgling Sandinista regime in Nicaragua.[8] Ironically, the Nicaraguan Contras also used profits from drug trafficking to finance their fight against the Sandinistas.[9]

But perhaps it's not really *that* ironic. As with the Taliban and Northern Alliance's experience, the drug trade is an equal-opportunity employer. If any place proves that, it is Lebanon. In the 1970s and eighties, while civil war raged, every faction—Muslim, Druze, Christian, even outside governments like Syria and organizations like the Popular Front for the Liberation of Palestine—had a hand in the drug trade, mainly cultivating and shipping hashish and heroin.[10] It was the only way to fund the ongoing fight against each other.

One terrorist outfit that profited particularly well from the dope rackets was Yasser Arafat's Palestinian Liberation Organization. Booted out of Jordan in 1970, the PLO holed up in Lebanon until the Israelis flushed them out in 1982. While the PLO did get financing from friendly Arab governments, estimates suggest Arafat and his cronies pulled thrice that subsidy annually from Lebanon's narcotics trade before its expulsion, about three hundred million dollars.[11] The US Justice Department confirmed in 1984 the PLO procured an estimated 40 percent of its light weaponry by trading hash, heroin, or morphine base.[12] After getting the bum's rush from Israel, the PLO increased its dependency on drug money, its treasury chief going so far as to say in a 1983 emergency meeting in Algiers, "the entire future of the PLO operation for liberation may hinge on our exporting more drugs throughout the world."[13]

Given this history, it should not be surprising that the Taliban and its most notorious ally, Osama bin Laden, would prosper from the trade.

Flower Power

In 1979 Soviet tank treads cracked the parched earth of Afghanistan as the Russian army marched in to occupy. While the Afghanis attempted to fight them off, Soviet money and military might far out-muscled the Mujaheddin. How was this ragtag militia, barely a week removed from the middle ages, supposed to fend off a global superpower? With flowers. The Mujaheddin took to cultivating opium poppies and funded their war effort with the proceeds of opium, morphine base, and heroin sales. The US certainly helped out—giving the Afghanis Stinger missiles and other forms of support—but the brave warriors could not have sent the Bear home bellowing without smack.

They kept going even after the Soviets pulled out. The money was just too good to let ground go fallow. British journalist James Meek does the math: "The seven kilos of [opium] seed required to sow a single hectare cost a million Afghanis, about £13. That hectare would be expected to produce roughly 10 kilos of khanka, the raw material from which heroin is made. Each kilo sells for up to 2m Afghanis. In other words, from planting in January to harvesting in July, £13 has become about £260."[14] Who's going to return to wheat with payoffs like that? "Ever since 1980, all the Mujaheddin warlords had used drug money to help fund their military campaigns and line their own pockets," writes journalist Ahmed Rashid in his acclaimed history, *Taliban*. "Publicly they refused to admit that they indulged in drug trafficking, but always blamed their Mujaheddin rivals for doing so. But none had ever been so brazen, and honest, in declaring their lack of intention to control drugs as the Taliban."[15]

More than a lack of intention to control, as the Taliban pressed its rule across the region in the middle-to-late 1990s, it began to actively profit from the trade, exacting up to a 20 percent tax on loads of opium.[16] Considering in 1999 Afghanistan produced more than 70 percent of the world's opium, the take must have been substantial. According to Congressional Task Force on Terrorism and Unconventional Warfare director Yossef Bodansky, the Taliban's estimated total annual income from the drug trade tallied eight billion dollars.[17] Even assuming that figure is grossly inflated, and some might suggest it is, the reality is that the Taliban was making a fair piece with poppies.[18]

Red flags might fly here. One would think that Islamic law—and the Taliban were sticklers for it—forbids profits from such nefarious deeds. Not a problem. As Shirley MacLaine tells Clint Eastwood in *Two Mules for Sister Sara*, given special circumstances, "the Lord grants dispensation."

"Specific fatwas from Islamist luminaries authorize these highly irregular, seemingly un-Islamic activities because they also contribute to the destruction of Western society," explains Bodansky. "The Sunni Islamist fatwas are based on and derived from earlier rulings of the higher Shiite courts issued in connection with operations of [Hezbollah] and Iranian intelligence. The logic of these activities was elucidated in the mid-1980s in the [Hezbollah]'s original fatwa on the distribution of drugs: 'We are making these drugs for Satan—America and the Jews. If we cannot kill them with guns, we will kill them with drugs.'"[19]

All well and good, but there was one immediate problem for the Taliban: Leader Mullah Mohammad Omar—Sheikh Smack—was not much of a money wiz. Rashid points out that Omar was known to run the Taliban's finances out of tin chests stuffed with cash under his bed.[20] To sort out that kind of money a person needs someone who can manage it beyond the mattress. Fortunately for Omar, Osama bin Laden was around. Bodansky notes that bin Laden administered the drug profits, "laundering them through the Russian Mafia—in return for a commission of between 10 and 15 percent, which provides an annual income of about a billion dollars."[21]

Bin Laden had other investments to be sure, but his narcodollars were vital in financing al-Qaida, and so was the Taliban's protection and support of his activities. As Rashid notes, bin Laden's terrorist organization "could not have spent the years of planning and organization that went into the [September 11] attacks without safe sanctuary where everything it needed was available—training, funding, communications, and inspiration."[22] Thanks to robust profits from the heroin trade, the Taliban became that sanctuary, a hub and haven for international terrorists bent on havoc and the destruction of the US and its interests.

While the Taliban is now mostly an unpleasant memory and al-Qaida's staging ground in Afghanistan is kaput, bin Laden's operatives and those from other Mideast terrorist shops are still afoot in the world and funding their ploys with drug money.

As of December 2002, DEA was investigating more than forty domestic drug cases in which officials believed proceeds were filtered back to Islamic terrorists.[23] In November 2002, US officials announced that they foiled a drugs-for-weapons scheme hatched by an American citizen and two Pakistanis. According to the indictment, the plan was to swap six hundred kilos of heroin and five metric tons of hashish for

Stinger antiaircraft missiles, which they intended to sell to members of al-Qaida. The trouble for these fellows was that they were unwittingly talking to the FBI and their discussions were being taped.[24]

Similarly, a series of drug raids in early 2002 by the DEA resulted in evidence pointing to Middle East men in the US smuggling huge loads of pseudoephedrine (for cooking methamphetamine) and funneling the funds back to the Middle East, where some of the money ended up in the hands of Iran-based terrorist organization Hezbollah.[25]

With the push by the federal government to put the kibosh on bogus charities and front companies, drugs' role in keeping extremists in the black is increasing. "Because there is pressure on the traditional funding sources . . . pressure on the money flowing to these groups, that leaves them to be entrepreneurs in how they will come up with the money for the different [terrorist] cells," said then-DEA chief Asa Hutchinson in late 2002. That, said Hutchinson, leads terrorists directly to illegal drugs. "That is the evidence we see and the trend that we see."[26]

And the trend can be seen all over, including our hemisphere. "One of the biggest bastions of terrorism is not a world away," says US Senator Zell Miller. "A two-hour flight south from Miami will land you in Colombia, the most dangerous and terroristic country in the world."[27]

Coke Central

"The political setting in Colombia is extraordinarily complex," explains the Cato Institute's Ted Galen Carpenter, which is too polite an appraisal. Colombia is a train wreck masquerading as a country, a 440,000-square-mile disaster with a national anthem. Carpenter is spot-on in explaining why: "[T]he government in Bogotá is involved in a struggle with no fewer than four factions. Explicitly arrayed against the government are two radical leftist insurgent movements, the Revolutionary Armed Forces of Colombia (FARC) and the National Liberation Army (ELN). Both have been designated as terrorist groups by the US State Department. Violently opposed to FARC and

ELN are the right-wing paramilitaries, most notably the United Self-Defense Forces of Colombia (AUC), also now designated by the State Department as a terrorist organization. . . . And finally there are the various narcotrafficking organizations," which Carpenter notes swing both ways, helping the insurgents or the paramilitaries depending which advances their business more.[28]

The important thing to the US government is not that Colombia is a piece of taffy with too many pullers; for Uncle Sam, the big concern is that Colombia is the heart of this hemisphere's cocaine and (since the mid-1990s) heroin trade. Coca and poppies are grown in the Andes Mountains, processed in Colombian labs, and disbursed to traffickers who smuggle it into the US, straight to the beckoning bloodstreams of willing Americans.

To halt this pursuit of chemical happiness, the US government has determined that it must go to the source and stanch the flow of illicit junk by convincing and coercing the Colombians to cut drug production. This is not an easy task—to some extent FARC, ELN, and AUC are all dependent on dope proceeds to pay for their various insurgencies and counterinsurgencies. They do have other means of raising money, to be sure: AUC extorts money from wealthy ranchers, promising to help them protect their properties from the *communistas*. ELN and FARC have been adept at lucrative kidnappings (thousands of abductees a year) and extortions of their own, which they call "war taxes," laying levies on bananas, petroleum, and whatever else people want to get to market—including coca. But, however diversified their portfolios, it is here in drugs where serious money can be made.

Coke's Revolutionaries

FARC is the largest of the guerrilla organizations and controls a rough and rural area in southeastern Colombia nearly the size of Switzerland (sixteen thousand square miles known as "FARC-landia"). FARC has been around in one form or another since 1949 and today boasts as many as eighteen thousand members. It started as a populist movement geared toward land reform, filling the chasm between the nation's rich and poor. From those early years, it took on a more Marxist flavor and, eventually, a terrorist one.

Instead of merely duking it out with government troops in traditional insurgency battles, FARC has led massacres of farmers not friendly to its cause, in at least one case hacking the victims to death with machetes; hijacked a Colombian senator's plane, kidnapping the senator; led a "large-scale mortar attack" on the Presidential Palace where the president was being inaugurated in 2002 (twenty one nearby residents were killed in the attack); and kidnapped and murdered three Americans in 1999.[29] Since 1980, FARC rebels have murdered at least thirteen US citizens.[30]

Involvement in the drug trade began by taxing it and offering protection from the government, establishing as early as 1982 a per-gram fee on coca-processing laboratories.[31] By then, subgroups in the FARC organization already had protection deals with members of the Medellín Cartel. A 1983 CIA intelligence estimate reported, "These guerrilla groups initially avoided all connections with narcotics growers and traffickers, except to condemn the corrupting influence of drugs on Colombian society. Now, however, several have developed active links with the drug trade, others extort protection money from the traffickers, and some apparently use profits from drugs to buy arms." Being the good socialists they were, FARC rebels not only taxed the coca trade, but as the CIA noted, "in some areas established quotas . . . wages and rules for workers, producers and owners of the coca fields."[32]

Over time, FARC's involvement became more pronounced, levying heavier taxes, additionally taxing the chemicals used to manufacture cocaine from the raw coca. Says Robin Kirk, "Soon they started buying *base* [the intermediary between coca and cocaine] themselves and sold it directly to traffickers."[33] Carpenter notes evidence exists that FARC and ELN are even more intimately involved. "The strongest evidence emerged from raids conducted by Colombian military forces in early

2001 that uncovered documents, eyewitness accounts, and financial receipts showing that the rebels were directly engaged in the production and export of cocaine."[34]

The close involvement pays off. US olfactories hoover up nearly forty billion dollars worth of coke annually. Between stateside septums and jungle-hunkered insurgents, there are many middlemen, but the take-home for Colombia's terrorist organizations is huge nonetheless. In the first year of the Reagan administration, FARC's member role tallied about one thousand. By the time Bill Clinton was cleaning Bob Dole's clock in 1996, FARC's ranks were fifteen times larger.[35] Its troops were well armed, sporting uniforms, and, in 2000, earning more each month than members of the Colombian army.[36] According to INTERPOL, just in its tax-slapping FARC pulls twenty dollars per kilo of *base*, thirty dollars per kilo of the fully refined stuff, plus twenty-five hundred dollars every time a trafficker wants to use a landing strip to fly blow either in or out at whatever stage of refinement.[37]

Adding more spice to the salsa, the Colombian government has arrested three members of the Irish Republican Army and confirmed the presence of Hamas and Hezbollah terrorists in the country, collaborating with FARC.[38]

Coke's Counterrevolutionaries

Battling FARC and company is the United Self-Defense Forces of Colombia, the loose-knit organization of right-wing paramilitaries founded as a direct counterforce to the Marxist guerrillas. But while they do not hold hands when it comes to politics, FARC and AUC do have something in common: AUC is up to its eyeteeth in the drug trade.

According to a confidential 2003 assessment prepared for the Colombian president Alvaro Uribe, "it is impossible to differentiate between the self-defense groups and the narco-trafficking organizations."[39] The *Washington Post*, which obtained a copy of the report, explained the way AUC's "budgeting" process works: "Through a handful of drug kingpins posing as paramilitary commanders, they control about 40 percent of Colombia's drug trafficking. The AUC 'sells its franchise' to regional drug traffickers, who rely on the group for security in exchange for a cut of profits. . . . [A]s much as 80 percent of the AUC's funding comes from drug trafficking."[40] According to the report, AUC's interests are geared more toward the advancement of its drug business than its fight against Marxist insurgents.

The prospect of fifteen thousand heavily armed combatants mainly concerned with advancing their interest in the dope trade is one about which the US government is less than keen. Before the month closed on the September 11 attacks, the Justice Department launched "Operation White Terror" and later uncovered evidence that AUC was cooking a deal "to trade $25 million cash and cocaine for weapons, including shoulder-fired antiaircraft missiles; 9,000 assault rifles; grenade launchers and nearly 300,000 grenades; 300 pistols; and about 53 million rounds of ammunition."[41]

The principal leader of AUC, Carlos Castano, is not secretive about the self-defense forces' drug-running: "Listen, that's the nature of the economy here. The FARC finance themselves with the same money. So I have to take their sources away."[42] It's just a question of squeezing out the competition.

Fighting Back

Naturally, the American government has been less than pleased with the troops supposedly battling narcoterrorists, being *narcos* themselves. The response to the problem has been to wring more tax money out of the federal budget and send it to the Colombian government so it will no longer rely on AUC forces to help battle the Marxist insurgents. President Clinton got the ball rolling with Plan Colombia, an outlay of $1.3 billion in military equipment and training designed to weaken the guerillas by decimating the drug crops from which they gain their funds. By summer 2003, the funds tallied $2.5 billion.

But for all the money dumped down this Andean-sized rat hole, success has been meager if not utterly elusive. First, there was the simple fact that drug warriors failed to get any traction; months after dropping the first hunk of funds into Colombia, crop eradication efforts had failed to budge the street price of cocaine. Had the efforts been effective, the price tag on a noseful of coke would have risen. It didn't. One possible reason: DEA vastly underestimated the amount of cocaine Colombia could produce. The feds figured up to 580 tons per year, but while that total is *double* what Colombia could manage in 1995, a report from the UN indicated that production capacity might really be closer to 800 tons.[43] No wonder antidrug forces found it difficult to make a dent.

Second, efforts to get locals to grow alternate crops have been a wash. Few other crops pay like coca. Bananas can't match blow for bucks; neither can coffee, rubber, corn, or much else. Depending on the licit crop, farmers can make ten times the lucre growing coca. Only opium poppies compete with those numbers.[44] By any measure, coca is an ideal crop for poor Andean farmers. Once planted, a coca bush will mature in just eighteen months, pumping out maximum yields in about three years. The bushes thrive in poor soil, provide as many as six harvests a year, and will live a quarter of a century provided they're well tended.[45] Further, with most cash crops, farmers heap up additional expenses just getting the goods to market—a difficult, costly task in the Andes. With coca, farmers report that buyers actually come to them.[46] "The notion that the potential income from bananas, maize, or citrus fruit can compete with the potential income from coca, marijuana, or opium poppies is about as realistic as assuming that a burger flipper at McDonald's can earn as much as a software designer for Microsoft," Carpenter sums up.[47]

Not only are alternate crops bad business for farmers, even with the ever-flowering array of various and sundry subsidies, in some cases alternate crops get poisoned along with coca fields in government spray campaigns. During just one Plan Colombia-sponsored spray campaign, pilots fumigated 9,000 acres of pasture land, nearly 3,000 acres of bananas, 1,300 acres of yucca, and poisoned some 200,000 fish.[48] They have to fly high to avoid guerilla antiaircraft fire, but the higher they go, the worse their aim. The destruction of legitimate crops has frustrated farmers and left them more willing to join organizations like FARC when their livelihoods and even health have been destroyed.

Third, there is the balloon effect. Since government cannot put equal pressure everywhere, when it pushes in one place, the trade expands in others. Like American jobs migrating to countries where the economics produce bigger profits, cocaine producers move to more profitable locales when the squeeze sets in. For instance, by March 2003, US drug czar John Walters was finally able to pronounce a "turning point" in Colombia. Cocaine production was down, according to government figures. But the success was mostly an illusion. While cocaine production was down in Colombia some 15 percent, it was back up in neighboring Bolivia and Peru. Further, it turns out that both Colombia and Peru are planting more productive varieties of coca, which means even though total acreage may be down, actual amounts of cocaine produced may increase.[49] And poppies have increased in Peru as well.[50]

In the end, Plan Colombia's success is a shell game. The "pea" has not been eradicated, it has simply migrated to more profitable environs, like Peru—where only a few years ago authorities were gushing with enthusiasm about declining coca production as the trade simply shifted to Colombia.

Rock the Kasbah

Afghanistan is in the same bind. While the Taliban is now gone and al-Qaida is limping along in other corners of the globe, the poppies are back and thriving. "If there was serious government pressure, the peasants would stop growing poppies, especially if they were given free fertilizers and free seeds for other crops," said one heroin smuggler from Kabul in November 2001—but then thought better of it: "Then again, the peasants might choose not to. When they're earning so much from the poppies, it's not very likely. People will still grow poppies in secret. People get richer quicker that way."[51]

Sure enough, in 2002, opium production jumped to thirty-four hundred metric tons, "making Afghanistan the source of three-fourths of the world's opium. . . ."[52] Last year was no different, except bigger. According to UN estimates, in 2003 production jumped to thirty-six hundred metric tons.[53] Despite the presence of thousands of US-led troops, UN figures show that poppies are being grown in twenty-eight of thirty-two provinces.[54] And the heroin stores created from these crops are tremendous.

In a January 2004 armed raid in Istanbul, Turkish police seized a solid ton of the stuff. Stuck between Europe and Asia, Turkey is the key trafficking route for heroin from the East, especially Afghanistan, and evidence indicated that the huge stockpile came from Afghanistan and Pakistan.[55] The same month, authorities in Pakistan found another 1.6 metric tons of heroin stashed in a cave near the Afghan border. From Pakistan, the drugs would have been smuggled through Iran on their way to Europe.[56]

And what's good for European junkies is good for Afghani farmers.

Like coca in the Andes, poppies out-compete alternative crops in a big way. In the mountainous regions, the hardscrabble terrain is well suited to poppies and little else.[57] They require less water than wheat, fetch twenty times the income of cotton, and because of opium's indefinite shelf-life, growers can either harvest and sell the opium right there in the fields or save it for a rainy day.[58]

In the province of Konar, the agriculture ministry has offered incentives to farmers who pull up their poppy crops—$1,625 per acre. Even someone who flunked Econ 101 can see the problem here: poppies pull in about $20,000 per acre, not that such numbers stop some from taking the government money and continuing to grow dope on the side.[59] Everybody's doing it. In the village of Jata, even the local mullah has a crop.[60]

Bankrolling Terror

Before 9/11, the various efforts to stamp out drugs and terrorism were seen as separate ventures. But the moment the al-Qaida terror fleet shattered our delusions, we saw the two for what they were—sometimes isolated, other times symbiotic scofflaws. "We have learned, and we have demonstrated, that drug traffickers and terrorists work out of the same jungle; they plan in the same cave and they train in the same desert," said former DEA chief Asa Hutchinson.[61]

The reason for this close relationship—as with almost everything in the drug trade—boils down to money. "Drugs are the currency of terrorists," in the words of one US attorney from Texas.[62]

And lest there be any doubt what that means in the practical world, North Carolina congressman Cass Ballenger cuts directly to the chase: "Americans must recognize that every time they buy cocaine or heroin, they are directly funding terrorists."[63] That has been the government line since shortly after September 11. As we all know, thanks to ONDCP's Super Bowl commercials, every heroin fix is a guaranteed deposit in First Terrorist Trust. But while many of the dots are there to connect, in the final analysis, the fundamental argument is bunk for one simple reason: Uncle Sam's finger is pointing the wrong direction. He's his own best suspect.

As with crime and corruption, the problem with the relationship between drugs and terrorism is not drugs. It's the *war* on drugs. The illicit industry created by prohibition provides opportunities for terrorists and insurgents to get involved at various stages of drug production and make money otherwise unavailable to them. FARC wouldn't be able to offer protection to coca-growers if the government were not coming after them with US-backed troops and materiel. Likewise, al-Qaida would have a hard time pulling in multimillions of dollars a year overseeing grain production; it is because Europe and the United States go to extreme lengths to keep their citizens' circulatory systems heroin-free that opium poppies are so lucrative for terrorist organizations.

Ditto for coca. It is even the same with cannabis in places like Morocco, Mexico, and Colombia.[64]

Currently, the rhetoric about terrorism and drugs comes down to fighting two wars: one on bad people, the other on bad plants. Few are apparently ready to admit that by ceasing the war on the bad plants, the bad people will lose an important source of funding for their bad operations. The flip side, of course, is that because of prohibition they can fund those operations, making the war on drugs and our government (even if unwittingly) instrumental in bankrolling terrorists.[65]

Says President Bush, "It's so important for Americans to know that the traffic in drugs finances the work of terror, sustaining terrorists, that terrorists use drugs profits to fund their cells to commit acts of murder. If you quit drugs, you join the fight against terror in America."[66] Given the economics here, it makes much more sense to reply, "If you quit prohibiting drugs and artificially driving up their prices, you join the fight against terror in America."

Destabilization

Some may object that terrorists' involvement in drugs goes beyond simply financing. Like Hezbollah's dope-slinging efforts in the 1980s, the terrorists are, so the argument goes, using drugs to destabilize the country, as a "weapon of mass destruction."[67]

Certainly, drug abuse does hurt many Americans, destroys families, and ruins lives. But the notion of the widespread nature of this menace is often a reflection more of our fear of drugs than reality. America did not have federal control of narcotics until 1914 with the passage of the Harrison Act. Similarly, marijuana was not illegal till 1937. Somehow the country went from newly liberated colonies to industrial powerhouse and world power all while dope was readily available at the corner—you guessed it—*drug* store. At various times and in various places many of these substances may not have been available, true, but one potentially destructive substance has been ubiquitous at all points in

American history: alcohol. And the time it most destabilized the nation was during the thirteen years it was *illegal*.

The destabilization argument is a desperately flung red herring. Drugs do not destabilize—at least, nowhere near as badly as prohibition does. As we saw in the first chapter, it creates crime and violence. As we saw in the second, it corrupts the very public servants we trust to protect our lives and property. As we will see in coming chapters, it wreaks havoc on the Constitution and traditional American liberties, provides government the right to rob people of their property, militarizes the police, and expands the size and scope of the state to frightening proportions.

If our goal is to defend Americans against terrorism, we're barking up the wrong coca bush. Our efforts must be directed toward scrapping drug prohibition.

4

SMUGGLERS' PARADISE

Prohibition doesn't deter trafficking; it pays the freight.

ANYBODY CAN DO IT," SAYS ZACHARY SWAN, AN EXTREMELY
successful smuggler, who before his bust in the late 1970s concocted
schemes galore to get cocaine and high-grade pot past the detection
of US Customs. With the stuff tightly compressed, he'd pack his
Peruvian nose candy in decorative rolling pins, carvings of various
Catholic saints, hand-wrought tribal heads, whatever worked. And
most things did work for Swan. He used the mail, cars, luggage, you
name it. There are "a million ways. . . . If you've got any brains at all,
smuggling is easy."[1]

Things have changed little since Swan's day, except today there are
more ways than a million, a fact that spells nothing but disaster for the
ongoing effort to keep drugs out of the United States.

Drug Warriors' Terminal Handicap

The reason drug warriors never really get the upper hand in the drug
war is that they are fighting entrepreneurs with bureaucrats. "The profit
opportunities created by prohibition will result in new methods of production, transportation, inventory, distribution, and marketing," says

61

economist Mark Thornton of the smuggler's advantage.[2] Such is not the case for bureaucrats, who are guided by rules, not profit margins. Some of the few exceptions exist solely because the bureaucrats and their enforcers turn noticeable profits—e.g., traffic tickets.

And what of the emotional capital of a job well done, making the busts and jailing the traffickers? Even the personal satisfaction many drug-law enforcers receive has a hard time competing with the deluge of dollars through which their adversaries wade after a short day's work. Naturally, some small-fry runners make small potatoes, but compared to the alternatives, often the money is nothing worth frowning about.

The ready and robust cash encourages drug smugglers to innovate and take risks. This keeps effective drug runners two steps ahead of the police, and by nabbing the second stringers, cops serve in a capacity for which the others are surely thankful: weeding out meddlesome competition. Yes, there are big busts. Yes, cartels are broken by diligent and longsuffering law enforcement. Yes, the guys in blue give it their all. But at the end of the day, the efforts amount to little genuine good.

The street price of drugs has been in steady decline over the years, regardless of major pinches. The purity is up. Some heroin dealers even microbrand their product, selling smack in color-coded vials, each hue indicating a different purity and price. Some vials are targeted specifically at upper-middleclass teen users, the heroin so pure it can be snorted.[3] When dealers sound more like business-school graduates than hustlers and brand their product like desktop PCs and designer-name chef's knives—all despite the best efforts of police—perhaps people should begin questioning whether those efforts actually serve any use.

Ain't No Ocean Wide Enough

Any time the law forbids people from getting what they want or taxes it beyond what they are willing to pay, the smuggler leaves a cold seat in the unemployment office. The job can be as simple as ordering wine and cigarettes online to skirt state tobacco taxes and liquor regulations, simple and hands-on enough for one to do the job himself. But some-times the goods to be smuggled require tactics more swashbuckling, risky, and demanding.

In 2000, Colombian authorities found a hundred-foot submarine under construction in a warehouse in the Andes. Why the vessel was being built so far from the coast is a mystery, but when completed, the twenty-five million dollar vessel would have been able to haul ten tons of narcotics. Colombians had used smaller minisubs in the past, but this was a big step up. With its double hull, protected propeller, and diving stabilizers, the sub was designed to descend as deep as 325 feet, which according to Captain Ismael Idrobo, projects director for Colombian Naval Academy, is deep enough to duck most sonar. The sub could stay at sea nearly two weeks and travel some two thousand nautical miles. "The guy who designed it knew exactly what he was doing," said Idrobo. "It took imagination and a lot of experience."[4] Elsewhere Idrobo admitted, "It was shocking to me to see how much technology illicit money can buy."[5]

Even worse for drug warriors, clues onsite tipped authorities to a long-suspected relationship between drug runners and the Russian mob. "That partnership worries security experts, who fear Colombian drug traffickers may be getting more than hardware from their Russian friends," explains *Los Angeles Times* reporter Juanita Darling. "They could be buying intelligence and counterintelligence services from spies who learned their trade in the KGB. . . ."[6] Colombians had tried to pur-chase an even bigger used Russian sub a few years before. The deal fell through, but the plan was to use the torpedo tubes to blast containers of drugs to the surface; traffickers would then rendezvous in speedboats and take them ashore.

Traffickers have made good use of semisubmersibles. Small enough to evade radar detection and so low to the surface that a difficult visual sight-ing is the best authorities can muster, they are virtually invisible. As reporter Paul Kaihla notes, the minisubs in this narconavy are sometimes used to "ferry drugs . . . to larger ships hauling cargoes of hazardous waste, in which the insulated bales of cocaine are stashed." Because of their dangerous cargo, these ships are rarely inspected.[7]

Drug runners are also running circles around interceptors on the surface.

Traffickers have developed boats they call "go-fasts," which fitted with multiple motors can skip across the water at fifty-five-plus mph and carry as much as 2.5 tons of cocaine and heroin. Fiberglass hulls make them hard to see with radar, and dull-blue paint makes them nearly invisible to the naked eye. "You can be in a customs launch, and the boat you're waiting to intercept can pass you 50 meters [150 feet] away," complained a Colombian intelligence officer. "You can hear it, but you don't see a thing." Once out of the reach of authorities, "Depending on their drugs' destination, smugglers dump them on an isolated beach, hand them over to local fishermen, or leave them floating at sea for a later pickup. The contraband is then shipped to the US mainland in freight containers, or carried on small planes or commercial airline flights."[8] Sometimes a boat and its crew will sit out in the open water for days, hiding under sea-blue tarps to avoid government detection from the air, waiting for a trafficker's plane to drop water-tight containers of coke nearby.[9]

The job is certainly dangerous. Traveling in an open boat with twelve-foot waves is enough to make a grown man soil his seat. But, as a mechanic of the boats, whose own brother died piloting one, told a reporter, "You have to die sometime. And for that much money, it's worth the risk." How much? Ten grand for a long trip (accounts do vary here; one *Washington Post* story claims a team of two or three go-fast boaters can make $250,000 for a successful voyage). "In this town of ramshackle houses, it is easy to imagine why a boatman might swap shrimp fishing for drug running," the reporter concluded.[10]

This puts the law at a big disadvantage, as megatrafficker Luis "Kojak" García explained some years back:

There are places [along the Florida coast] where the water is two feet deep and less, and the channels that you have to use are unmarked. Now, a good doper knows those channels because he studies them. He's also making ten, twelve, fifteen thousand dollars—it depends on the load—for four hours' work, and for that kind of money he's expected to take the risk of getting it wrong. The guy chasing him is making maybe a hundred bucks a shift, on which he's going to pay tax, and if he hits that sandbank at sixty miles an hour he isn't going to collect his pension because he's going to be dead. Now, you're in the Customs' boat heading for that sandbank: Which way do you want to push the throttle?[11]

It's those sort of incentives that keep traffickers ahead of the anti-narcotics game—not only in willingness to take risks and push the limits, but because of the big loot, also in upgrading the tools needed to pull it off successfully day in and out. "The drug smugglers make so much money, they are going to be on the cutting edge of technology," says a US official involved in antinarcotics efforts. "Whatever's the biggest and the fastest, they're going to have it—before we do."[12] Advanced spy and encryption technology, communications, cutting-edge radar tracking systems—drug runners use everything they can to stay out of arm's reach.[13]

Under Your Nose

While not as romantic as speedboats and submarines, simply stashing and disguising drugs inside things is common and profitable if done well.

There's the longstanding favorite: false-bottomed thises and thats. Smugglers also stash items in labeled containers to throw officials off the scent—baby food, canned tomatoes, etc. Often just a few containers in an entire load will have the drugs, making it virtually impossible to detect. Other times it will be part of a person's attire—sewn inside a jacket or brassiere seam, for instance. The heels of shoes are popular. Ditto for umbrella handles, books, pens, medicine bottles, and toys. One guy tried stashing pot in a hollowed-out wooden monkey.[14]

Food works well, too—heroin hidden inside fake pears, little lumps of pressed marijuana disguised as almonds, prescription drugs secreted away in Oriental pastries, and cocaine stuffed inside papier-mâché avocadoes, cocktail sausages, and hallowed-out passion fruit. "We don't know the exact technique used," said a police spokesman about the last. "You couldn't tell the [fruit] had been damaged." Authorities only became suspicious because they thought the fruit looked "unusually ripe."[15]

Smugglers sometimes hide behind phony business logos—or rather, genuine ones. Border Patrol has to keep a close eye on utility and delivery trucks, falsely labeled and lugging drugs inside.[16] In Britain where tobacco taxes are preposterously high, smuggling cigarettes is a multibillion dollar industry—one known for subterfuge and craft. Smugglers bringing an illicit load from Eastern Europe, for instance, utilized a set of hydraulics to hide cigarettes between the body panels of a delivery truck. When officials figured out the trick, they flipped the switch to watch the outer shell of the vehicle rise five feet and display its freight of forbidden fags. "It was like something from a James Bond film," said a customs spokesman. The price tag was sexier still—£1 million for the single load.[17] In 2003, pot smugglers were busted using a stolen late model Dodge Durango and Ford Expedition to sneak almost nineteen hundred pounds of pot into the US. What made the run unique was that the vehicles were near-perfect Border Patrol dummies, decked out with the BP logo, paint stripes, and even government license plates.[18]

Diplomatic couriers can also be successful drug couriers. The sealed pouch is a hot potato for anyone not charged with carrying it, and the immunity they possess can be an emboldening thing, like a stiff drink before a fist fight. The fights rarely come, of course, as the pouches are not inspected by Customs; couriers are considered to be acting on official business. Sometimes they most definitely are not. In 1985 the chancellor of the Belgian embassy in New Delhi, India, was busted at La Guardia International Airport with ten kilos of heroin worth some forty million dollars in his official pouch.[19] "At one time . . . it was such a widespread method of avoiding detection that customs officers in both

Europe and the USA wryly suggested that the initials CD (meaning *Corps Diplomatique*) should stand for *Contrebandier Distingué*," says opium historian Martin Booth.[20]

Positions of power are easily abused to smuggle. According to the DEA, a Saudi prince used his personal plane to smuggle more than two tons of cocaine from Venezuela to Paris. Taking the two thousand kilo total and using a wholesale figure of sixteen thousand dollars a kilo, that makes the prince's load worth thirty-two million dollars. Once it's divvied up among street-level dealers, bump that to two hundred million dollars. The DEA says the prince, who is supposedly not in the line of succession, met with smugglers in 1998 and agreed to fly the load the next year. Because of his office and position, it seemed as if things would go off without a hitch. It didn't. But though he was nabbed in the end, more than half the load had already been distributed. French and Spanish authorities pinched only the remaining nine hundred-odd kilos.[21]

Little Big Small-Timers

On the flip side of such a massive load, because of heroin's high price relative to its volume, secreting away even tiny amounts can be very profitable. Inside earrings, under the stones of rings, inside hearing aides—the places a few pinches of powder can hide are endless. Booth mentions a case where two-ply postcards were separated, a small amount of heroin placed in-between, and the plies reglued—post office, at your service, Mr. Smuggler.[22] This also means that smugglers can more easily hide drugs in or on their own persons. People strap drugs to their thighs, under their arms, and between their butt cheeks; women strap packets of drugs under their breasts.

Some people actually lug drugs internally to get their dope through airports, into prisons, across borders, wherever it needs to go. "Stuffers" shove "chargers" full of heroin up their rectums or—in our equal opportunity age—vaginas and remove them at their destinations. "Swallowers" go the opposite route and ingest plastic or rubber packets of dope to be excreted upon arrival. The average load is between seventy and eighty packets, the big concern for the courier being that a balloon may rupture and kill him.[23] A massive influx of cocaine or heroin into one's system is not a happy way to die. Still, considering the payoff, it's worth the risk for many.

Hair is also a popular place to stash. Contraband is hidden under wigs, heroin rubbed into hair to be shampooed out later. The latter works especially well with towhead blondes or people with gray hair. If some of it shakes out, it may look like nothing more than dander.

Dissolving drugs—mainly heroin and coke—is also an oft-used tactic. With cocaine, for instance, the drug will be dissolved in a tub full of alcohol. An absorbent item, e.g., a suit or a blanket, will sop up the drug-laced liquid dry and be ready to have the drugs removed once safely across. One smuggler was able to carry an entire kilo of heroin this way in his jeans and shirts.[24] Another tried getting ninety opium-soaked tablecloths through customs at O'Hare in Chicago— once processed into heroin, the load would have been worth five million dollars.[25] While it can be successful, the problem with this method is that the smell can sometimes tip the smuggler's hand.

Thanks to one method, smell is not a problem at all—neither is a customs agent staring straight at the substance. Cocaine traffickers have figured out a way to put their stash right out in the open, disguised as spas, auto-body parts, toys, anything really. The trick is to mix powder cocaine with plastic or fiberglass resin. Turning the combo into, as the DEA calls it, a "$1,000,000 bathtub" or any other commercial good is as simple as dropping it into a mold. Presto! Odorless, inconspicuous cocaine. This is an improvement of an older tactic of passing off molded or carved chunks of opium as *objets d'art*. Since one cannot readily snort a bathtub, once across the border the items are chemically treated and the cocaine extracted, ready to be sold for heaps and hoovered in kind. Better still for smugglers, "there is no way an enforcement agent can deduce the presence of the drug without chemically testing each fiberglass item."[26]

Because of how the 2000 movie *Traffic* treats this innovation, it may come across as relatively new, but in 1992 authorities found smugglers made portable dog kennels out of the stuff.[27] So it's been in use at least a decade. There's no way of knowing, but the DEA figures "tons" of nose candy makes it into the US this way, and with NAFTA-encouraged trade between North and South, it will only increase.

Run for the Border

America shares some two thousand miles of border with Mexico, more than five thousand with Canada. There are hundreds of official crossing points, which even before NAFTA processed some five hundred million legal US entries every year.[28]

High-grade pot from Canada, "BC Bud" as it's known, is carried across the border in the boots of automobiles and hiked overland by backpackers. "Smugglers are using kayaks, horse trailers, Army trucks and even a cage holding a live bear to sneak it into the United States," writes Shannon McCaffrey for the *St. Paul Pioneer Press*. "They tuck packages into fish meal or coffee to avoid drug-sniffing dogs. Private planes dip into US airspace and drop hockey bags filled with the stuff to couriers waiting in the woods on ATVs."[29] In British Columbia, the trade is estimated at $2.8 billion annually—making it more valuable than legitimate crops grown in the area, all of them combined, in fact. And given that a pound of BC Bud goes for upwards of six thousand dollars by the time it migrates to Southern California (a price comparable to the same weight of cocaine), it is not surprising to hear that the trade is escalating greatly.

Because of its quality, the DEA says Canadian-grown weed can be twenty times more expensive than the stuff stamped "hecho en Mexico." But what our Southern neighbors lack in quality, they make up for in quantity. Using US Customs data, McCaffrey points out that while in fiscal year 2002 authorities snagged nearly twenty thousand pounds of pot coming from Canada, they got their hands on 1.2 million pounds coming from Mexico.[30]

It's no mystery as to why. One crossing alone, definitely the single biggest, San Ysidro in San Diego, California, racks up forty million served each year. The task of processing all these people is mind-boggling. "Think of screening the population of Spain in a traffic jam, every year," writes columnist George Will.[31] Across the twenty-four lanes that connect Tijuana with Southern California, thousands of cars make their way into America every day, some with drugs. The biggest fear is the drug-sniffing dogs, which have sense of smell better than the mother of a teenage boy—some seven hundred times more acute than the rest of us. On a good day, they can sniff drugs vacuum-sealed, hidden in fish, submerged in oil, you name it. Of course the dogs don't get a chance to get close and personal with every vehicle. There are just too many. Nixon once tried carefully checking every car coming in. It wasn't just a speed bump in cross-border traffic. It was a wall. The border ground to a halt and virtually shut down. It didn't take long to give up on the idea of 100 percent inspection—can't be done.

Intelligence plays a big part in foiling Customs. "With stakes so high, smuggling syndicates go to great lengths to keep tabs on what is going on at San Ysidro; when, for instance, shifts are ending, how many rovers are deployed on a given day, which canine units are employed."[32] Remember, they don't have to get many cars through—it's just a question of timing. Standing on the Mexico side with binocs and cell phones, traffickers help guide cars into lanes where they think they will fare best.[33]

What plays the biggest part, however, are drivers willing to simply pull up, look the inspector in the face, and smile like they don't have ten kilos of cocaine under their seat. "We get up to 60,000 cars a day, and you have to keep in mind that 99 percent of the passengers are honest travelers," says supervisory Customs inspector Robert Hood.[34] Customs cannot check everyone. They even have time limits on how long they can hold up traffic.[35] "So the bad guys come straight at us. And if we intercept a few loads, that's just a tax they factor into the cost of doing business."[36] Things in this situation couldn't be worse for officials: Let's say nine out of ten couriers make it through, which considering the interdiction stats is about right. Because of the big number of couriers, the odds are good some will get caught, but for the individual, the odds are good it won't be him. And for the drug organization coordinating all the runs, a few busts is just part of the game—a tax on the trade. No biggie.

Thanks to the Bush administration, working to comply with the NAFTA, things promise to get even more interesting. While striving on one end to batten down the hatches in the effort to protect the US from terrorism, President George Bush has also labored to open the borders further—namely signing legislation in late 2002 allowing Mexican commercial trucks greater access to US highways. How many trucks are we talking about? Right now, some fifty-seven thousand tractor-trailer rigs enter the US daily—only some of which can be personally checked for drugs.[37] "President Bush has made good on his commitment to open the border to international trucking and cross-border regular route bus service. This will help increase trade between our countries," said transportation secretary Norman Mineta.[38] Yes it will. No prizes for guessing what kind.

And what about pedestrians? More than twenty thousand flatfoot it across the border *every day* at San Yisdro. Hollow out the soles of your tennies, fill them with heroin, and you can buy not only a new pair of shoes but a new luxury car to match.[39] When Dominic Streatfeild was researching cocaine smuggling at San Ysidro, Customs told him that twelve walkthroughs a day were busted. Could the other 19,988 really be clean, he wondered. He calculated that about twenty cars a day were busted for drugs. What about the other tens of thousands?[40]

Keeping Score

How much do authorities actually snag? In 2002, reporter John Stossel asked then-DEA headman Asa Hutchison the question and got a less than stellar answer. "What we're doing is increasing the risk to the traffickers," said Hutchinson. Stossel's rebound: "Is that a way of saying we don't stop much?"[41]

Yes, according to Hutchinson's own testimony before House Subcommittee on Coast Guard and Maritime Transportation in October 2001, where he was a bit more frank: "Well, in reference to interdiction of assets, the national strategy provides that we should have an 18 percent rate of interdiction. And if you look back in 2000, the seizure rate was 10.6 percent."[42] Hutchinson went on to say that the goal for 2002 was 18 percent as well. Considering the lack of reported whoopee, I'm assuming we struck out again then, too.

The numbers are impossible to figure with any certainty anyway. As many observers have noted, it's not as if smugglers are very scrupulous about filing honest tax returns and reporting their income. Further, no one really knows how much drugs are being produced or moved in the world. But even if we give the government the benefit of the doubt and say it scored its 18 percent goal, do drug warriors actually wake up in the morning and feel good that only 82 percent of drugs are getting in thanks to them?

Pandora's Boxes

Drugs hit US soil by other means as well. Between five and ten thousand pressurized rail tank cars enter the US every day from Mexico; because they are sealed shut and officially accounted for, they go unsearched upon entry. As such, they are natural hiding places for drug shipments and possibly worse things. "These sophisticated and effective terrorist/drug cartel networks have extensive knowledge in how to use North American railway systems to transport whatever they wish," says former Customs special agent Darlene Catalan.[43] Estimates flag between five hundred and one thousand cars as likely holding drugs. In one investigation, Catalan herself uncovered thirty-four kilos of coke and eight thousand pounds of pot from one such car. Worse, the old standby of smugglers, the payoff, seemed part and parcel of Catalan's discovery. She blew the lid on "massive scale" narcotics involvement among Customs agents who were allowing large numbers of these cars to enter the US laden with not-so-goodies.[44]

More than just drugs can enter America stashed in train cars. Sometimes illegal immigrants enter the US amongst goods destined for US markets. In late 2002, eleven decaying bodies thought to be Mexican nationals were found in a grain car in Des Moines, Iowa. The plot probably went awry when the car traveled far beyond the American Southwest and out of the control of the immigrant smugglers, "coyotes," as they're called. With cars en route to Texas, Arizona, New Mexico, and California, keeping track of cargo is a bit more manageable—and if it's drugs, the good thing is that coke and heroin have a longer shelf-life than migrants without adequate water, air, and food.[45]

Mixed in with all the cheap toys, bananas, and dress shirts at the docks are plenty of drugs, as well. In the day of containerized shipping, in which dozens of massive ships bigger than Navy destroyers hit the wharfs with millions of pounds of cargo daily, hiding drugs amongst the legitimate freight is far from unlikely. In fact, given the odds, it is more than likely. "We look at less than two percent," says one high-ranking Customs official.[46] Author Mike Gray notes,

> Los Angeles alone will land 130,000 containers this month. Customs inspectors will examine 400. The other 129,600 will pass through without so much as a tip of the hat. And as this tidal wave of heavy machinery, cameras, car parts, and cuckoo clocks moves off the wharf on endless lines of semitrailers and flatcars, it's worth remembering that the entire annual cocaine supply for the United States would fit in just thirteen of those steel boxes. A year's supply of heroin could be shipped in a single container.[47]

Border Bustle

Beyond the hundred legal points of entry, there are millions of *unofficial* points of entry. America has more than twelve thousand miles of coastline. Fishing boats and other vessels can swing in and drop dope for pickup.

Low-flying planes can dodge radar or duck into the US with little incident. "At one stage," writes Streatfeild, "twenty Mexican drug planes were crashing over the border every month. Not flying, mind, but *crashing*. Twenty! Imagine how many got through."[48] Even after September 11, planes still make runs, even though they don't always have to. Oftentimes pilots will not take the risk of crossing. Instead, they land on the Mexico side and drop off the dope in the desert at a predetermined location. A few guys in a truck will drive across, grab it, and hit the road before dawn. "How do you stop people doing this when they can do it anywhere in a desert over two thousand miles wide?" Streatfeild asks. Simple—you don't.

In a study for the Defense Department, Peter Reuter of RAND Corporation pointed out that given the viability of small heroin shipments, drug traffickers could—if they are not already—use radio-controlled model airplanes to fly drugs across the border. Easy to get, smaller than a buzzard, and nearly impossible to see, many of these little shuttles could fly a sizeable load into the US with no hassle at all.[49] This is hardly a stretch considering that smugglers have trained pigeons to fly packets of drugs across borders.[50]

If that sounds too much like child's play, you can also hike across an unmanned area of the border with a backpack full of contraband and a loaded rifle. Illegals often schlep a sack as payment for passage into America. Rancher Bill Winkler of Elfrida, Arizona, has encountered armed drug runners on his property a number of times. "First time, there was seven of 'em, with packs," Winkler recounts. "Four had assault rifles—looked like AK-47s. . . . The next time, there were four in the same arroyo. Three had assault rifles and all were wearing big packs."[51] A neighbor of Winkler has had similar experiences: "there are the drug smugglers wearing camouflage and carrying assault rifles. They cross right through our ranch carrying millions of dollars of cocaine, marijuana, heroin and methamphetamine on their no-good backs. There is a whole drug-smuggling network on our roads and in our pastures."[52]

Indeed, when Ranch Rescue, a private group of US citizens who monitor the border armed to intercept alien and drug smugglers, nabbed nearly three hundred pounds of pot near Lochiel, Arizona, Customs was unimpressed. "Well, so what?" dismissed Kyle Barnette, an agent stationed in Arizona. It's not that difficult. "I could stand in the parking lot of my office, hit a 3-iron in any direction and hit a dope load on any given day."[53] In 2001, US Customs agents busted nearly two hundred thousand pounds of marijuana in the Grand Canyon State alone (and that, remember, doesn't count what local police nabbed). "People in this environment realize this is no big accomplishment," Barnette said. Drugs are so plentiful, "I would suggest I could train a chimpanzee to catch 300 pounds of weed."[54]

Of course, the chimp might get shot.

Dodging Bullets

Increasingly, drug smugglers are firing at border agents on patrol. Agents in El Paso, Texas, were fired upon during a bust that netted three suspects and 158 pounds of marijuana. Five suspects were spotted—two split across the *Rio Grande* into Mexico and shot at the agents from the Mexican side. [55]

"Besides the Border Patrol, federal officers of many stripes have become targets for drug lords who are offering rewards, reportedly as high as $200,000, for every US Drug Enforcement Agency officer or other federal agent trying to keep the twin tides of illegal drugs and immigrants from flooding the states," reports Jon Dougherty for WorldNetDaily.com. In 1999 alone, he says, there were five hundred violent assaults against federal agents at or near the border.[56]

Because of the vast stretches of land to patrol, it is impossible to catch more than a crumb of what breaches the border. "[Smugglers] keep us running like you can't believe," says Detective Sergeant David Cray, who heads an antidrug unit of the Tohono O'odham Nation Police Department. Tohono O'odham is a massive Indian reservation in Arizona, 2.8 million acres. Cray estimates that three thousand pounds of pot weekly pass through just one breach in the border fence, the Itak Gate. Thirty backpackers minimum, he says, may hike through the area on any given night, lugging up to a hundred pounds of weed each. "They have two-way radios, night-vision gear, body armor and carry automatic weapons," says the detective. "They've put people on the hills to act as lookouts and use portable solar panels to power their communications equipment. They have powerful four-wheel-drive vehicles and are under orders not to stop—to shoot their way through if they have to."[57]

And shoot they do. "There have been more firefights on the border in recent weeks than there have been in Bosnia," said Republican congressman Duncan Hunter in 1997, before passage of a bill giving President Clinton permission to deploy up to ten thousand American troops at the southern border.[58]

Mexico is also sending troops to the border—but in less official functions. In 1998, the DEA claimed senior members of the Mexican army were complicit in drug-trafficking. The corruption was so far-reaching, US agents refused to work with their Mexican counterparts, who might very well be undermining their operations. A year later, "Mexican military officers assigned to an elite antidrug smuggling group had been arrested in Mexico City on charges of drug trafficking and alien smuggling. Among those arrested were several captains and majors, all of whom had been assigned to the Mexican Attorney General's Office as antinarcotics agents."[59]

Some of these Mexican troops have actually crossed the US border and fired at US agents. In one instance, they came across in two Humvees and sent some zingers past American border patrolmen. In another, Mexican military inside US territory fired at a clearly marked Border Patrol helicopter.[60] The US has documented more than a hundred such incursions in the last five years.[61]

"There's no doubt Mexican military units along the border are being controlled by the drug cartels, and not by Mexico City," said Republican congressman Tom Tancredo after a trip to the border. Tancredo says the Mexican military not only protects but sometimes delivers drug shipments. "There isn't a soul down there on that border . . . who do[es] not believe that is exactly what the Mexican military is doing," he said. "US law-enforcement personnel actually have watched the Mexican military unload drugs from their Humvees to awaiting vehicles for transport into the United States."[62]

It's true: Since the September 11 terrorist attacks, the borders have been tightened a good deal. But the result hasn't stopped the inflow of drugs so much as proven that profits trump rules. Barnette's 3-iron comment was made after border-cinching, so the efforts haven't been nearly as effective as some might be led to believe, and drug runners are always cooking up new and more efficient methods of getting drugs to their customers. Market economics: What works for Hewlett Packard works for hash slingers. Even if it means getting low and playing dirty.

Digging Deeper

With increased border security and the resultant trouble in getting drugs across overland, some smugglers are taking them underground, a fact evidenced by an increasing number of tunnels discovered by police on both sides of the US–Mexico border.

While probably an overstatement to say that smugglers have turned border regions into gigantic prairie-dog towns full of narcoschlepping rodents, it is not far off. At least sixteen tunnels have been found by officials along the southern border in the last decade—and six of those since December 2001. One found in April 2002 actually opened up in a parking lot close to the US Customs office in Nogales, Arizona.[63] While small-timers up-top get nabbed with fifty kilos of coke in their trunks, thousands of kilos make their way through these tunnels with no more than the gophers to complain.

Many of these tunnels are humble affairs—less than a hundred feet long, not too deep or too wide. But some would bring nothing but awe and envy to the hearts of Colonel Hogan and his heroes.

One tunnel discovered in 2002 at a pig farm in Tierra del Sol, California, connected south of the border to a fireplace in a house outside of Tecate, Mexico. The discovery started with a closet on the

American side. Inside was an empty safe, but underneath the floor was the entrance to "one of the most lucrative drug-smuggling mechanisms ever discovered along the US-Mexico frontier," as one reporter phrased it. Decked with ventilation ducts, electric lights, and wooden walls, the twelve-hundred-foot tunnel was four-foot square and had five hundred and fifty pounds of pot packed and ready to roll when discovered. "They used this tunnel to smuggle billions of dollars worth of cocaine, marijuana and other drugs into the United States for several years," said Errol J. Chavez, special agent in charge of the DEA's San Diego office.[64] Authorities figure the underground dope route was at least ten years old—possibly twenty.[65]

If the Otay Mesa tunnel had been completed, Tecate might have had some considerable competition. The longest dig ever discovered—1,416 feet—the tunnel went sixty-five feet beneath a Tijuana industrial compound, was reinforced with concrete, and sported ventilation and lighting systems. Nearly finished when discovered in 1993, the intended tunnel terminus was a cannery in California, from which trucks hauling legitimate goods could be freighted with tons of narcotics. Amid all the normal truck traffic, no one would have been the wiser. "They would have operated with impunity," said one DEA agent.[66] Mexican police found the tunnel as a part of an unrelated investigation. A similar tunnel was found in Arizona in 1992, leading authorities to guess they were designed by the same engineer.

But smaller tunnels are nothing to turn a nose at. Authorities figure an eighty-five-foot tunnel found in December 2001 in Nogales had been used to shuttle more than twenty million dollars worth of cocaine and pot into the US. And the figure is likely lowball, as it is based on a somewhat dubious claim by Customs that *all* the drugs smuggled through the tunnel had been seized, some 956 pounds of cocaine and 839 pounds of marijuana. Considering the tunnel was in operation for five months or more, bunk meters should be at tilt.[67]

The tunnel—at least the eighth found in Nogales since 1995—was thirty feet below ground, four-feet high, supported with timbers, strung with electricity, and had tracks for dope-laden carts to quickly move along. Traffickers were extremely cautious to not be detected. "Drug smugglers would break a hole in a concrete drain in Mexico to get to the tunnel and after every drug shipment, the hole was patched up to avoid discovery by Mexican authorities."[68] It was "one of the most complicated we've seen," said Customs agent Vince Iglio, who compared the tunnel to a previously discovered, three-hundred-footer found in 1990; concrete-lined, electrified, and supporting a hydraulic lift, it was used for some serious trafficking.[69]

Nogales is a prime target for diggers because of its footprint on the map. As post-WWII Berlin's American cousin, the town is bisected by the border with Mexico with a wall running between the two countries. Beyond being able to possibly lob a baggy of dope over the border, many smugglers opt for taking it underground—and previous city planners were happy to oblige, even if inadvertently. The town is built atop a massive system of canals or "arroyos" that drains the frequent and heavy summer rains into the Santa Cruz River. But because the arroyos join the US and Mexican sides of the city, a lot more than water travels through them, despite efforts to stem the tide.

The problem is simply that the drug smugglers are too quick with too many routes to get drugs from there to here. With some seventy storm-drain intakes on both sides of the border, Dominic Streatfeild says it's common for drugs to be carted through the waterways to rendezvous with a false-bottom van up-top. Using a hydraulic jack to bust the manhole cover, the drugs can be quickly passed through and the transfer done in minutes. Running drugs through these canals can be preposterously lucrative, and it's not like smugglers have to hang around for months to take good advantage. "[H]ow much marijuana could you push through an arroyo wide enough to drive a car through in a week—if no one was watching?"[70] How about cocaine? Or heroin?

Plenty. And, as Streatfeild points out, the law is not taking this sitting down:

To combat [smugglers] the Americans installed giant steel doors in the arroyos. They didn't last long. Mexican traffickers took down oxyacetylene torches and cut their way through. Soon the US found itself having to send repair parties down into the arroyos twice a week to fix them. Once down there, they noticed something strange: extra tunnels that didn't feature in the original blueprints. They called in US Customs, who traced a tunnel all the way from Mexico into an old church next to Burger King on the American side. Two more popped up on Oak Street. Another emerged on Loma Street. . . .[71]

Finding the tunnels taxes authorities on both sides of the border. "We can't go around doing seismic graphs," said a DEA spokesman in San Diego, "and we can't check without a search warrant."[72] The only answer is to root them out as part of routine investigations, which makes keeping a lid on tunnels no small chore. While existing tunnels are in use, new tunnels are being dug, and sometimes old ones are reopened. The tunnel discovered in December 2001 was back in the swing of things shortly after it was sealed. "[Santa Cruz County Metro Task Force] heard that the tunnel may have gone back into business, and after obtaining a search warrant, they discovered that the tunnel had indeed been tapped into, probably by the same group," said the local sheriff.[73] The diggers went to considerable effort; whoever was using it had to create a new crawl space and dig around twelve feet of concrete.

"We don't know for sure how long the tunnel has been used since it was sealed, but our rough estimate is late January," said Lieutenant Raul Rodriguez of the Metro Task Force. With its rediscovery in March, that means the tunnel was shut down for a month and operated again for at least two. Nearly eighteen hundred pounds of nabbed narcotics were linked to the tunnel before it was shut down—including a single bust of nearly one thousand pounds of cocaine.[74] And that's just what the feds *knew about*. It's anybody's guess how many tons of drugs went through before the initial discovery and since its reopening.

Post September 11

Not even the post–September 11, security-heightened state has helped much. In the four months after the attacks, tighter security at airports, shipping yards, and border crossings bumped up total drug seizures 66 percent. Customs blushed enthusiastically as it hyped how seizures among commercial traffic along the Canadian border were up 326 percent.

"There has been a definite unintended consequence of the effort against terror: We are doing a better job of keeping illegal drugs out of the United States," gushed Customs commissioner Robert Bonner. But are they? "Experts have no clear evidence that the increased seizures have created a shortage of drugs on the street or raised their price there," notes *New York Times* reporter Fox Butterfield.[75]

The connection between more seizures and less drugs on the streets only holds true if you assume that incoming supplies of drugs are static. They don't appear to be. For one thing, more seizures mean that heightened security isn't scaring off traffickers. You'd expect seizures to decline if Customs' teeth were adequately sharp. Instead, a boom in narconabbing might simply signal that traffickers are tossing more product at the borders to make up for what they expect to get pinched. This is certainly in keeping with their previous behavior, regarding seizures as simply costs of doing business, like rent. "Law enforcement officials are uncertain whether the increase in seizures means only that they are intercepting a larger proportion of the narcotics . . . or whether the traffickers are . . . increasing the number or size of their shipments as a way of overwhelming the tighter security," writes Butterfield. The trend over the past decade indicates that the latter is more likely.

Global Illicit Drug Trends 2001, one of those info-clutter publications from the United Nations, shows how genuinely meaningless the seizures are. The UN says that total potential production of illicit opiates (raw opium, heroin, morphine, etc.) in 1999 was 576 metric tons, nearly double what it was in 1989. The amount seized has ratcheted up as well, from 9 percent in 1989 to 15 percent in 1999. But that still leaves 491 metric tons of illicit opiates available for consumption—182 metric tons more smack than when the first President Bush was reassuring the nation that the US would prevail in the war on drugs. Yes, we're grabbing more, but only because there's so much more to grab.[76]

Two simple graphs in the UN report make this embarrassingly clear. The first shows global seizures of heroin and morphine from 1989-99. The number of seizures more than doubled, with twenty-seven metric tons seized in 1989 and sixty-one in 1999. Keep that in mind as we flip to the next chart, which tracks the wholesale and retail prices of heroin over the same period. Where a gram of heroin would cost you more than $275 in 1987 (using 1999 dollars), twelve years later the same gram would set you back less than $50. While less dramatic, the downward slope for cocaine is just as obvious.[77]

Even the short-term seizure gains after 9/11 weren't terribly promising for drug warriors. Traffickers made up for shortfalls the way they always do—by simple redirection. Because the Coast Guard shifted its efforts away from interdiction to antiterror duties, cocaine seizures went down by one-third, and marijuana seizures were only a fifteenth what they were in 2000. The drugs were still getting in, just by different routes. If seizures continue to go up while the price continues to fall, the only sensible answer is that drug production and trafficking are going gangbusters, and the feds can't bust the gangs.

Pipedreams

Nothing has changed in the world. During Prohibition, "liquor flowed across the borders in a stanchless deluge," John Kobler writes in his book, *Ardent Spirits*. "Under fake bills of lading, deceptively packaged and often with the connivance of Customs officials and shipping clerks, it entered the States by railroad, truck, passenger vehicle, speedboat."[78] Kobler provides examples of a number of innovative smuggling methods, including freezing clear bottles of booze in ice shipments and another scheme of donning priest's garb to get the waive from a reverent Customs official.[79] "The smugglers plumed themselves on their ability to devise new tricks of concealment as fast as the old ones were exposed."[80]

If there is a single thing to be learned from interdiction efforts is that they fail more often than Hollywood marriages. And things only get worse for drug warriors when considering the domestic green-thumbs and homebrewers. While cocaine and heroin predominately come from South America, the lower forty-eight generate plenty of dope *inside* the borders of the US.

Vast amounts of the marijuana smoke filling the lungs of Americans, for instance, come from homegrown weed, cultivated in small patches in woods, hollows, and fields or grown indoors under grow lights. Estimates on sales of domestic pot are more than thirty billion dollars a year.[81] A big percentage of the weed smoked domestically comes from just three states—Kentucky, Tennessee, and West Virginia—making pot Appalachia's biggest cash crop. The pay is such that with National Guardsmen finding and burning 50 percent of a crop, growers still count themselves successful.[82] The same payoffs also keep people tilling the soil in states like California and Hawaii.

To avoid asset forfeiture problems and maximize yield, growers plant pot in the vast national and state forests across the country, setting up booby traps and even guarding the patches with firearms to prevent wayfaring hikers and "patch pirates" from spoiling their profits.[83] Of these forests, the central Sierra in California is well widely known for its pot. "Thanks to the mild climate, rich soil and a lengthy, March-to-October growing season, California cultivators routinely produce 10-ft.-high specimens worth up to $4,000 each," writes Margot Roosevelt for *Time*. "Some of these California pot farms"—many operated by Mexican drug gangs flouting the post-9/11 border beef-up—"stretch over several hundred acres and have as many as 50,000 plants."[84]

In 2003, the central Sierra also became known for its poppies (and not the state flower). A crop of forty thousand *opium* poppies—almost two acres worth—were discovered by a backpacker in the Sierra National Forest.[85]

Methamphetamine is widely produced in the US, from Appalachia to the rugged woods of Southern Oregon. In 1999, an antidrug task force in Oregon's sparsely populated Josephine County busted forty-two meth labs.[86] Over just three years, cops discovered and dismantled nearly two hundred labs in Missouri's Mark Twain National Forest.[87] In places like North Carolina, tapping into the preexisting moonshine culture, meth has become a cottage industry, with thousands of labs popping up across the state. Made with everyday materials and highly portable equipment, meth cookers are not easy to find, and crank makers are highly incentive-driven to cook tweak on the sly—a two thousand dollar investment can reap profits of twenty thousand dollars.[88] Eastern Tennessee is similarly experiencing a glut of labs; in 2003, Anderson County authorities busted at least forty-five.[89] In the Missouri Ozarks, where meth has taken off in recent years, law enforcement laments the difficulty in keeping up with the cookers. Said one drug enforcement detective, "Dopers don't quit."[90]

Antidrug forces cannot compete with the fantastic and corrupting profits of narcotraffickers and domestic producers. Because of the simple economics of prohibition, they never have been able to, and they never will.

Instead of facing up to this reality, however, drug warriors delude themselves into thinking every kilo matters, every seizure is a battle won. Drugs are produced at such a small cost and the profits pulled from distributing them so great, there will always be ten more kilos coming for every one seized. When a drug lord is knocked off the hill, five new guys step in. Pablo Escobar's death was considered a great victory for drug warriors, ditto for the dissolution of the Cali cocaine cartel, but more drugs than ever come out of Colombia and surrounding countries. A drug lord getting knocked off his throne isn't a victory; it's a job opening. But instead of seeing this as evidence of a war unwinnable, prohibitionists foster fancy and eschew anything that might constitute a negative vibe.

This is why we hear so much talk along those lines of Hutchinson's lame "increasing the risk to the traffickers" answer to Stossel's straight-forward question about how much dope gets seized. "What you do is you try to minimize, reduce, and then contain, and that's really where our focus has to be. Because if we set unrealistic goals, we will not achieve them, and people say these battles have failed," says Congressman Mark Souder in another common annunciation of the view.[91] Of course, if you compare that with the rhetoric of total eradication heard from officials since Nixon began the war on drugs, it is easy to peg these as convenient defensive positions, taken by many who are simply unwilling to quit a war they now realize cannot be won—many who a decade ago thought just a few more billon dollars would do the trick. For them the drug war has become more like the Cold War. No big blowouts, just holding the line.

True Believers

Of course, it was the free marketeers who won in the last Cold War; the Soviet's socialism couldn't keep pace. Now the roles are reversed. The US is the economic sloth in this battle, and the drug traffickers are at the advantage, kings of the hill on a very steep incline.

"The US government's goal for interdiction mocks any claim to protect America from the scourge of illicit drugs," writes James Bovard, who points to comments made by Clinton administration attorney general Janet Reno that federal experts estimate that "to have any impact on drugs in America you would have to interdict 75 percent of the stuff and that would be economically prohibitive."[92] The United Nations International Drug-Control Program agrees that officials must pinch "75% of . . . shipments for the drug bosses to start feeling much pain."[93] Well, they are not seizing anywhere near that—they are not even getting 25 percent. My guess is that federal drug cops are still around 10 percent for total seizures, and that still says nothing for the impossible task of stopping everybody's Uncle Jim from growing a few plants for personal use in the basement.

Still, there are plenty of true believers. Despite the insurmountable odds facing drug warriors, they remain steadfast in their aims—inscrutably cheerful, always earnest—victims of an incredible antipipe pipedream. The very nature of the game and how it is played dictates their failure. Still, they maintain a delusion of victory. Drug warriors bluster and bellow about how the latest seizures are some sort of triumph, but as the numbers demonstrate, it is all a show. By jailing a few drug runners and pinching their product, drug warriors can continue to claim their well-loved token successes while drug dealers continue to claim the real ones.

5

BUTTING IN

Prohibition increases government invasion of privacy.

IN AN UNMARKED CAR, A MAN WAITS FOR HIS CONNECTION. AS he tells it, she's delivered before—the opiate painkiller Lorcet and Xanax, an anti-anxiety drug. Both are illegal without a prescription, and this woman is hardly a doctor. When she shows, the woman has one of her children. The man gets out of the vehicle and approaches her to make the deal, buying some drugs and making plans for another illicit exchange in a few days.

Once the money and dope have switched hands, the man lets the woman in on a secret: He's a cop. Worse for her, he's Picayune, Mississippi, police chief Jim Luke.

"Are you kidding?" she asks.[1]

Just her luck. He's dead serious.

Busting Offenders

For obvious reasons, smuggling is a secretive thing. Most activities related to crimes are. But prohibitionary crimes, such as transporting and selling contraband like prescription painkillers and pot, have an added dimension of secrecy—namely the lack of a victim.

When someone is victimized by a crime—say, burglary or assault—there is a person wronged who can go to authorities and alert them to the crime. With this person's insistence and cooperation, police can sometimes nab a bad guy red-handed. If the offender has escaped, the victim's eyewitness account and assistance can help authorities corroborate details and begin piecing together the evidence that will hopefully point to the perpetrator. With prohibitionary crime, however, there is no victim.

To see this, consider the way the purchase would have played out if Chief Luke had been a user instead of a cop: The buyer wants drugs; the woman wants money. Through the black market, they find each other and arrange a deal. The scene is identical to the one above. The man is as anonymous as possible. The woman, cautious, stays back and waits for the buyer to approach her. Bringing along her child helps her activities look somehow less illegal. Both breaking the law, neither party attempts to be conspicuous. The transaction is fast, and arrangements for a future meeting and deal are made before departing.

And that's it.

Neither springs it on the other that one is a cop; neither one is arrested; and both go on their merry way, free to meet in a few weeks and run through the scenario again—this time perhaps on a different street, up a different alley, behind a different building, mixing it up to keep things as unsuspicious and untraceable as possible.

Unlike a mugging or car heist, finding a victim in this picture is hard. If there is a victim, someone actually harmed, it is the very people who've chosen this for their lifestyle. It's a harm they've brought on themselves. Obviously, the inclusion of the child here is tragic, but countless more people transact the same business without bringing children into harm's way. We don't consider such people victims—possibly fools, but not victims.

Drug warriors don't see it this way. Says former drug czar William J. Bennett, "don't listen to people who say drug users are only hurting themselves: They hurt parents, they destroy families, they ruin friendships."[2] Yes. Then again, so do people with inordinately high measures of pride, selfishness, and vanity—things that have damaged countless more relationships than all the crack in Chicago. So do people who do all sorts of *legal* things every day.

Bennett and others miss the point entirely when discussing so-called "victimless crimes." No one is saying that Aunt Ruth isn't distraught because of Nephew Jim's heroin use. She may feel victimized by it; his use may hurt the family reputation, may strain relationships. But that could be just as true if Jim became a worker's comp attorney. What is meant by "victimless crime" is that in the commission of the act, no one is harmed or defrauded *in real terms.* Disliking what someone has done with his life doesn't count. Neither does disruption to a marriage or family because of a pernicious drug habit. These things are bad, no doubt about it, but they do not produce victims in the criminal sense. The issue is simply one of consensual transactions—and this is where law enforcement runs into a problem. Due to the secrecy of the crime and lack of a victim to fink to the fuzz, nabbing narcotics violators is an extra special challenge.

"Because the drug industry arises from the voluntary transactions of tens of millions of people—all of whom try to keep their actions secret— the aggressive law enforcement schemes that constitute the war must aim at penetrating the private lives of those millions," explains Stephen Wisotsky in a paper for the Cato Institute. Police are forced, instead of *reacting* to the report of a victim, to *proactively* ferreting out offenders by methods that inject government right into the daily lives of even the most law-abiding among us: invasive searches, courier profiles, roadblocks, pretext stops, snitches, and undercover cops. "[B]ecause nearly anyone may be a drug user or seller of drugs or an aider and abettor of the drug industry," says Wisotsky, "virtually everyone has become a suspect."[3]

Sadly, we've been through this before.

Writ and Wrong

"The high duties which have been imposed upon the importation of many different sorts of foreign goods . . . have in many cases served only to encourage smuggling," the great economist Adam Smith wrote in *The Wealth of Nations*, published in 1776. "Heavy duties being imposed upon almost all goods imported, our merchant importers smuggle as much and make entry of as little as they can."[4]

One merchant whose actions perfectly illustrated Smith's thesis was John Hancock. Known best today as the American founder who penned his outlandish signature on another important document published in 1776—the Declaration of Independence—Hancock swore to never drink wine repressively taxed by the Crown. But neither was he a teetotaler. Instead, he dodged the tax and became a smuggler. In one of the galvanizing events in the decade prior to the Revolution, after smuggling some 126,000 gallons of Madeira, Hancock's ship, the *Liberty*, was seized by customs officials. Riots ensued, and British agents were attacked.[5]

But Hancock's situation was only a sample of the crackdown being undertaken by the king's agents and the anger it incited. Faced with widespread smuggling, the Brits did not take the sensible tack advised later by people like Smith. Instead of lowering import duties and taxes, the Crown authorized customs agents "to break by force, if necessary, into any ship, warehouse, dwelling, or store [that] suited their whim."[6] Since commerce in contraband was so widespread and the perpetrators so hard to find, British officers could obtain general search warrants called Writs of Assistance, which entitled them to browse through just about anybody's house, books, and dirty laundry as aimlessly and indiscriminately as they chose. As one writer described the outrage in 1772 for the Massachusetts Committee of Correspondence, "our houses and even our bedchambers are exposed to be ransacked . . . and plundered by wretches, whom no prudent man would venture to employ even as menial servants," adding that these writs deprived the people of "domestic security."[7]

Writs of Assistance were issued without the requirement of probable cause or specified place to be searched; neither did the writ have a time limit or requirement to return it to the court. It was, in short, a perpetual license to harass. That's certainly the take of James Otis, an important American lawyer and pre-Revolutionary founder.

"Every one with this Writ may be a tyrant," he protested in a 1761 hearing, stating that "it is a power that places the liberty of every man in the hands of every petty officer." If a man has one of these licenses to harass, said Otis, he "is accountable to no person for his doings. Every man may reign secure in his petty tyranny and spread terror and desolation around him. . . ."[8]

Otis's protests went unheeded by the Crown, and abuse intensified. In fact, the official sanctioning of these flagrant infringements led directly to the Revolution. "[I]t was an outrage that brought with it corrupt officials, lawless seizures, selective enforcement, and fabricated evidence," write law professors Eric Blumenson and Eva Nilsen. "From these complaints, John Adams later said, 'the child Independence was born.'"[9]

Erecting a barrier to government invasions and intrusions, the founders later codified their intolerance for such maltreatment in the Fourth Amendment:

> The right of the people to be secure in their persons, houses, papers, and effects, against unreasonable searches and seizures, shall not be violated, and no Warrants shall issue, but upon probable cause, supported by Oath or affirmation, and particularly describing the place to be searched, and the persons or things to be seized.

As we'll see in the following chapter, the Fifth Amendment's regulation on forfeiture also finds its roots in these abuses by the British. Sadly, however, the drug war has caused something of a memory flush regarding many of the lessons learned and taught by our nation's framers.

Drug prohibition has forced the courts and law enforcement to engage in a troubling tug of war with the Fourth Amendment, yanking its meaning to the point that most any intrusion and invasion necessary to successfully wage the drug war is allowed. The result is that the founders' hard-fought protections of the citizen's right to property and privacy have in many cases been qualified and redefined to the point of meaninglessness.

Search And Seizure

Getting product to market requires conveyances. Toy manufacturers cannot let their goods sit in a warehouse forever. At some point they must go via boat, truck, or train to where customers can take possession of them. Drugs are identical, which means that dopers must use various types of transportation—public and private—to move their goods to market. To root them out, the courts have approved a variety of far-reaching tactics, near dragnet schemes that ensnare and harass countless innocent citizens.

A search, as far as the courts are concerned, is pretty much any invasion of a person's expectation of privacy. Think of it this way: If an officer can see something in plain view on a person's front seat, it's not a search. But if he must jimmy the lock on the glove box before looking at what's inside, that's a search.

A seizure is when the officer takes possession of either person or property.[10] If, for instance, he finds a stash of marijuana in that glove box, he can seize it. To justify a seizure, police need at minimum what the courts call reasonable suspicion; an officer must be able to articulate specific facts from which a reasonable person could infer that criminal activity may be underway.[11]

Naturally, the mere visible presence of pot is enough for a reasonable person to infer that criminal activity may be underway. But the pot is not usually visible. With other drugs, such as cocaine or heroin, the relative volume of the product means it's even easier to conceal. Ditto for LSD blotters and ecstasy tablets. Ditto for illegally procured prescription pain meds. As we saw in the previous chapter, dopers pride themselves on their ability to escape detection. This means that for an officer to more easily and efficiently detect criminal activity, the definition of "reasonable" has to be stretched.

Elastic with the expediency granted by courts, reasonable searches can be justified by such things as drug-courier profiles.

Unfriendly Skies

While often tied to racial politics and civil-rights imbroglios, most profiles have nothing do with race or ethnicity. Courier profiles are really just character compilations that supposedly provide law enforcement a rough picture of what a drug trafficker looks like. They are ideally designed to narrow the scrutiny of cops to those most likely schlepping dope in their satchel. "But in practice," writes Georgetown University law professor David Cole, "the drug-courier profile is a scattershot hodgepodge of traits and characteristics so expansive that it potentially justifies stopping anybody and everybody."[12] One federal circuit court judge wryly noted that DEA profiles sport a "chameleon-like way of adapting to any particular set of observations [made by officers about suspects]."[13]

Trolling through court cases and law journals, Cole has assembled a broad list of traits that federal agents have used to support their arrests. A sample is in order. Variously, officers have *reasonably* inferred criminal activity was afoot because suspects:

- bought a coach ticket *or* a first-class ticket
- bought a one-way *or* round-trip ticket
- paid for a ticket with cash—big notes *or* small
- traveled alone *or* with a companion
- arrived late at night *or* early in the morning *or* in the afternoon
- were first *or* middle *or* last to deplane
- made eye contact with officer *or* avoided eye contact
- wore expensive clothing and jewelry *or* dressed casually
- left airport by—take your pick—taxi *or* limousine *or* private car *or* hotel courtesy van[14]

Still other profiles assert that landing in a city known as a major source for drugs might supply an officer with reasonable suspicion of illicit goings-on. Never mind that every city with a major airport is considered by authorities to be a major source for drugs.[15]

Police watching buses and trains do the same, a sort of geographical profiling. When Vietnamese immigrant On Hoang Thach—whose case we'll explore briefly in the next chapter—was stopped aboard Amtrak in Albuquerque, part of the reason cited by authorities for their suspicion was that he paid cash for his ticket and traveled from Los Angeles. No drugs were found.[16] In 2001, New York's highest court tossed a conviction of a man caught in Albany aboard a public bus from the Big Apple with a load of coke. Police boarded the vehicle and questioned its riders precisely because it "came from an area with illegal drug activity. . . ." Though the case was thrown out in New York, the inspector in charge claimed the practice of geographical profiling was in wide use across the country.[17] Despite its widespread use, as investigative journalist James Bovard notes, "When the Founding Fathers created the Fourth Amendment, they were not thinking of 'going to Detroit' as 'reasonable suspicion'. . . ."[18]

For this reason explains Cole, "Such profiles do not so much focus an investigation as provide law enforcement officials a ready-made excuse for stopping whomever they please."[19]

It's just as bad on the roads.

Drive Me Crazy

Police in different states have justified their suspicions of drivers both by pointing to traveling in excess of posted speed limits and "scrupulous obedience to traffic laws."[20] "Overly cautious" operation of a vehicle can also get a person in trouble. Further, even though its drivers were violating no traffic laws, one sheriff's deputy followed a U-Haul "because it was a U-Haul, and because it had been his experience that U-Haul's carry narcotics."[21] Apparently, it never occurred to this deputy that they also carry sofas, lampshades, and boxes of books.

In *Police Patrol Operations*, author Mark R. Miller lists several broad profiling factors for officers involved in traffic stops. Police should keep there eyes out for: nervous driver and passengers; poor identification; cell phones and pagers; no luggage; fast food trash; air fresheners; road maps; excessive mileage. Miller adds that "None of the items above are probable cause in themselves to search for drugs. They are simply warning signs. . . ."[22] Warning, apparently, that drug couriers have characteristics that are identical to the rest of us. Depending on what's going on in my life, I fit most of these factors, including others that Miller lists, such as sleeping items in the car. After being stranded one night along a remote road with only a throw rug to keep me warm, I started carrying a few blankets with me, always a sleeping bag. And, further, Miller isn't entirely correct. While it may be right by the rulebook, policing isn't always done by the rulebook.

David Cole notes the Supreme Court has ruled that profiles alone do not constitute adequate suspicion for stopping someone. But in practice, "courts frequently defer to the profile and equate it with reasonable suspicion."[23] He quotes the conclusion of one judge after conducting a review of profile-related court decisions: "Many courts have accepted the profile, as well as the Drug Enforcement Agency's scattershot enforcement efforts, unquestioningly, mechanistically, and dispositively."[24]

Even if police cannot conjure enough genuine suspicion to warrant a stop, courts allow them to make a type of pretext stop to fish for more evidence. Say an officer thinks something illegal is going on but he's got little more to go on than a hunch. Piece of cake. All he has to do is follow the driver until he commits the inevitable traffic violation and the officer is free to stop the car. With any luck, he'll turn up something that will produce articuable suspicion, and he'll be good to go. Given that some one hundred million Americans commute daily in private cars and that it is nearly impossible to comply a hundred percent with traffic codes, that means an officer can remain within the law and still pull over just about anyone he likes, should he so desire.[25]

Coupled with a 1996 ruling, this is even more insidious. Deciding it would be "unrealistic to require police officers to always inform detainees that they are free to go before a consent to search may be deemed voluntary," the Supreme Court opened the door for widespread suspicionless harassment. If there is no reason to keep a stopped motorist, an officer can leave the driver in limbo by not telling him he's free to go and at the same time let him believe that the officer is not yet finished with him by asking for permission to search the vehicle.[26]

Of course a person can always decline the search. This is a perfectly legal course of action. A motorist can ask the officer what his probable cause is to search, rattle on about his Fourth Amendment rights, or keep it short and simple—just say no. While most folks don't have the moxie to push it this far, for those who do, the police have another lever. "If you tell me no, I'll just go get a warrant," they might say. Refusing to cooperate with police is not technically suspicious in itself. Cops aren't supposed to take it personally if someone has a beef with them. But they do. "I think 99 percent of people would be cooperative," said one Louisiana-based DEA spokesman. "As for people who are uncooperative, you cast all your suspicions on them."[27] That's convenient. As Bovard explains, "a citizen's refusal to allow himself to be searched creates grounds to get a search warrant—a Catch-22 that gives police officers the de facto right to search anyone."[28]

The DEA and other law enforcement swear by profiles, touting their widespread success. But as Yale law professor Steven B. Duke and writer Albert C. Gross note, "profiles are self-fulfilling. If the profiles are based on who is searched and found guilty, the guilty will necessarily fit the profiles."[29] The obvious problem is that drug traffickers are not space aliens—they share many characteristics that everyday, law-abiding citizens do. Couriers are increasingly encouraged and recruited by trafficking organizations to blend in as closely as possible. So even though the profiles are patterned after couriers, they encompass traits and characteristics common enough to all of us that many innocent people's right against unreasonable search and seizure is violated daily across the country. That's the rub.

Since we are not carrying drugs in our luggage or trunks, for most of us it matters little whether a court will defer to a profile. We'll never see the inside of a courtroom because we've done nothing illegal. What does matter greatly, however, is that these profiles are used to stop and harass innocent citizens every day—people who are doing nothing more inherently suspicious than anyone else but who are stopped and sometimes searched because the courts have chipped away at Fourth Amendment protections against government invasion and of property and person.

Something else here warrants passing note: Let's say a man is wrongly hassled by the law, unjustly treated, and sues. Let's further say that he wins and is awarded damages. Right has been done, correct? Yes, but it is a victory of small consolation. Because of the misdeeds of police, even if the man wins, we all lose. His payment comes out of the taxpayers' pockets.[30]

Checkpoint Charlie

On the roads, the rights erosion is ongoing, even in spite of apparent victories. The Supreme Court signaled its approval of random roadblocks to bust illegal aliens up to ninety miles from the border in 1976. In 1990, it gave its blessing to sobriety checkpoints. But things looked like they might come to a halt when, in 1998, Indianapolis police took a page from the playbooks of other cities and states and began randomly stopping cars looking for dope. Officers would demand the drivers' papers and spy the interior of the vehicle while a drug-sniffing dog made a circuit of the car.[31]

"The checkpoint was not based on any particularized suspicion," as reporter Robyn Blumner points out, "anyone driving along that road could be detained until he satisfied police of his innocence." Indianapolis police used the tactic for four months before being challenged over it. In that time 1,161 cars were stopped, fifty-five of which led to drug arrests.[32] Supporters of such stops cite that figure as evidence that they work. Many others are simply shocked that they violated the rights of well over a thousand innocent motorists.

In November 2000, the high court ruled six to three against the checkpoints, saying the obvious: they violated the Fourth Amendment by randomly stopping scads of drivers in an attempt to ferret out ordinary criminal wrongdoing. The argument in favor of sobriety stops had always been one of traffic safety—immediate threat to life and limb. No such problem here. Drug checkpoints are simply unconstitutional dragnets.

Interestingly, the three dissenting justices were Chief Justice William Rehnquist, and Justices Anton Scalia and Clarence Thomas. What's interesting is not that the conservative trio backed pro-drug war practice. In most cases, that's sadly predictable. What is interesting is that while Rehnquist and Scalia saw the drug checkpoints as basically consistent with the 1976 and 1990 rulings upholding random stops for immigrants and dipsomaniacs, Thomas threw doubt on the whole legal package. He went along with Rehnquist and Scalia for consistency's sake but then questioned whether the previous two rulings shouldn't also be overturned: "I rather doubt that the Framers of the Fourth Amendment would have considered 'reasonable' a program of indiscriminate stops of individuals not suspected on wrongdoing."[33]

Thomas's statement reveals the shallow nature of this Fourth Amendment victory. Police may no longer conduct random drug stops, as such, that's true. But, as Jacob Sullum writes, "drug checkpoints could be rejiggered to meet the Supreme Court's objection. If police offered rationales the Court as approved, declaring that the primary purpose of a checkpoint was to get drunk and unlicensed drivers off the roads, they could then look for drugs incidentally." It's similar to pretext stops that use everyday traffic infractions as evidentiary fishing expeditions. "Given some of the Court's other rulings," writes Sullum, "the upshot might be the same as allowing drug checkpoints officially identified as such."[34]

If a cop can't enter the Fourth Amendment's front door, he can always try going through the bathroom window.

Immediately following the Supreme Court's ruling, for instance, a Missouri lawman proclaimed he would continue using the roadblocks by simply arguing that his stops were different. How? They were phony.

Law enforcement "would typically set up a sign warning of a drug checkpoint ahead, but allow motorists the opportunity to exit between the sign and the supposed checkpoint," explained one report. But the checkpoint was a ruse. "The checkpoint was actually at the bottom of the off-ramp. Under the police logic, drivers who take the exit, especially those with out of state plates, are deemed to have created reasonable suspicion to be stopped and possibly searched."[35] Never mind that the exit might actually be the one the driver meant to take regardless of the posted drug checkpoint sign.

Other agencies in other states have pulled the same juke. "Narcotics checkpoint, one mile ahead" and "Narcotics canine ahead"—so read signs posted by police during the 2000 Telluride Bluegrass Festival in Colorado. There was no checkpoint, of course. Instead, police donned cammies and hid out waiting to see if drivers would toss things out their windows, presumably drugs, or simply turn around to dodge the check-point entirely once they saw the sign. The mere hassle of thinking one would have to stop and endure some sort of inspection apparently doesn't count as a legitimate reason for trying to avoid a checkpoint. Given the Supreme Court's ruling that such stops are an infringement, such a justification is apt. But by the outcomes of cases in Colorado and Oklahoma, it appears as if merely not wishing to come under police scrutiny is adequate cause to assume a person should be scrutinized. It's a no-win situation, and it's all legally kosher. "The posting of signs to create a ruse does not constitute illegal police activity," ruled the federal Tenth Circuit Court of Appeals after one case.[36]

For those that do get stopped, things got dicier in 2003. Late last year, the Supreme Court handed down a ruling that bodes ill for passengers of vehicles in which drugs are found. Rather than demonstrating that drugs were owned by any particular party, if drugs are present, an officer can essentially arrest everyone if the owner doesn't come forward.

Previously, a Maryland state appeals court ruled that the "policy of arresting everyone until someone confesses" was "constitutionally unacceptable." The Supreme Court disagreed. As Charles Lane writes in the *Washington Post*, the decision "means that, in such cases involving drugs, officers may now err on the side of arresting the innocent without violating the Constitution."[37]

Erring on the side of the State is fundamental to the successful waging of the drug war. Hence, the rare rollback of unconstitutional powers.

Go back to the Supreme Court's roadblock ruling in 2000. Contained in Rehnquist's dissent is a dangerous implication, one that is indicative of drug warriors' attitudes on the drug war and the Constitution, the former responsible for the latter's increasing demise: "These stops effectively serve the state's legitimate interests; they are executed in a regularized and neutral manner; and they only minimally intrude upon the privacy of motorists." So as long as a violation of the Constitution serves the benefit of the State, all people are violated equally by it, and it is considered only a minimal intrusion, then it's acceptable. By that logic, the State could begin stopping and frisking pedestrians with no cause, too.[38]

No doubt James Madison corkscrewed in his coffin a few times at Rehnquist's words. Any action undertaken by the State to enforce its laws is arguably in its "legitimate interests"; that's why it finds any action worth doing. The problem is that what is best for the State is not always (perhaps not usually) good for the citizen. That's the reason the Bill of Rights was written, to protect citizens from the government's overreach.

Rat-Fink Nation

In 2001, the White House pushed for what it called the TIPS program, which would have officially enlisted millions of Americans into an army of finks. The plan was so egregiously invasive that, even in a period of heightened concern over terrorism, it was shot down. But while the TIPS program was broad and far-reaching, others in different spheres are encouraged to rat on their fellows in the name of the drug war.

New Jersey state troopers, for instance, pay hotel workers a thousand dollars bounty for ratting on their guests. "The program," reported the *New York Times*, "has enlisted at least two dozen inns, mostly near Newark Airport, where troopers are regularly allowed to search through guests' registration forms and credit card receipts without warrants or subpoenas. Troopers have conducted seminars to train hotel employees to report guests who fit the profile of drug smugglers: those who pay with cash, receive frequent visitors or phone calls, or drive recreational vehicles."[39]

While police are limited by the Fourth Amendment, hotel clerks and maids are not. Any suspicious or illegal activity they encounter, they can report. Since the 1990s, police in cities such as Los Angeles and New Jersey have encouraged them to do so, and if they spot anything funny, the law provides financial incentive to snitch.

The owner of the Days Inn near Newark Airport refused to rat on his guests. "It's like a tactic out of some dictatorship," he said. "When a person checks into a hotel, he or she has a reasonable assumption that the place of business will protect their privacy, not treat them like a criminal."[40] Perhaps they shouldn't. Similar programs are in use across the country, including Wichita, Kansas; Mesa, Arizona; and Columbia, Missouri.[41]

Thanks to the Bank Secrecy Act (BSA) of 1970, bankers have also been morphed into the eyes and ears of the State. "Money laundering is essentially a paperwork offense," says Solveig Singleton of the Competitive Enterprise Institute, "the crime of trying to conceal the proceeds of a crime."[42] To stop such paperwork crimes, the federal government enlists financial institutions to squeal on their clients when they suspect illicit business.

The BSA requires banks to report all cash transactions over ten thousand dollars and file "suspicious activity reports" for transactions half that if they have "no apparent lawful purpose or are not the sort in which the particular customer would normally be expected to engage."[43] Things like money withdrawn to pay for a medical procedure? Things like money from a personal used car sale? Could be. How's the bank to know what's going on in a person's life? When I cashed the first half of my advance for this book, it's not as if I told the clerk about my business. It's no surprise, then, that only the slimmest margin of those investigated are ever convicted for illegal activity. Between 1987 and 1995, for instance, banks filed some seventy-seven million suspicious activity reports. Only 580 money-laundering convictions resulted. For every twenty-five thousand reports, the government busted 0.2 offenders.[44]

Naturally, the law would skewer more innocent than guilty. Just as gun laws penalize innocent gun-owners far more than violent criminals, so do anti-money laundering laws. By definition, law abiding citizens play by the rules, and so they conduct their transactions and (provided they know about them) don't even think of evading the reporting regulations. But by definition, crooks do not play by the rules and have an added incentive to avoid being caught up in the law, so they make sure to steer wide of reporting their transactions.

They "smurf" dealings, making many small transactions under the reporting threshold. They launder money through casino winnings, purchase money orders with cash, and pay cash for high-expense items registering the assets under different names. They pay cash for securities, wire funds to offshore bank accounts and front companies, and—as they do with cops—sometimes buy off bank employees to cover for illegalities.[45] In other words, dopers take much of their business under the radar of formal financial reporting measures, leaving few but the law abiding for the feds to ogle. A classic dragnet.

"You're getting so much data on people who are absolutely legitimate and who are doing nothing wrong," John Yoder, director of the Reagan administration's Justice Department Asset Forfeiture Office told reporter John Berlau. "There's just so much paperwork out there that it's really not a targeted effort. You have investigators running around chasing innocent people, trying to find something that they're doing wrong, rather than targeting real criminals."[46]

Just as troubling, once reported, the information is out there and in the hands of the government, regardless of the subject's innocence or guilt. Nearly sixty different law enforcement agencies are privy to information in the Suspicious Activity Reports database, and probable cause is not needed to take a peek. Singleton notes that many agencies download the files as a matter of routine and hold on to them for unspecified future use.[47]

Sometimes info gathered on citizens is used immediately—the entrepreneurial side of law enforcement—as when Amtrak ticket salespersons in Albuquerque provide the DEA with information about passengers in exchange for 10 percent of any cash seized from suspected couriers. For a while, the local DEA had a direct computer link to Amtrak ticket information. This window on travelers' souls allows drug enforcement agents to scan ticket buyers' names, their itineraries, when they bought their tickets, and whether they used cash or credit. Red flags? "What they are doing raises serious issues about invasions of privacy, about Fourth Amendment protections against unwarranted search and seizures, and about equal protection rights related to profiling by racial or income types," said the ACLU's Peter Simonson.[48]

The DEA, of course, didn't see it in that light. "I don't consider that to be an invasion of privacy," said Steven Derr, assistant special agent in charge of the Albuquerque DEA office, answering charges coming from civil libertarians like Simonson. "The whole idea of why we do it this way is so we're not randomly stopping people."[49] Great response—if you don't mind someone playing looser with the English language than Bill Clinton before a grand jury.

Privacy, let's recall, implies confidentiality, a limit on the spread of a particular piece of information. How "private" is it when Amtrak allows the DEA to spy its passenger manifests without letting you know? At the point the eyeballs of someone other than the people directly involved in the transaction roll across the ticket information, it ceases being private—by the very definition of the word.

And how about "random"?

Random implies lack of care in selection, no rationale. A few years back, before taking Amtrak from Sacramento down to San Jose, I called the capital city DEA office to find out about profiles used to sniff out couriers traveling by train. The agent I spoke with told me that a sure tip-off to a drug officer would be someone buying a ticket right before getting on the train. As it happens, I always buy my ticket at the station minutes before boarding. Next, the agent said that carrying no luggage was a good clue for a narcotics cop. "Whew," I thought, "I've always got at least one suitcase." Apparently reading my mind, he then said that another tip-off was carrying just one bag.

"What we looked for are the consistent factors [that] all the seizures we've made have in common," said Albuquerque DEA agent Kevin Small. "And those factors are usually one-way cash tickets bought within three days of the date of departure." So buy with credit, right? Wrong. Derr says the DEA watches credit card purchases made shortly before departure time as well.

Not random? Like the insanity with profiles in the airports, you can tip off the narcs if you carry one bag—or no bag; if you pay with cash—or you don't; if you buy tickets, one, two, or three days before hitting the rails. It may not be random in the quantum physics sense of the word, but it sure seems random in the common English sense. "By the DEA encouraging this kind of action, they put under criminal suspicion people who have no reason to be confronted with a search by the DEA," said Simonson.[50]

After a heavy raft of bad press, Amtrak killed the computer link, but the government-funded operation still finks to the feds and others. "We cooperate with law enforcement agencies, including the DEA, and will continue to do so in the future," said Amtrak police chief Ernest R. Frazier Sr.[51]

Things aren't much better in the air. The DEA "maintains confiscation squads at major airports and has turned airline and airport employees into informers by awarding them 10 percent of confiscated assets," explain Paul Craig Roberts and Lawrence M. Stratton in *The Tyranny of Good Intentions*.[52]

Kids are even roped into this national tattletale enterprise. The widely touted Drug Abuse Resistance Education program, more popularly known as DARE, is designed to teach children in government schools about the dangers of narcotics. It also teaches them how to fink on friends and family. Writes Diane Barnes in the *Detroit News*, "Children are asked to submit to DARE police officers sensitive written questions that can easily refer to the kids' homes. And you might be surprised by a DARE lesson called 'The Three R's: Recognize, Resist, Report,' which encourages children to tell friends, teachers or police if they find drugs at home."[53] Drug arrests in a number of states have been tied directly to children ratting on parents. The reason is simple enough: DARE classes are taught by cops, who are then duty-bound to follow up on tips from kids. The *Wall Street Journal* reported two Boston cases in which "children who had tipped police stepped out of their homes carrying DARE diplomas as police arrived to arrest their parents."[54]

Rat-fink kids are institutionalized by other means as well. In February 1999, three high schools in Portland, Oregon, kicked off a program to pay students who snitch on their friends (or enemies) a thousand dollars for drug offenses on school property. Armed with a direct hotline to school police. "This turn-in-your-friends-for-cash scheme at Judas Iscariot High School is a stark example of how Drug Prohibition has warped the morals of this nation," said Libertarian party national chairman Steven Dasbach. "Instead of treating drug abuse as a medical problem that requires concern and compassion, this program treats drug abuse as an opportunity to earn 30 pieces of silver by ratting on your schoolmates."[55]

Life's a Snitch

Relying on generally law-abiding citizens like hotel maids and children to fink on wrongdoers in their midst is not hugely practical for law enforcement for one reason: Most wrongdoing does not go on in their midst. Drug buyers and sellers don't enjoy being discovered. As a result, if cops really want the inside dirt on who's doing what, they've got to go where the dirt goes down; they've got to get where the action is. This they do in one of two ways: undercover cops and snitches.

It's always been this way with prohibition. In the Islamic Ottoman Empire, tobacco smokers were on the outs. Murad the Cruel, who ruled the vast empire between 1623 and 1640, was particularly rough on tabagophiles and made smoking a capital offense. Death being an undesirable thing, tobacco users tended to be secretive about their habit, but their sneaky statesman had a trick up his robe. Writes Iain Gately in his sweeping history, *Tobacco*:

> Murad's habit was to roam the streets of Constantinople in disguise, feigning an urgent craving for a smoke then beheading any good Samaritans who offered relief. Contemporary records state that he himself killed or had put to death . . . in excess of 25,000 suspected smokers. Murad's example was followed in Persia, where merchants caught selling tobacco were executed by having molten lead poured down their throats.[56]

The punishments today are lighter, but the methods of smoking out the culprits are much the same.

New Jersey state police officer Jack Cole was working undercover with a snitch who went by the name Fast Eddy. In a rough neighborhood of Paterson, New Jersey, the pair pretended to be junkies looking to score some heroin. The going wasn't easy. Getting into a scuffle with a few guys trying to rob them, Fast Eddy's hand was cut with a knife before Cole could chase them off with his sidearm. Just then, a young man came across the two—Fast Eddy bleeding like mad. He retrieved some bandages from his home to take care of the wound. A college student trying to work his way out of the ghetto, the Good Samaritan didn't approve of drugs but felt pity for Eddy and Cole, who kept feigning the need for a fix, and took them to a dealer who wouldn't cross them. In the estimation of an old colleague, New Jersey state police lieutenant Fred Martens, Cole is "probably the best undercover agent I ever worked with." It was his personal mission was to "rid society of the evils of drugs. . . ." Naturally, he busted the Good Samaritan.[57]

Going undercover is a much-used method of getting into the middle of unfolding criminal situations. By carefully working an investigation, big busts can result. For instance, with the combined help of the FBI, state agents, and ten local agencies, a small undercover investigation in Ohio that started with a single cocaine purchase in 2002 ended up netting some $3.6 million in street drugs and $685,000 in cash when the cops lowered the boom in January 2004.[58]

But these kinds of busts are really the rare ones. More typically, successes are meager, and the activity of undercover cops more like ongoing maintenance operations. In February 2004, the sheriff's office in Beaufort County, South Carolina, released the semiannual report of its Multi-jurisdictional Drug Task Force. The report flagged 102 indictments and 613 drug-related charges filed in 2003. Simple marijuana possession made up the bulk of the charges: 153. As one reporter had it, "Drug dealers who are put in jail are easily, and often, replaced by others looking to make an illegal buck. The [task force] continues to make undercover 'controlled drug buys' and take dealers and users off the street one at a time, but it is admittedly a frustrating, perhaps neverending, effort, said Sheriff P.J. Tanner."[59]

Beyond putting police into drug dealing situations incognito, drug cops also rely heavily on informants—both professional and informal—who can weasel their way into the lives of drug dealers and exit with evidence of criminal activity.

Roy Parrish, an ex-con informant employed by Hays County Narcotics Task Force in Texas, worked diligently to befriend his neighbors, throwing parties and welcoming minors to drink from his beer-freighted fridge. One person he sidled up to was Alexander "Rusty" Windle, a young man who was working to turn his troubled life around. A local middle-aged couple provided the support Windle needed to get his life set straight. "He sobered up, got a job as a short-order cook, and then drove a Pepsi truck for several years before becoming an electrician's apprentice. . . . He developed a reputation as a quiet, extremely dependable, even-tempered young man."[60] But he was also a mark.

Parrish "asked everybody to get him pot," said a close friend of Windle, "he practically begged you for it." At Parrish's prompting, Windle procured him some—just enough to qualify for a felony—and then, a week later, the cavalry arrived. The warrant shows that Windle had a hard time coming up with the stuff. When he couldn't get the half-ounce Parrish wanted, he managed to get a few grams. He felt so bad, he refused payment. By any reading of the events, Windle was just trying to do a favor for someone he thought was a friend. That didn't stop nine officers from the task force converging on Windle's home for a predawn raid and shooting him dead after he answered the door with a rifle.[61]

But drug suspects are better alive than dead. Here's why: When the feds caught up to David Perkins, he was deeply involved in moving cocaine and the prescription painkiller OxyContin. The DEA had detailed information about Perkins's dealings because an associate of Perkins rolled after he was busted. To get easier treatment for gun and drug charges, the associate snitched on Perkins. So did a handful of other former friends and clients. By the time Perkins was in hand a while, he flipped as well, ratting out his brother. "I told them about [him] and that pretty much f—ed me with my family," he said.[62] It's the information meat grinder that keeps churning out drug convictions. Police count on people like Perkins rolling on their associates.

Thanks to mandatory minimum sentence laws passed in the 1980s, "the feds can work miracles along the lines of Jesus feeding a crowd with five loaves and two fish," writes Cynthia Cotts. "The trick is to take a single conviction and, after debriefing the defendant, turn it into a flow of indictments, seized assets, and trial publicity."[63]

Who knows, with any luck Windle might have lived and turned snitch on friends and family. The whole idea is that, once lassoed by law enforcement, suspects can be enticed to turn around and set up someone else for a bust to get off or receive a lighter sentence. It's like a multilevel marketing scheme for the criminal underground—the more people in your downline, the better chance you can cushion your legal fall. All you've got to do is breathe and know the identities of a few offenders. "Typically they're given a quota," said an attorney about snitch deals in the Texas county where Windle lived. "Go out and get anyone you can until you've made 'X' number of cases."[64]

After nabbing a beautiful young blonde in Kerrville, Texas, on a minor drug possession bust, police made her an offer as attractive as her looks: If she helped the cops pinch five more offenders, she would dodge prosecution. An ACLU report sums up the way it worked: "Police told her to sit in a bar, flirt with men, then ask whether they could get her marijuana."[65]

It doesn't even have to be the offender. Tit for tat is all that counts. When his son was busted for selling LSD, James Settembrino was told by the US Attorney's Office that if he helped set up another dealer he could get time knocked off his son's ten-year mandatory minimum sentence. It was up to him to raise the money and locate the seller.[66]

The problem is that, faced with the hope of mitigating or eliminating their sentences, many dopers are willing to play around with the truth. "It's not unusual for informants to be bulls— artists, encouraged by prosecutors who are eager to make the case," writes Cotts. As one attorney put it, "these informants aren't deacons in their churches."[67] Staring down the business end of a long mandatory sentence makes lying, even about friends, begin to look attractive. Take a mental jaunt back to Chapter Two for a moment. If otherwise honest *cops* are willing to lie to bust someone, what about these guys? Under the circumstances, lying seems like a given.

Police readily admit that informants are untrustworthy. Said the commander of the Southwest Mississippi Narcotics Enforcement Unit,

A lot of informants are people that are selling dope themselves. It's a game. We've come back and even made cases against informants we've used. We're making a case on them while they're making a case on someone else. It's a big game. Informants love to play agencies and law enforcement against each other.

The biggest problem is that they don't listen to what we tell them to do. They think that they can do things their way. It's almost like babysitting, to stay on top of them, to make sure they're not breaking the law.[68]

Says former DEA agent Michael Levine, "These informants are criminals and liars and they will create crimes to make money and, at the same time, get the protection of the people they are working for." So why do police put up with them? "Informants run the drug war. Ninety-nine percent of all drug cases start off with a criminal informant."[69]

Informants know their worth to police. Some squeal specifically for the purpose of having the police on their side. The quid pro quo is essentially that the drug dealer is allowed by the police to operate as long as he's balancing his crimes with busts the police need to keep prosecuting the war on drugs.

Former San Miguel County, Colorado, sheriff Bill Masters mentions the case of small time drug dealer "Rick the Stick" with whom he set up busts. "Stick would . . . work for me doing dope buys from other dealers when he was short on cash or wanted to stick it to his competition," remembers Masters. Stick's cooperation was rewarded. "In my zeal to bust dope dealers, I easily overlooked Stick's own dealing. . . . All this worked out really well for Stick. He got some money form the sheriff's office and helped bust his competition. With every arrest, Stick raised his prices. He even increased his inventory prior to the fall of a competitor, knowing that he would have to supply more customers."[70]

Depending so heavily on informants puts police in the position where they are willing to suffer a lot of shady business on the part of their snitches. Writes criminologist George F. Cole, "In exchange for cooperation with the police, addicts are sometimes rewarded by being given small amounts of drugs, freedom from prosecution for possession, or police recommendations for leniency should they be sentenced. These practices result in a paradox: the police tolerate certain levels of vice in exchange for information that enables them to arrest other people for engaging in the same behavior they tolerate in the informant."[71]

For the Children

Kids get sucked into this deceptive mire as well—though it's usually undercover cops doing the bust, not convicts. Early in 2001, parents in Northern California's Yuba County were alerted to "rampant drug use and sales," specifically at Lindhurst High School. Lowering the boom, the sheriff's office sent in an undercover cop to flunk a few locker-side dealers. An attractive twenty-seven-year-old female agent of the state Alcohol Beverage Control was enrolled in classes and began attending on a daily basis near the start of the semester. After racking up a total of twenty-one marijuana, ecstasy, and diet-pill sales, the agent was pulled out, and days later the arrests made. In all, eight offenders met the business end of the law.[72]

One such criminal, Richard David Rodney, was the only adult hit by the sting, as he turned eighteen shortly before the bust. At the agent's request, he sold her two ten-dollar bags of marijuana, pot which the judge in the case later declared to be "extremely poor" in quality. But Rodney was hardly a dangerous dealer. "All parties agree that the two marijuana sales were an effort by the defendant to impress the female operative, and did not appear to be part of an ongoing profit-making enterprise," said Judge James Curry in his decision about the case, specifically citing Rodney's "naiveté." She asked him to get tougher stuff—cocaine and methamphetamine—but he wasn't able to find it.

By any reasonable standard, the case was entrapment. Sure, the officer didn't *make* the boy break the law, but she certainly cajoled him to—and, with the hormonal charge of a teenage male looking to score with a girl clearly more "mature" than any other senior on campus, the whole scenario almost inevitably led to his grabbing a few dime bags for her.

The ACLU responded to a similar Los Angeles case in which a high school football player, egged on by his "girlfriend's" insistent demands for drugs, was arrested after finally succumbing to her pleadings. Chalk it up to dumb jock luck: she was an undercover cop. "When other adults try to get young people involved with drugs, we call it contributing to the delinquency of a minor," the ACLU noted. "When the LAPD does it, we call it the school-buy program."[73]

Originally, Rodney faced two counts of felony transportation, distribution, and importation of marijuana. If convicted, he could have spent the next four years in jail. Instead, he got forty-five days in the clink after a plea bargain to a single misdemeanor charge of possession.[74] As for the others busted, it was a first offense for all but one of the other seven. No heavy drugs like coke or speed were involved, as authorities expected. As it turns out, Lindhurst's "rampant drug use and sales" problem consisted of a single repeat offender and seven rookies out of a student body of 1,250. What's more, twenty-plus known drug sales were instigated by the police.

Interestingly, when fifty students were arrested earlier this year in a single orchestrated sting at six North Carolina high schools, some students suspected they knew who the mole was. "They say she was a white girl named Cindy," reported the *Burlington Times-News*. "She was always asking other students about where to buy drugs. To get sympathy, she told everyone that her grandmother had died." But pot for pity wasn't her only gambit. Back to tripping up the boys, one female student "said that Cindy would dress provocatively and play easy to get. 'She flaunted it' . . ."[75]

It's more than troubling that with genuine criminals on the prowl, people inflicting damage to life and property, law enforcement officials deem it worth scarce time and resources to root out offenders that have to be prodded, pushed, and sometimes lured on emotionally and sexually to break the law—especially kids.

And the lesson for today, class? That this is one more way in which the criminalizing of drugs has made our society more closely resemble the criminal subculture. When trust is oft betrayed, people trust less. Criminals are used to this already. But as the dragnet goes out across society more generally and common folk are encouraged to snitch on their fellows, the very notion of society is undone. The tendrils of trust that hold communities together are undermined, and the bonds of neighbors and friends are as well. This is why the snitch, the fink, the rat, the stool pigeon, and the tattletale are regarded as the divisive, hurtful creatures they are.

War on People, War on Rights

After busting the young man who helped Fast Eddy with his bleeding hand, Cole saw him in jail. The Good Samaritan exclaimed, "Man, I was just trying to be your friend." The statement shook Cole because it was the first time he realized that he was busting a person, not just some dealer. It ate away at Cole for years. Today he's an outspoken opponent of prohibition.

"The 'War on Drugs' is a total failure. There's no way we can fix it," he says. "This isn't a war on drugs—it's a war on people. Their lives are being destroyed."[76] So are their freedoms.

The purposeful blurring of the lines between the war on terror and the war on drugs (while ignoring prohibition's responsibility in both) will only worsen things in the months and years to come. Various intrusive surveillance techniques permitted by US law for the express purpose of countering terrorists are being used on more general lawbreakers, including dopers.[77] With the nonstop harping about the drug connection to terrorist finance, it's not hard to imagine those invasive investigative practices in defense of national security being used to pursue even the commonest drug offenders.[78] And it does no good to believe that a benevolent, well-meaning administration won't abuse its draconian powers. All governments do. For all its supposed goodness, a much worse administration might be just an election away, and then all bets are off.

"We're trading our paranoia to get rid of these drugs for our constitutional rights," says attorney Dennis Knizley, "and we're making a terrible mistake in doing that."[79]

6

RENDER UNTO SEIZURE

Prohibition allows the police to steal your stuff.

JACOB A. KING JR. OWNED A MOBILE CARWASH WITH HIS fiancée's father, Robert Faulkner. In the summer of 2000, the two had a scheme to buy a custom 1964 Chevy in Phoenix and drive it back to Omaha where Faulkner would restore it. The pair would then sell the vehicle at a profit and use the proceeds to buy additional equipment for their business.

Everything cooked along fine until the airport.

At Eppley Airfield, while King was waiting to board with his fiancée and one-year-old daughter, drug agents got their hands on him and, more important, his money. After King paid cash for his ticket, a sheriff's deputy approached and questioned him about the size of his roll. King claimed he brought $7,221 with him so he could purchase the car without the hassle of waiting for a check to clear on his Omaha bank. But the deputy wasn't buying. Worse, he was taking. After a drug-sniffing dog gave the pile a whiff, agents turned the money over to the DEA.[1]

King was never arrested, and no drugs were ever linked to him—on his person, in his luggage, anywhere. The only "incriminating" item he had was the cash. "I didn't think $7,200 would cause a red flag," he later said. He was wrong. Cash isn't green for drug cops. It's crimson. And any large sum is pretty much assumed to be connected to drug trafficking. In Nevada drug cases, for instance, "state law allows police to consider any cash in excess of $300, found in a suspect's possession, to be considered the product of criminal activity," explains *Las Vegas Review-Journal* reporter Chris Di Edoardo.[2] Once that connection is made, the money is fair game for law enforcement; it can be seized and forfeited.

What of the drug dog's contribution? Consider another case in which canine cops played an important role: In February 2000, federal drug agents seized $148,000 from Vietnamese immigrant On Hoang Thach on an Amtrak train in Albuquerque. The feds claimed that because he had no credible answer for how he got the money—Thach said he was a lucky gambler—they should be able to keep the cash. No drugs were found, and Thach was not charged with any crime. Thach paid cash for his ticket, was traveling from Los Angeles and was carrying a cell phone—all of which were cited as reasons for nabbing the money, because it's apparently common knowledge that only drug couriers leave Los Angeles with cell phones and pay cash for train tickets.[3] As for the money itself, two dogs ran noses over it; one signaled dope residue on the bundles of cash, while the other did not. Hardly a resounding "affirmative," considering that 50 percent positive is still 50 percent negative.

Then there's the simple fact that vast amounts of money in circulation have drug taint, between 85 and 90 percent.[4] Micrograms are all it takes for a dog to notice, and considering the preposterous sums of cash that flow through the hands of drug organizations and then back into circulation, it's not surprising that in one test in Florida, drug residues were even found on the bills from the pockets of, among others, Jeb Bush, the Archbishop of Miami, and Janet Reno.[5] "It is conceivable," said Sunshine State Circuit Judge Robert Lance Andrews, "that anyone in South Florida who was carrying US currency would 'alert' a narcotics-sniffing dog."[6] That's true the nation over. In one case in Atlanta, prosecutors washed money seized from defendants and found cocaine. Unimpressed, the defense hired a local toxicologist who performed the same stunt with a bale of shredded money from the US Federal Reserve District Bank.

Like Moses in his showdown with Pharaoh's magicians, the defense one-upped the prosecution by also finding cocaine in the wash. After seeing that, the government returned the money.[7]

The government also returned Jacob King's money, but not because it saw the light. After filing a claim with the US Attorney's Office and meticulously proving the cash was lawfully earned, King received his money only because a federal judge ruled the government failed to meet a deadline in the forfeiture process.[8]

Saved by a bureaucratic bungle.

Pleading the Fifth

The founders would never have countenanced a person's property being only as sacred as a bureaucrat is inefficient. While forfeiture was used to finance the State in the early days of the nation, it was rooted in legislation geared toward enforcing tariffs (which before passage of the Sixteenth Amendment in 1913 was the principle source of federal funds) and was severely limited compared to the present-day forfeiture bonanza.[9] Forfeiture was mainly seen as a tariff-enforcement threat—duck the fee, lose your boat.

The Constitution's framers were highly respectful and protective of property rights. Fresh from the sting of British tyranny, the founders feared forfeiture abuse and flagrant disregard for personal property. Law professors Eric Blumenson and Eva Nilsen paint the historical backdrop: "Financial incentives promoting police lawlessness and selective enforcement, in the form of the writs of assistance, were high on the list of grievances that triggered the American Revolution." Mentioned in the previous chapter, these writs "authorized customs officers to seize suspected contraband, and retain a share of the proceeds, often a third, for themselves and their informants. From the viewpoint of the Crown, this incentive could help insure that goods landing in American ports were taxed or, if prohibited, confiscated."[10] The colonials hardly saw it that way—for them it was despotism, plain and simple.

Having successfully kicked the British back to their side of the ocean, the founders worked to ensure that such abuse would not take root in the new republic. During the constitutional debates, one Pennsylvanian anti-federalist pinpointed forfeiture proceedings as "modes of harassing the subject," recognizing their bounty as "objects highly alluring to a government. They fill the public coffers and enable government to reward its minions at a cheap rate."[11]

Addressing such concerns, the founders added the Fourth and Fifth Amendments to the Constitution. As we saw in the previous chapter, the Fourth proscribes "unreasonable searches and seizures." While most people think of the Fifth as providing "weasel protection"—or, more nobly, protecting a person from self-incrimination—it also strives to guarantee that "[n]o person shall be . . . deprived of life, liberty, or property without due process of law; nor shall private property be taken for public use without just compensation."

Notice how it never says, "Unless we're talking about dope, in which case the cops can take whatever they want." Unfortunately, that is exactly how drug warriors read the amendment today, and their interpretation has opened America up to some of the worst drug-war abuses ever.

California Schemin'

After the Sixteenth Amendment, forfeiture fell largely out of use. It experienced a quick comeback during Prohibition and was used to go after rumrunners, but after the nation woke up from this nightmare, it quickly went the way of bathtub gin and the jake trot. Its rebirth came years later.

Before President Nixon, no one really conceived of a war on drugs. Narcotics had been illegal since 1914, and there were agencies that targeted their importation and use, but enforcement wasn't a big priority. People had more pressing things to worry about: WWI, the Depression, WWII, the Communist subversion, and the recently kick-started Cold War. Beatnik heroin shooters weren't a big deal; neither were black users in the ghetto. But suddenly a convergence occurred in the late 1960s. Middle class white kids started smoking dope, and despite the fact that crime is a local problem, Nixon ran for office with a strong anti-crime plank that he promised to use on the behinds of drug addicts and their supposed scourge. "I have found great audience response to this [law and order] theme in all parts of the country," Nixon wrote his mentor, former President Eisenhower, "including areas like New Hampshire where there is virtually no race problem and relatively little crime."[12] And that's why we call him Tricky Dick. Stoking fears of Junior toking on funny cigarettes and being jacked by a cash-strapped junkie, Nixon promised a war on drugs if elected. Come Election Day, the voters bought. And Nixon delivered.

His presidency brought about a massive realignment of the government's antidrug priorities and activities, including the formation of the Drug Enforcement Agency and the passage of the 1970 Controlled Substance Act. The new law contained a provision for the forfeiture of a person's property connected to the narcotics trade. In those drug-war salad days, asset forfeiture was seen as an important tool—largely punitive—to fight big-money dope lords in places like the rural woods of the Golden State.

Northern California plays host to many profitable pastimes: hunting, fishing, skiing, camping, hiking, growing pot. Humboldt Country is particularly well known for the latter.

Leftover hippies and Haight-Ashbury refugees flocked to the rugged and remote landscape in the 1970s, setting up camp in the canyons and woods, holing up in ramshackle cabins and shacks, living out of VW buses and campers. With most of the timber jobs gone, their arrival sparked an economic shift toward botany of a different caliber. High-grade weed could fetch between one and three thousand dollars a plant; by the pound, pot sometimes pulled up to a grand.[13] Generating that kind of jack, it didn't take long for the free-love socialists to become free-market capitalists. Soon, marijuana plantations both big and small dotted the fertile landscape. Increasingly, so did armed guards, shooting at those who wandered too close to the action. One local was even blown up in a booby trap.[14]

Once the picture of rural serenity, the situation in Humboldt did little but worsen as the Reagan administration eclipsed Jimmy Carter's. "They call this the lawless area, and they're right," said Humboldt district attorney Bernard DePaoli in 1982. "It can't be anything else when the usual deterrent to the crime of growing the drug is a $5,000 fine and maybe six months in the county jail. All the defendant has to do to pay the fine is sell six plants." With all the money growers were making, DePaoli said, "taking away their land is the only thing that will work."[15]

The feds' solution to the problem in Humboldt was to partner with state authorities in a forfeiture scheme designed to nip growers in both the proverbial and literal bud. Stripping away any advantage their wealth might offer in riding out prosecution or surviving a bad sentence, once local cops busted a grower and charged him under state law, a federal agent would step in and seek a forfeiture order from a federal judge, using the Controlled Substance Act. If he succeeded, growers could kiss the back forty goodbye. "The idea of it is scaring the hell out of them already," said DePaoli.[16]

Considering what was coming down the pike, it should have scared the hell out of a lot more people. It was certainly more than Nixon planned for. More than a weapon against dealers and traffickers, thanks to an obscure medieval doctrine, forfeiture was about to become a budgetary boon for police, skewing law-enforcement priorities and threatening property owners everywhere.

Jailing Junk

At some point during Dennis and Denise Schilling's career as indoor pot growers, the authorities got wise and let loose the sword of Damocles that hangs precariously over the head of every illicit greenthumb. In May 2002, cops raided the Schillings' Big Bend, Wisconsin, home and found about 6½ ounces of marijuana, twenty-one plants, along with twelve grams of hallucinogenic mushrooms. The tally was not extraordinary. Neither were the Schillings' possessions.

Unlike the high rollers' loot DePaoli was concerned with, assets listed for the Schillings included $1,500 in various accounts and a handful of uncashed checks: a $7,300 bank check, a $629 payroll check, a $143 refund check from the Department of Workforce Development, and a $3 Gallo wine rebate. Other than their $118,000 home (on which they still owed nearly $50,000), the couple could lay claim to two heavily used automobiles and a pile of assorted debts. Following the arrest, the couple's financial situation was so desperate that Dennis had to borrow money from his daughter and prematurely pull cash from a retirement account to cover attorney costs.[17]

In this, their case is no more tragic than those of many others who are busted and have their property threatened with seizure. The big difference: Five days after the seizure order, Dennis and Denise, wildly distraught, went to a Madison motel and hanged themselves, ending their criminal prosecution by default.

But the fact that the Schillings couldn't be found guilty for a crime meant squat to the circling feds looking to pick the bones of the meager estate. For almost twenty years, such technicalities hadn't mattered. In 1984, Congress passed the Federal Comprehensive Forfeiture Act (part of the larger Comprehensive Crime Control Act of the same year). The legislation allowed the feds to also nab "derivative proceeds" the same way they nabbed narcotics—civilly. And I don't mean well mannered. The distinction is based on how the forfeiture is conducted, as a criminal or civil proceeding.

In the late 1970s and early 1980s, federal prosecutors were very hot on the use of forfeiture to curb drug crime, but even a decade after the Controlled Substance Act had been written, it had rarely been used against dopers. This made the forfeiture flurry in Humboldt unusual. The problem with the law was that grabbing assets was contingent upon a criminal conviction—some sort of strange, archaic notion that someone should actually be found guilty before you punish him. Worse, prosecutors had to prove in a criminal proceeding that the man was not only guilty of the crime but also that the stuff to be forfeited either facilitated the crime (e.g., a plane used to smuggle pot) or was the fruit of it (e.g., a house bought with drug money). Sure, it was doable, but what a hassle. The better deal would be one that allowed authorities to nab a guy's stuff *without* proving he'd been involved in a crime.

At the dawn of the Reagan years, convictionless forfeiture was the Holy Grail for drug warriors. Better yet, it was Excalibur, a powerfully destructive weapon that could cleave dopers to the quick. Though thoroughly medieval, this weapon would prove much less mythic.

The first step is to take the forfeiture out of the criminal domain entirely. Instead of taking a man's ill-gotten gains as part of a criminal punishment, the new scheme would be to prosecute the property itself. In short, cops jail a man's junk, not him. In a sense, this wasn't new. Police had always been able to confiscate and destroy contraband. If cops find a bale of marijuana, they don't take it back to the lost and found and wait for the rightful owner. Because the item itself is illegal, there is no such thing as a rightful owner. Police can seize and destroy the pot. Extrapolating from there, as mentioned above, in 1984 legislators passed the Federal Comprehensive Forfeiture Act. The legislation allowed the feds to also seize and forfeit much more than mere dope. Now almost any property "tainted" by contraband was also contraband.

"Let us give law enforcement every single tool" to pursue drug dealers, said a young Republican congressman riding herd on the bill. Dan Lungren, who later became California's attorney general and a failed GOP gubernatorial candidate, argued that nailing and jailing traffickers wasn't enough to stem the tide of illicit dope flooding the country. He and others insisted that lawbreakers' property should be forfeited to the State.[18] The only way to hit the pushers where it hurt was in the purse. The legislation allowed the government to seize any property connected to a drug crime—a dealer's car, a buyer's house, whatever. Covering most of the bases, the bill specifically listed filchable assets as "aircraft, vehicles, or vessels, moneys, negotiable instruments, securities, firearms, raw materials, products, or equipment, controlled substances, paraphernalia, and books, records, and research."[19]

With the bill's passage, suddenly police were empowered to grab not only that bale of pot in the back of the pickup truck but also the truck. If the truck drove to a house to unload the goods for further distribution, the authorities could also grab the house. They could do this without a criminal conviction. The owner could be innocent of any wrongdoing, but it wouldn't matter because the property was the problem, not the person.

With the feds pushing the legal envelope, states were encouraged to follow suit and did. State forfeiture laws could be more restrictive on law enforcement than the federal law, but they boiled down to much the same thing: The punishment was being meted out against the property the same way it was against the pot.

This wasn't something Lungren and company pulled out of thin air. The precedent in the West goes back at least as far as the Middle Ages. Litigation attorney Stefan B. Herpel explains the dubious origin of the modern-day practice of civil forfeiture: "The old English rule was that an inanimate object causing the death of a person was forfeited to the king . . . The rule proceeded from the legal superstition that an inanimate object can itself be guilty of wrongdoing . . . [P]remised on the guilt of the property itself, property was forfeitable regardless of the guilt or innocence of its owner."[20] The big difference today, as Herpel points out, is that the law is far tougher than its mediaeval predecessor. For the government to seize an apartment building, the structure doesn't have to kill someone, it only has to be used in a drug sale.

Going after the property in what's called an *in rem* procedure ("against the thing" rather than *in personam*, "against the person") reduces the relevance of a property owner to something of a third party. Sometimes, as with the Schillings, something much less. In a civil forfeiture action, warm bodies count for nothing. They can be sitting in a cell, dangling from a rope—what's the dif? Property doesn't need a pulse to prosecute.[21]

The feds had the Schillings' house sold off and, after a *compassionate* arrangement with the probate attorney, took only $26,009. Taxes and debts threaten to suck the remainder dry.

The Lord Giveth, the Police Taketh Away

It's easy for folks to feel little pity for the Schillings' situation. After all, they were growing weed, right? But what about the Joe who's not slinging smack or profiting from pot? As Paul Craig Roberts and Lawrence M. Stratton explain in *The Tyranny of Good Intentions*, you can't "leave suspected drug traffickers unprotected by traditional safeguards of criminal procedure . . . without also leaving the innocent unprotected." As Roberts writes elsewhere, "Conservatives did not realize that the main result of their efforts would be the routine confiscation of the assets of the innocent."[22]

An example provided by Roberts and Stratton is the case of Helen Hoyle, an elderly black woman in Washington DC who "lost her home because of police suspicion that one of her grandchildren once had drugs in the house." Another: Donald A. Regan of Montvale, New Jersey, picked up a hitchhiker in need of a lift. Authorities seized the car when they found drugs, unbeknownst to Regan, in the passenger's possession.[23]

Hoyle and Regan are not alone.

Spotting a listing for a used Corvette in Missouri in January 2000, Rudy Ramirez and his brother-in-law rented a car and drove to Kansas City from their home in Edinburg, Texas, with $7,300 cash to purchase this Odin atop the American pantheon of muscle cars. Everything was going fine until the KC police pulled them over. They asked if he had any money; Ramirez said yes. "I didn't think they would take it away. I had nothing to hide." But, as writer Kyla Dunn explains, "the trajectory of the rental car, and the piles of cash, suggested otherwise to police." They suspected he was hauling dope from Mexico. Though a thorough search of the vehicle turned up no drugs, police were convinced he was a trafficker and seized six thousand dollars of his money before turning him loose. Though he was later able to prove the legitimacy of the loot, authorities refused to return the now-forfeited money.[24] The mere charge was all that mattered.

"If [a suspect] is charged with intent to distribute, you take the money, you take the car," said police lieutenant Arthur Brodeur of Marlborough, Massachusetts. "As far as we're concerned, they bought the car or are keeping the payments on the car with drug money." Thus, it's not about what's established in court. It's about the biased assumptions of police—precisely why the founders insisted on jury trials, so a person's peers, and not the authorities alone, could establish the facts of the matter. In asset forfeiture, justice too often takes a backseat to finances. And it's a vicious cycle. Brodeur says most of the money he seizes goes to fund further investigations. It's like an entrepreneur reinvesting in his business.[25]

But unlike the free market, in which wealth is expanded through mutually beneficial trade, forfeiture is a zero-sum game, and far too often the presumption of guilt means the innocent get the shaft. Even when they prevail, they can still get gouged. Disabled retiree Delmar Puryear almost lost his thirty-seven-acre farm after police found five hundred marijuana plants growing on the property. As we saw in Chapter Four, covert pot plantations are common in places like Kentucky, Tennessee, and West Virginia. If a grower thinks he can use someone else's land to avoid seizure of his own property, he'll do so. A jury saw reason and refused to convict Puryear of any criminal wrongdoing, but that didn't keep the feds at bay. With the old man over the barrel, the government pressed for the forfeiture of the farm until Puryear finally agreed to fork over twelve thousand dollars, an extortionist's fee.[26]

US attorney James DeAtley seized Houston's Red Carpet Inn in 1998 because employees said they thought guests might be dealing drugs. No genuine evidence was needed to make the grab; instead, the government argued that hotel owners gave "tacit consent" to drug dealing and other crimes by not following police counsel on operating their business: hiking room rates, hiring security guards, not renting to locals, among other points of advice. Why a hotel owner would listen to a cop about how to run his hotel is puzzling enough; that the police would actually shut him down and take his business for not taking the advice is, however, nothing short of grotesque and outrageous.[27]

Henry Hyde certainly thought so.

Day in Court? Ha!

Property rights are basic to the issues of drugs, prohibition, and forfeiture. The very question of drug use is fundamentally a property-rights question: *Is that roach yours, or isn't it?*[28] But while some may recoil at the notion that the right to life, liberty, and property also means a man has the right to snort a line of coke or fire up a blunt, they should be able to see the astounding hypocrisy of a government constituted in part for the protection of property actively working to undermine that right.

Henry Hyde saw it. In 1993 the Republican congressman from Illinois had something of an epiphany regarding asset forfeiture abuse. By that year, several exposés had been written on the topic in such papers as the *St. Louis Post-Dispatch* and *Pittsburgh Press* and by columnists such as the redoubtable *Chicago Tribune* pundit Steve Chapman. Convinced that the "Kafkaesque" side of the law was far too pronounced, that same year Hyde introduced legislation to end the worst of these abuses.[29] As we'll see victory has remained illusive.

Since the passage of the Federal Comprehensive Forfeiture Act of 1984, Americans have been subject to confiscations of their property—with or without warrants—based solely on probable cause. Actual proof of wrongdoing is for the courts to figure out, which, despite all the grand images of Blind Lady Justice, is a boon to police. Once seized, the property can be reclaimed only by suing the government in civil court, a situation that greatly favors the government. The burden of proof in civil proceedings is much lighter than in a criminal case: Police can establish guilt based on a mere "preponderance of the evidence"(which means at least a 51 percent chance), rather than meeting the much stricter standard of "beyond a reasonable doubt."

Speaking at a 1999 conference on asset forfeiture reform hosted by the Cato Institute, Gordon Kromberg, assistant US attorney for the Eastern District of Virginia, defended civil forfeiture precisely on the basis that it can be used to punish people when a prosecutor cannot muster enough evidence to prove guilt. Reporter Michael Lynch sums up the argument thusly:

> Prosecutors are busy. Way too many bad guys are running around for them to help catch with stings and convict in court. Some outlaws are even pretty smart. [Kromberg] admitted that he currently had 10 money laundering cases in which he couldn't figure out how the people were washing the dough. But still, he knew these people were guilty and was certain they needed to be punished. Should we let these people get away, he asked, before answering in an illuminating way: Not if we can punish them through other means. . . . He bluntly declared that people like him ought to be able to punish individuals they believe are guilty, even if they can't prove that guilt in a court of law.[30]

Others have said as much. "If we can put together a criminal case, great," said Franklin County, New York, prosecutor Derek Champagne. "But if we can't, for whatever reason, we're going to go after who's doing it or the person who owns the property as a civil case."[31]

By lowering the burden of proof, the government makes it much easier to keep a man's stuff. Eighty percent of forfeitures are never challenged in court. Defenders of forfeiture argue that this shows property owners are guilty, but it does no such thing. More obviously, it shows that few people can afford to fight the State with the deck stacked against them.

Getting word his mother was stricken ill in Mexico, Anastasio Ortiz Vega bundled up his life's savings—$23,600 earned from long, hard hours of masonry in Nashville, Tennessee. After hiding the money in a spare tire, Vega hit the road. But the money never made it further south than West

Memphis, where a cop pulled him over and seized his purse. Vega's boss vouched for his employee, who put in as many as eighty hours working seven days a week. "I assure you that was very hard-earned money," he said. "He just works like a dog." Vega was able to prove he lawfully earned more than $54,000 the year the money was grabbed, but the Crittendon County prosecutor had Vega right where he wanted him. With time and leverage on his side, the prosecutor held out till legal bills forced Vega to settle. Vega recouped $16,500 of his money—the government kept $7,100.[32]

Even if claimants make out better than Vega in a forfeiture contest, those who can afford to fight city hall and win still suffer. Beyond legal bills and lost time, often the government will try to make contesting a seizure even more prohibitive by using a lopsided loser-pays model. In Nevada, for instance, "most forfeiture complaints specifically [ask] the court to award the county fees and costs against all unsuccessful claimants in the case."[33] If a person wins, it can still come back to bite them. In 1998, the South Florida Impact Task Force nabbed thirty thousand dollars from the bank accounts of an Orlando epoxy manufacturer based on a transaction with a single Colombian client. After the case crumbled, the task force returned the money—less six thousand for its legal costs.[34] Similarly, after fighting three years to save her home from a "drug nuisance abatement" forfeiture in Seattle, Etta Mae Franklin was billed by the city for the cost of filing the civil action.[35]

Facing a criminal charge only makes matters worse. Because asset forfeiture is a civil proceeding, defendants cannot plead the Fifth when asked questions that might incriminate themselves, and any statements or admissions made in the civil trial can boomerang the defendant in his criminal trial, thus dissuading many from contesting a seizure.[36]

And, as Ramirez's Corvette-hunting misadventure in Missouri proves, innocence is no guarantee of returned property. After the Brunswick County, North Carolina, Sheriff's Department confiscated a total of $7,633 from two men, Ernest Hill and Morris Hill (unrelated), in separate drug raids in late 2000, authorities were unable to prove the pair had anything to do with illegal drugs. The charges were duly dropped but the money kept. The sheriff's office had sent the cash to the US Marshal's Office for forfeiture. Once the feds have possession of the money, any legal wrangling to have it returned must be done on federal turf. But by the time Hill and Hill jumped through the necessary hoops and discovered this, the deadline to contest the seizure was past. Instead of getting their money back, the Justice Department kept 20 percent and sent the remaining 80 percent back to the sheriff's department to be disposed of as it best saw fit.[37]

Little Orphan Forfeiture

Such a split is very common. In what's called "adoptive forfeiture," state and local agencies turn seized property over to the feds to be processed through federal statutes. The reason for this is that many states have restrictions on how police treat seized assets. A few states, for instance, require that all seized loot be deposited in the state's general fund; others insist it be devoted to education. But there's a loophole: If the feds are involved in the seizure either by physically being there at the time the property was grabbed or by having the local agency hold the goods until a later time for the feds to officially seize it, then the feds and locals split the money. The federal government usually keeps 20 percent and sends the remainder back to the local agencies responsible for the bust. Such sums create a strong incentive for police to treat drug cases not like law enforcement, but like fundraisers and budget boosters.

In 2000, the California legislature passed a bill that would have ended this practice. It required local and state police to petition the state court for permission to transfer seized property to the feds. "Despite major asset forfeiture reform a decade ago, our local law enforcement agencies have circumvented state due process laws, allowing them to seize a person's assets without that person ever being convicted of a criminal violation," said state senator John Vasconcellos. "The lure of increased revenue has blinded local law enforcement to their responsibility to abide by our state policy and to protect the due process rights of our citizens."[38]

Giving the middle finger to the resounding bipartisan support for the legislation, Governor Gray Davis vetoed it.

Asset forfeiture reform has been a hard fight from day one. Despite the gross mistreatment of seizure victims, Henry Hyde was shot down year after year. It took seven laborious orbits around the sun before night set on some of Hyde's targeted abuses. Until he was able to get passed his Civil Asset Forfeiture Reform Act of 2000, before a person could sue to get property returned, he had to post a bond of five thousand dollars or 10 percent of the property's value, whichever is lesser. Claimants actually had to pay for the privilege of trying to get their property returned. Unfortunately, while the bond is gone, someone contesting a seizure can still take it in the wallet: "If a judge determines a claim is frivolous, the owner can be subject to a fine of $250 to $5,000," writes *Kansas City Star* journalist Karen Dillon.[39] The burden of proof was also totally out of whack with the framers' idea of due process. The burden was on the person contesting the seizure; he had the preposterous job of proving to the government that his property was innocent. Hyde turned this around, though his bill couldn't toughen up the standard of proof past a preponderance of the evidence. Before Hyde, claimants also had very limited time to file their claim. If the forfeiture had not been contested in the short allotted window, you could kiss goodbye any chance of seeing your stuff again—unless a police chief was driving it to work. The sad thing was that Hyde's bill wasn't able to hem in adoptive seizure or the police's direct profiting from seized cash and property.

That's the real dirty side of asset forfeiture: Police are given incentive to seize property because they profit from forfeiture.

Finders, Keepers

The government stacks the forfeiture deck against citizens as much as possible for one basic reason: It gets to keep what it takes. Seized funds are assimilated Borg-like into the budgets of federal and local law enforcement. This is partly why it took Hyde seven years to get any reforms of this nightmare passed. Drug warriors have a highly lucrative vested interest in seeing the laws are not messed with, and anyone trying to handicap the goose that's laying the golden egg will not find it an easy job.

And these eggs are golden, indeed.

In 2001, authorities in Cook County, Illinois, seized a total of $14.8 million. Almost $12 million of that was in cash. Nearly six hundred cars were seized. Additionally, nearly $20 million was sent upriver for deposit in the federal government's asset forfeiture fund for the state.[40]

In 2002, the Tuscaloosa County, Alabama, Sheriff's Department seized almost $2.9 million; more than $1.9 million of it ended up in department coffers.[41]

Police in Michigan are prospering all the same. "In Oakland County, Farmington Hills Police Chief William Dwyer said drug forfeiture funds have been used to purchase in-car video cameras, computers, weapons for the South Oakland Narcotics Intelligence Consortium (SONIC), training, intelligence equipment and a public seminar on drugs in the workplace, among other things," reports the *Detroit News*. "The Oakland County Sheriff's Department has used drug forfeiture funds to buy Taser stun guns, a mobile command post and an all-terrain armored vehicle." Things are similar elsewhere in the state. In 2002, the budgets of Macomb County police agencies received an infusion of nearly $1.5 million in forfeiture money.[42]

It's the same across the country.

"The Comprehensive Forfeiture Act of 1984 has been good for prosecutors and police, who now drive seized luxury cars in place of government-issue automobiles," write Roberts and Stratton, elaborating, "Gold Rolexes have replaced Timexes, and seized cash now finances tennis and health club memberships for law enforcement personnel." Ashland, Massachusetts, police chief Roy Melnick used seizure money to buy "new gold and silver badges for his officers, which he also presented to selectmen and the new town manager as gifts, encased in lucite with names inscribed."[43] Melnick said he bought the badges to boost morale. They cost sixty-six hundred dollars.

Beyond being used to bolster basic police opulence, drug dough sometimes goes to thoroughly ridiculous items, as well. An audit in Kansas turned up a record of forfeiture money going toward drug-education coloring books and crayons. The same audit found that several hundred dollars of forfeited cash went to buy a remote-control door opener for a police dog.[44] One Missouri sheriff put seizure money to dubious PR use, buying a pamphlet entitled "Your Friend the Sheriff."[45]

And abuse, as usual, is not unheard of. "One agency actually had disposed of drug money before a judge declared it legally confiscated," reported Dillon in the *Star*. "Another agency improperly deposited state and federal money into a local bank account instead of its law enforcement trust fund, as the law requires."[46]

Fixin' for Forfeiture

"Police have become addicted to seizure money," says former police chief of both San Jose, California, and Kansas City, Missouri, Joseph McNamara, needing the additional funds to help finance their ever-growing budget expenditures.

Some in law enforcement are perfectly frank about their forfeiture jones. "I could never fund my narcotics unit properly with the budget I get," said Framingham, Massachusetts, police chief Steven Carl. "The majority of undercover and narcotics work comes out of the drug law enforcement funds. We have a very large budget for personnel and operations, but it does not allow for extras. . . . [T]he narcotics trade is not going away and we need to always have resources."[47]

Roberts and Stratton highlight a 1990 Justice Department memo for US attorneys that emphasized the importance of seizures: "Every effort must be made to increase forfeiture income during the remaining months of 1990." And they were raking in the dough. Between 1984 and 2001, the federal forfeiture take was $7.3 billion.[48]

This addiction to forfeiture money has twisted law enforcement priorities. Blumenson and Nilsen write, "Economic temptation hovers over all drug enforcement decisions: methamphetamine distribution may demand more enforcement, for example, but targeting marijuana deals is usually far more profitable because methamphetamine transactions tend to occur on condemned or valueless property." The two professors quote a Justice Department study that shows cash as a key focus: "[I]t will be useful for task force members to know the major sources of these assets and whether it is more efficient to target major dealers or numerous smaller ones."[49]

Blumenson and Nilson point to another problem—one that mirrors the larger problem of police going after petty drug offenders to the neglect of more serious property-crime violators: "[B]y linking police budgets to drug law enforcement, forfeiture laws induce police and prosecutors to neglect other, often more pressing crime problems. They make business judgments which can only compete with, if not wholly supplant, their broader law enforcement goals. The Department of Justice has periodically made this practice official policy, as in 1989 when all US attorneys were directed to 'divert personnel from other activities' if necessary to meet their commitment 'to increase forfeiture production.'"[50] As former New York City police commissioner Patrick Murphy explained in testimony before Congress, the result is that forfeiture laws "created a great temptation for state and local police departments to target assets rather than criminal activity."[51]

Go no further than the case of Malibu multimillionaire Donald Scott to see this in action. As covered briefly in Chapter Two, police secured a warrant to raid Scott's ranch home by juking a judge with false and misleading evidence. Scott was killed by police in the raid, and no drugs were found. But stopping a drug kingpin was never really the goal of the operation. A later investigation turned up evidence that the seizure of Scott's substantial estate was the primary motivation for the raid.[52]

Another lesser but more widespread and thus insidious example of this is the practice of busting drug buyers on the streets. Recalling a study mentioned in Chapter One, dealers are usually the ones that pack heat. Smalltime buyers rarely carry guns. This makes busting customers less risky than busting dealers, who are the greater threat to a community's safety. It's easy to justify this misdirection of effort, however, because while they don't usually carry guns, drug buyers do carry cash. If cops bust dealers, they get something essentially worthless—dope which must be destroyed. But if they bust buyers, they get their wallets.

Sometimes risking the violence is worth the payoff, even if it puts innocent townspeople possibly in harms way. With dollars on the mind, at least one law enforcement agency in Florida distorts the cost/benefit scheme to the extreme; more than simply taking advantage of the fact dopers are doing business in its jurisdiction, the Sarasota Police Department has its officers pose as dealers and entice dangerous international drug buyers to venture into the town, then bust them and grabs their goods once inside Sarasota jurisdiction. Yes, cops—those sworn to fight crime—actually invite out-of-town criminals to create *more* crime, not less. "The main point is to get bad guys off the streets," said a lead detective who wished to go unnamed. "My job is to lock bad guys up." But even though residents think they've got plenty of homegrown baddies and ne'er-do-wells, the Sarasota PD insists on luring violent criminals from as far away as England, Venezuela, and Panama for no more glorious reason than the payoff. Raking in more than $1.3 million since 2001, Sarasota cops are able to use the money for training junkets to Orlando, Panama City Beach, and Las Vegas, among other things, including squad-car computers that automatically print out traffic tickets.[53]

While Hyde's reforms fix some of the more egregious abuses, they are only helpful on the federal level. Despite the machinations of big-government centralists, there are still fifty states, and many of them are still fouled up in the forfeiture category. Back in the early 1980s, when using federal statutes to bust Humboldt pot farmers, DEA agents encouraged states to craft their own forfeiture laws. As soon as they began to see the tremendous profits involved, not only states but also local municipalities cranked up the forfeiture machine.

Local Loco

The drive from Humboldt to Oakland only takes about five and a half hours, though possibly longer if you're waiting by a curb trying to hitch-hike—which, if you actually go to Oakland, might be how you get home, depending on what the police think you're doing when you're in town.

Apparently awash in hash and hookers, city elders took the forfeiture ball and ran it as far upfield as bureaucratically possible. If a junkie or john prowls the streets in search of fix or female, the police are empowered by city ordinance to not only arrest the suspect, but take his car, too. Oakland police "conduct their car seizure operations, called 'Operation Beat Feet,' in various neighborhoods about twice a month. About 80 percent of the cars seized belong to alleged drug buyers, and the rest to alleged johns."[54] In the first three years of the program, the city confiscated 350 vehicles and auctioned off more than 280 of them.

While hustling to have a similar measure enacted across the bay in San Francisco, Supervisor Amos Brown cited people's "right to peace, tranquility and safety in their neighborhoods" and called for cars used in drug buys to be labeled "public nuisances" and subject to confiscation and sale. How much of a public nuisance are these cars? Brown, who is also a Baptist minister, likened the vehicles of drug users and sellers to the chariots of Pharaoh's army. And his proposed ordinance? According to the *San Francisco Chronicle*, Brown compared his plan to God's knocking the wheels off those chariots.[55]

When Brown's proposal came up for a vote, the board of supervisors—in a rare bout of sensibility—hammered it, voting to send it to the place where bad ideas go when they die. "In this ordinance," said Supervisor Leslie Katz, "the forfeiting of vehicles runs the risk of forfeiting those rights we must hold dear, and that is my primary concern. The presumption of innocence is one of the primary tenets of American jurisprudence." Brown, of course, was bummed. "We've listened to the people who conveyed their fear, their trauma and their personal pain," he offered in justification for the measure.[56] Apparently, however, he never listened to someone who has had his property wrongfully filched by authorities and had to sue the city to get it back even though charges were either not filed or substantiated—someone like Eric Kinney.

Kinney's car was nabbed when he was caught in a 1999 sting operation, allegedly trying to score two grams of ganja. Oakland police seized his 1989 Ford Ranger on the spot; the vehicle was worth about five thousand dollars. He eventually got his truck returned, but it was a very tough fight that in the end cost him two thousand dollars in legal fees. What's more, he was never convicted of any wrongdoing.[57] He wasn't even charged.

While an Oakland official tries to reassure the public that car-snatching "is not a big moneymaker for us," by fall 2000 the city had raked in some $321,000 since the program started in 1997.

The previously mentioned South Florida Impact Task Force is another practitioner of bounty hunting. While praised by drug warriors like General Barry McCaffrey, the heavy-handed tactics of the Coral Gables-based force draw fire from even the Justice Department and DEA. With seizures dubbed "overaggressive" by some, between 1993 and 2000 the organization nabbed more than $140 million in suspect funds. "This is not too much different from the Sheriff of Nottingham, except we don't have any Robin Hood," said Robert Bauman, a former Maryland congressman and boardmember of Forfeiture Endangers American Rights, an organization dedicated to reforming forfeiture laws.[58] Instead of robbing the rich and giving to the poor, the task force robs from whomever and gives to itself. As the Drug Reform Coordination Network summed it up, the South Florida Impact Task Force "is an entirely self-funding operation. In other words, to survive it must seize assets. Asset forfeiture is both its reason and its means for existing."[59]

Reform? Takin' It to the States

But it is also at the state level that the best hope for reform can be seen. Carol Thomas of Millville, New Jersey, had her 1990 Ford

Thunderbird seized when her seventeen-year-old son used the car to sell marijuana to an undercover cop. Regardless of the fact that no drugs were actually found in the car and Thomas had no clue her son was using the car to pitch pot, the police kept the automobile. Humorously enough, at the time of the bust, Thomas was an officer with the Cumberland County Sheriff's Office and had actually worked on the same narcotics team that filched her T-Bird.[60]

With the help of the Institute for Justice, a civil liberties law-firm based in Washington DC, Thomas sued to have her car returned. What was really stunning—and important—was the argument. IJ argued that New Jersey's practice of turning over forfeited money to police and prosecutors violated the due process clause of the Constitution. The judge agreed, and Thomas won her car back along with the fifteen hundred dollar bond she was required to post to contest the seizure.[61] But Thomas wasn't done yet.

After she won her case, the judge allowed Thomas to advance a counterclaim that called into question the legality of the state's forfeiture laws. Thomas and IJ succeeded again. Calling it a "rotten system," in December 2002, Superior Court Judge G. Thomas Bowen ruled that the bounty-hunting aspect of forfeiture obscured police priorities enough to jeopardize citizens' due process rights; he declared the law unconstitutional.[62] While never before litigated in court, that basic argument has been fundamental to legislative and initiative-based reform efforts in other states such as Oregon, Missouri, and Utah.

The nutshell version is that police shouldn't profit from seizures, and so forfeited money should be deposited in the state's general fund or particular programs that do not benefit law enforcement directly.

When Colorado worked to reform its forfeiture laws in 2002, two sheriffs were vocal supporters. Said San Miguel County sheriff Bill Masters, "The public needs to be able to trust law enforcement, and clear forfeiture rules that protect the innocent and reduce monetary incentives will help to restore some of that lost trust." Pitkin County sheriff Bob Braudis told the *Aspen Daily News*, "To continue to finance the war on drugs with seizures from people who are never convicted of a crime is not only counterintuitive, but unfair."[63] When the dust cleared and the politicking was finished, the successful reforms prohibited police from directly profiting from seized loot and—better than Hyde fared—bumped the standard of proof past a "preponderance of the evidence" up to "clear and convincing" proof the assets were involved in the drug trade.[64]

Getting these sorts of reforms state to state and in force at the federal level is vital if the founders' vision of property rights and due process are to have any weight in modern America. But then, the drug war is at odds with much of what the founders' expected from government. Hyde isn't particularly hopeful. "I've been around Capitol Hill long enough," he says, "to know that no legislation has a realistic chance of becoming law that will take hundreds of millions—indeed billions—of dollars away from . . . the war on drugs."[65]

7

BIG GUNS

Prohibition turns police from public servants to soldiers.

THE TOUGHEST COP IN THE NATION, SHERIFF JOE ARPAIO OF Maricopa County, Arizona, has a tank. The sheriff's Web site calls the howitzer, donated by the US Department of Defense, "the ultimate weapon in the war on drugs." Painted black and emblazoned with twin lightning bolts, a badge, and the words "Sheriff Arpaio's War on Drugs," the howitzer fires pyrotechnics from the barrel to excite kids before antidrug classes and events.[1]

What's troubling is not so much the use of military surplus to grab the attention and applause of children. It's the continuing militarization of the nation's police in attitude, weaponry, training, and tactics. And while amping up the bellicosity has enabled cops to nab more dopers, the tradeoff for this full-metal jacketing of law enforcement has been the increasing loss of traditional American rights and liberties.

Storm Troopers

Getting ready for her government job in downtown New York City the morning of May 16, 2003, Alberta Spruill walked into the main room of her Harlem apartment as a dozen officers from the city police's

Emergency Service Unit and regular patrol converged on her home. Told by a confidential informant they'd find a cache of guns and drugs, guarded by dogs, the ESU team battered open the front door and chucked a stun grenade into the room Spruill had just entered. The device, also called a flashbang, is intended to distract suspects. This one exploded with a concussive, deafening bang above a glass-top table, instantly shattering it amid a blinding white flash. Then, with whipsting speed, six tactical officers rushed the dwelling and handcuffed a coughing and screaming Spruill.

Up to this point, the raid went flawlessly, but police were soon puzzled to find neither guns nor drugs in the home of the fifty-seven-year-old, churchgoing grandmother. The snarling guard dogs had apparently taken a powder as well. As it turned out, the informant had been less than accurate; the cops had the wrong apartment. Realizing their mistake, the police apologized and asked if Spruill needed any medical attention. She did, but the paramedics could not save her. Spruill died of a heart attack less than an hour and a half later.[2]

When the sheriff's office of Preble County, Ohio, got word from an informant that residents of a rural farmhouse were peddling pot, it conducted a three-day investigation and then sent its Emergency Services Unit on a late-evening, no-knock raid. Because police thought there might be more than a dozen men at the farmhouse, they deployed a heavily armed team of fifteen. The result, besides what the *Dayton Daily News* referred to as "a small amount of marijuana, pipes and a bong, papers used in rolling the drug, and weapons," was a dead suspect, Clayton J. Helriggle, whom police shot as he came down the stairs with a 9mm handgun.[3]

Helriggle's mother admits it was regular practice for her son and the men at the house to smoke pot in the evening after work. But was such a raid necessary? Police said they found materials used to distribute marijuana, true, but sandwich bags are also used to wrap up a ham and cheese on rye. The other items found indicate nothing more than use of the drug, which was found only in "a small amount"—hardly worth sending in the big guns. (In Ohio possessing less than 3.5 ounces of marijuana is an infraction punishable by a hundred dollar fine.[4]) As for possession of weapons, *it was a farmhouse*. What farmhouse doesn't have a few rifles and other firearms? Given that fact alone, Helriggle's death is likely the police's fault more than anything. When the police raid a house at twilight, it's perfectly predictable that a suspect would pick up a gun and come down the stairs to face the intruders. Responsible homeowners and renters should be expected to defend their families and homes from invaders.

After the raid, Helriggle's father said, officers "high-fiv[ed] each other." "They were so busy celebrating and everything. It was like a carnival to them," he said. "They all got to use their new guns and stuff." The sheriff's office denies the celebration, but Helriggle's father watched the jubilation with his wife from a nearby field, presumably unaware then that their son had been killed by the celebrants.[5]

There was certainly no celebration going on the morning of October 17, 2002, on Marcella Monroe's block. Hoping to nab a sizeable stash of cannabis from a major cultivation operation, an awe-striking total of fifty-nine officers converged on the Whiteaker neighborhood of Eugene, Oregon, targeting three homes Monroe co-owned. The officers' use of an armored tank-like vehicle borrowed from the National Guard set the tone for what was to follow—a down-home version of the invasion of Normandy. Storming through the properties and securing the area, police blocked traffic and guarded alleyways while other officers burst through doorways in a massive show of force, setting off stun grenades and bringing to bear an impressive and imposing display of firepower.[6]

Once inside, police yanked four people from their beds, cuffed them, and kept them detained in a room for several hours. One woman was pulled from bed in only a T-shirt and underpants, the other completely nude. Increasing the degradation, police covered Monroe's head with a black hood until she agreed to cooperate.[7] Not that cooperation produced much. No marijuana plants or weapons were found anywhere on the properties. One tenant was found with less than an ounce of pot—a misdemeanor in Oregon and hardly a cache requiring the services of the

Eugene-Lane County Metro SWAT team, Springfield SWAT, the Eugene Rapid Deployment Unit, Portland police, and the pair of National Guardsmen needed to drive the armored vehicle.[8]

Bespeaking the total failure of the raid, no charges at all were filed against the property owners, and the misdemeanor charges against the tenant were later dropped.[9]

As with Spruill, sometimes even the most innocent are at risk from overeager, militarized police. Early on the morning of May 14, 2003, officers broke down the door to sixty-eight-year-old Timothy Brockman's apartment, tossed in a stun grenade, blitzed the residence with guns, gas masks, and shields, and ordered the old man out of bed. Surprisingly, they found no weapons or drugs on the former Marine and retired factory worker. Perhaps not too surprisingly, considering the quality of the investigation. There was one informant who identified the wrong apartment building, another who didn't exist, confusion about the apartment address on top of the misidentified building, little or no double-checking of evidence, and no checking at all of various key assumptions. Still, armed with much more determination than preparation, the officers rushed in like the Delta Force of dope.

"They threw some kind of bomb in here," Brockman said after the raid. The flashbang grenade set fire to his carpet, and the concussive ruckus so terrified his neighbors that they split the building with their kids still decked in pajamas, thinking a terrorist had struck their building and fearing for their lives.[10]

"The police—they're all right with me," said the good-natured Brockman. Occasionally suffering from seizures, the elderly man is grateful when officers are out and about and can help him up when he falls afflicted in the street. "You have people who say, 'The police are dirty, this and that.' I can't find any fault with them that I know of. They got a job to do. But I don't know why they came and broke into my house," he said, betraying at least a slight fracturing of his faith. "I don't see any right in that. If they have me under surveillance, they would watch me and see who's coming in and out. Not to come in like storm troopers."[11]

Consider it an unfriendly handshake with the drug war—where metaphor is reality, where crack troops go after crack dealers, where cops act more like soldiers than police, and where innocent people like Brockman, low-level offenders, and others are trapped in the crossfire.

Going Commando

Explaining the tactics of the Eugene raid, the city's special operations chief, Captain Steve Swenson, said, "We rely on the element of surprise and speed . . . and an overwhelming display of force when you come through the door." While he admitted that the tactic "sounds bad," Swenson added that "it prevents problems. We don't know who we're dealing with when we go through the door."[12]

The sudden door-kicking display of brute force is routine in such raids. No-knock, dynamic entries are the *modus operandi* of drug enforcement. "Particularly in narcotics warrant service, to make their entry as dynamic and overwhelming as possible, SWAT teams often use the swarm or saturation method," explains tactical policing authority Robert L. Snow in his book, *SWAT Teams: Explosive Face-offs with America's Deadliest Criminals*. "This technique involves the immediate flooding of the inside of a location with police officers. Doing this gives the officers immediate control of the inside of the location, discourages thoughts of resistance, and prevents the destruction of any evidence. The idea behind the technique is to immediately dominate the site with officers and firepower."[13]

If police knock on a drug hustler's door, identify themselves, and wait around a minute or so for the fellow to greet and let them in, the suspect may have time to not only flush his stash down the john but also hide behind the couch with his two best friends, Messrs. Smith and Wesson. If, on the other hand, officers bust the door open and storm the house like special-forces troops, they stand a better chance of catching the dealer off-guard and red-handed, before he has a chance to reach for his peashooter.

But Snow points to an important problem with storming a residence: "This tactic . . . has a certain inherent danger level should any shooting break out, since officers could very easily be caught in the cross fire."[14] Interestingly, Snow doesn't seem to share the same concern for the suspects—even plainly innocent ones. He mentions only police being accidentally shot. The reader is left with the impression that if the residents are "caught in the cross fire," then *c'est la guerre*.

They're only criminals, right?

Attack Teams

Tactical or paramilitary policing was the brainchild of Daryl Gates, who later became the celebrated Los Angeles chief of police. The idea at the time was a police unit tough enough to take on rioters and the various armed rabble-rousers of the 1960s. Such teams also would be used in hostage situations or the rare instances when snipers were needed. But the ready firepower possessed by these units made them an easy fit for rousting heavily armed drug dealers and serving narcotics warrants at houses where cops figured suspects were extremely dangerous.[15]

Gates originally conceived of these units as "Special Weapons Attack Teams," or SWAT. (If that seems inordinately bellicose, don't forget that this is the same Gates who told a Senate committee that casual drug users should be rounded up and shot because "we're in a war," and even occasional use "is treason."[16]) Unsurprisingly, that name gave Gates's superiors the willies, portending PR disasters ahead. Accordingly, the knife-edged contents of the acronym were blunted to "Special Weapons and Tactics." Today paramilitary police teams also go by names like Emergency Services, Special Response, Tactical Operations, and Violent Crime Suppression Units. There are more than thirty thousand such units operating in jurisdictions across the country. Fundamentally, they all amount to the same thing: high-power, military-style policing.[17]

Had it not been for the twin catastrophes of the Johnson and Nixon administrations, use of these teams probably would have remained limited to big crime-ridden urban centers. But militarized policing thrives on the vine of big government (there is a reason they're called "police states"). And so liberals like President Johnson, having little respect for the traditional division of power between the states and the national government, created not only the Bureau of Narcotics and Dangerous Drugs to more effectively federalize the drug war but also the Law Enforcement Assistance Administration. The purpose of LEAA was Great Societyesque: dole out federal money to solve local problems—in this case, crime. Welfare for cops. If their city or county couldn't come up with the goods, local police could put in for federal grants for training and hardware, including radios, high-power weaponry, new squad cars, even helicopters. In its first year, LEAA's budget was seventy-five million dollars, which was much more than milk money at the time, though still not overwhelming.

Then came Nixon.

Tricky Dick also ignored the basic fact that most crime is local. Having run on an anti-crime platform, he greatly increased federal drug enforcement, building the Drug Enforcement Administration on the BNDD's foundation and hugely inflating LEAA's budget. Recounts journalist Dan Baum, "In a single jump, the LEAA . . . grew from a $75 million mouse to a half-billion-dollar-a-year lion."[18] Throughout the seventies, LEAA would cost taxpayers more than a billion dollars a year.[19] Now, regardless of actual need, police across the nation could afford to outfit themselves like Gates's SWAT team. And soon they'd also have an important legal tool.

About the same time Gates was getting his big guns, Republican House Judiciary Committee counsel Don Santarelli started advancing the idea of no-knock raids, an idea he later pushed in the Nixon administration. Traditionally, when police served a warrant, they would come during daylight hours, knock, and announce themselves, allowing the resident time to reach the door and see the warrant. But a no-knock raid is just what it says: Cops don't knock, they just barge in—waving guns, shouting, throwing people on the ground, and roughing up the furniture. None of the Sheriff Andy Taylor brand of politeness here.

This was quite a departure. For a search to be constitutionally kosher, it must abide by certain strictures. One of those is the knock-and-notice principle. As it is currently codified in US law, "The officer may break open any outer or inner door or window of a house, or any part of a house, or anything therein, to execute a search warrant, if, *after notice* of his authority and purpose, he is refused admittance. . . ."[20] In other words, police shouldn't just blurt "Police!" and then go Dirty Harry on the door with a boot or battering ram.

This is an old standard. The principle of knocking and providing notice before busting a citizen's door latch and tossing a stun grenade through the bathroom window goes back long before stun grenades were invented and rests on the traditions of English common law. The idea is linked to the same sentiment which provides the basis for the Fourth Amendment to the US Constitution—namely, the principle that folks' property and homes are not to be messed with by the authorities without a very good cause. The legal doctrine was as true as the cliché: A man's home is his castle.[21]

With such a radical deviation from traditional policing, drug warriors needed special circumstances to justify the new no-knock raid tactic. That tactic would be, ironically enough, safety. Said Nixon administration attorney general John L. Mitchell, "We are dealing with clever and ruthless drug peddlers, who have no hesitation about taking the life of an agent."[22] So officers can bust the baddies without becoming casualties of the war, cops have to burst in the door before dopers can respond with all that ruthlessness for which they're so well known. But even Mitchell knew the PR problem here; he wanted to go with the euphemistic moniker "quick entry," which sounds much more efficient than flat-out dangerous.

The story hasn't changed much over the years; with the populace sufficiently dulled to the reality of no-knocks, proponents are noticeably less skittish about defending such a radical policy. Tactical policing experts such as Snow give the nod to SWAT teams in drug warrant service "because drug dealers have so increased their affinity for violence in the last few years"[23] and courts have justified raids by ruling that "unannounced, dynamic entry" could minimize the "possibility for violence."[24]

The question is, minimize violence for whom?

Home Invasion

Before the clock struck midnight on August 9, 1999, the El Monte, California, Police Department Special Emergency Response Team struck the home of Mario Paz. Police shot the locks off the front and back doors, tossed in a flashbang grenade, and proceeded through the house to the bedroom where the elderly man had been sleeping with his wife. Within minutes he was dead, shot twice in the back.[25]

Explaining the shooting, the police said that gramps was reaching for a gun. Who wouldn't? According to Brian Dunn, the attorney representing what's left of the Paz family, Mario thought it was a home invasion robbery. Considering the tactics used by officers, it'd be easy to confuse a raid with a robbery; as we will see, it's a common confusion. When jolted awake by armed men storming his house, a person doesn't have much time to evaluate the situation, ask questions, and request to see warrants and badges. He reacts on impulse and adrenaline. If he's lucky, he's subdued by the officers before he can pose a threat to them. If he's mobile and quick, he might be able to reach for a gun to defend his home from the raiders. If so, *adios.*

In the case of Paz, what the cops were looking for—drugs—they didn't find. They did find a few guns and ten thousand dollars, which they seized, even though the family said they kept the guns for protection in their high-crime neighborhood and had the bank withdrawal slip for the money.[26]

Other elements of the story also point to police error, one of which concerns whether Paz really reached for his gun. "The Sheriff's Department, which routinely investigates officer-involved shootings, has provided three explanations for why officers fired at Paz," reported the *Washington Post.* "At first they said the El Monte officers believed

Paz was armed. Later they said that he was reaching for a gun. The latest statement said officers saw Paz reaching for a drawer where guns were found."[27] Good stories don't change that frequently.

"The reason why Mario Paz is dead is the manner in which his house was searched," said attorney Dunn, who painted the incursion as a "full-scale, military commando-style raid" in the *Post* story. "Those kinds of tactics should not be used against law-abiding people."[28]

What kind of tactics, in particular?

"We throw flash-bang grenades. We bust open the doors. You've seen it on TV," said El Monte assistant police chief Bill Ankeny after the fatal event, conjuring up images from the television show *Cops*. "We do bang on the door and make an announcement—'It's the police'—but it kind of runs together. If you're sitting on the couch, it would be difficult to get to the door before they knock it down."[29]

Sometimes even if the feeble announcement doesn't run together, it doesn't matter much, as a nighttime raid in autumn 2000 on the house of sixty-year-old Juan Mendoza Fernandez makes clear. As reported in the *Dallas Morning News*, while Juan and his sixty-four-year-old wife, Josefina, were watching Spanish-language TV near midnight, they heard an explosion, which they assumed had something to do with a drive-by shooting. They should have been so lucky. Actually, it was a grenade tossed by police at the front of the house. Outside, men yelled, "Open the door!" according to Juan's eleven-year-old granddaughter, who was startled from sleep by the clamor.[30]

"They were screaming and banging on the door," Josefina told a reporter in Spanish. "We thought they wanted to come in and kill us." Juan bolted to the rear of the house to protect his frightened granddaughter, according to the accounts of Josefina and the girl, huddling over her to shield her from gunfire.

Once police had entered the house, officers detained Josefina in the living room and headed to the rear of the house, where they confronted Juan and his granddaughter. Police say that Juan leveled a large-caliber handgun at them—an action which was answered by gunfire. According to the police account, the lead officer fired at Juan, who fell but continued to point the firearm. The lead officer and a second officer shot Juan again. "When he turned around, they shot him," said the granddaughter while hugging her mother the day following the raid. "Then they got down and shot him, I think, four more times."

The family contends that at the time of the raid Juan was unarmed, a claim that, for purposes of justifying the shooting, may be relevant to some but is, in a sense, of little concern. Even if Juan were armed, as police claim, few people could blame him for it.

"We didn't know it was the police," said Josefina, who thought the men banging on the door were robbers. As with the Paz story, the confusion is understandable. When a troop of black-clad men storm a person's driveway and try battering down the front door—sometimes announcing themselves as police, other times not—can people be blamed for thinking they're about to become victims of a home-invasion robbery? "Mistaking police raids for robberies is a common theme in SWAT killings," explains Christian Parenti in his book, *Lockdown America*. "Tactical officers often fail to follow the law and properly identify themselves during raids."[31]

A Muncie, Indiana, woman who allegedly shot a police officer near the groin during a raid claimed precisely that. "According to arrest records," one paper reported, "[Jillian D.] King . . . told police that she heard a noise, looked out a window and saw men with masks and camouflage trying to open a door, so she went to her bedroom and grabbed a gun."[32] Home invaders have even played on the similarities between police raids and robberies, hoping for the same results the police expect, that their victims will be cowed by the high-impact raid. Five thugs in an Edinburg, Texas, home invasion robbery reportedly wore clothing emblazoned with the word "Police."[33]

In Juan Fernandez's case, the police identification was simply inadequate. According to family members, neither Juan nor his wife were fluent in English (Josefina speaks none at all), and, even though officers announced themselves and wore clothing identifying them as police, the couple did not understand what was going on.

Given the time of day, that's hardly surprising. These raids are most commonly conducted in the early morning or late at night, precisely when people are the least alert, coherent, and rational. This increases the danger for those involved, something seen clearly in the case of Juan, who simply acted the way terrified people sometimes do—defending themselves and the lives of their loved ones as best they can, given what they know about the rapidly unfolding situation.

In the end, however, few people will cry for Juan, as officers came away from the fatal raid with almost a pound of meth, an ounce of cocaine, and a tad more than five grams of marijuana. "They are pumping the drugs into the city of Irving [Texas]," said one officer of Fernandez and other members of the family, "and we are going to do everything possible to stop it."

Including introducing Juan to the hereafter.

Forcing the Confrontation

Raids of this sort "are a bad idea at early hours or late at night," Timothy Lynch, director of the Cato Institute's Project on Criminal Justice, told me shortly after the incident. Given the time of day, "People are startled, which increases the chances of misunderstanding and violence." "Startled" is a bit of an understatement; "terrified" is more like it. That is especially true if the suspects speak little or no English and have a child in the house. Of course, if police are correct in charging that Juan was selling drugs, no doubt he brought this danger upon himself and his family, as such a risk would be known to anyone dealing in drugs. The question is, does that justify the raid?

A narcotics team surveilled the Fernandez home before Juan arrived at about 11:20 P.M. Why, someone might ask, couldn't they have arrested him upon arrival—when family members wouldn't have been placed in danger—and served the search warrants after neutralizing Juan? Instead of this or some similar tactic, they charged into the house, a high-risk situation for all involved, and *permanently* neutralized Juan.

While some will no doubt respond by saying Juan was a drug dealer and knew the risks of the trade, Lynch counters by saying, "Even with someone who is a drug dealer or user caught up in the raid, we have higher expectations of how the police conduct themselves in these situations." The fact that the granddaughter was present should have been enough of reason for officers to pull back and try it another day. The family of eleven-year-old Alberto Sepulveda of Modesto, California, can explain why. Only weeks before the Fernandez incident, a Modesto SWAT officer accidentally shot Alberto dead during a raid targeting his father. In the early-morning hours of September 13, 2000, police crashed into the Sepulveda home and rounded up Alberto's father, mother, and brother. Ordered to lie face down on the floor next to his bed with his arms outstretched, the boy did just as he was told. Innocent, obedient, and then dead. A few seconds after Alberto complied with the order, a SWAT officer training his shotgun on Alberto accidentally discharged the weapon, killing him.[34]

"With a nighttime raid at that hour and with this language barrier, it just sounds like an awful operation from the word 'go,'" observed Lynch about the Fernandez case. "Most people will recognize certain circumstances where no-knock raids are necessary," he added, "but it is the government that has to justify this sort of military-style raid. . . ."

The justification the government gives is often stunningly inadequate. In January 2003, for instance, police in Spokane, Washington, decided to raid a home based on the sale of a single twenty-dollar rock of cocaine, putting at risk not only the officers but also the three boys and a woman who lived there. Worse, they found no drugs.[35] Getting the bust was so important that it was worth creating a life-threatening situation in which police stormed a home not even knowing that they'd find drugs inside. Picture it this way: Playing poker, a man slides a twenty-dollar crack rock into the pot; sitting across the table, the police see the bet and raise him a family.

Or consider a 1990 raid in Dallas. As University of Georgia School of Law instructor Donald E. Wilkes Jr. recounts it, police chucked a stun grenade through the window of Juan Garcia's home before forcibly busting inside:

> Inside the residence are a man and his pregnant common law wife and the 2-year-old child and 9-month-old baby they are babysitting. The stun grenade lands and explodes in an empty baby stroller just three feet from the man. The baby had been removed from the stroller only minutes earlier.
>
> The explosion breaks all the plates in the china cabinet, pulls the sheetrock one and a half inches out of the ceiling, and burns a hole in the sofa and the carpet. The detonation burns and shatters the stroller.
>
> The pregnant woman soon begins bleeding and four days later miscarries.[36]

"Is it worth putting an entire family at risk for what is sometimes a small amount of drugs, or small-time dealers?" asks Peter Kraska, criminal justice professor at Eastern Kentucky University. While his answer is clearly "no," drug warriors seem to think the answer is "yes." According to Kraska's figures, between 1980 and 2000, deployment of tactical police increased more than 900 percent.[37] Once a rarity, calling out SWAT for drug warrants has increased to the point that today it is routine, often no matter how small the reward.

Taking it back to the Fernandez case, none of this discussion is to say he was innocent—just needlessly slain. The police, no doubt, could have put the raid off until better circumstances existed or conducted his arrest in a different manner, one that didn't risk the lives of his wife and granddaughter. Instead, they forced a confrontation that shoved Juan into the position of defending his property and family from armed men he most likely did not even know were police. If Juan was armed and threatening them, as the police say, they were justified in killing him. But police must shoulder some responsibility for creating the confrontation in the first place.

The Paz raid is even worse. While the police now acknowledge that Mario had nothing to do with drugs, they didn't have any evidence even before the raid. "We didn't have information of the Paz family being involved in narcotics trafficking," assistant police chief Ankeny told the *L.A. Times.* Worse, he told the paper, in what was probably a flank-covering maneuver, that "he was unsure if his department's narcotics unit even knew whether the family was living at the Compton home when it was raided by the SWAT team. He said the team of up to 20 officers . . . was looking for evidence that could be used in a case against Chino drug suspect Marcos Beltran Lizarraga, who had been released on bail the morning of the raid."[38] Why, after all, would you burst in on the house of a man you couldn't link to drugs? Simple: They didn't know he was even there. But what does that say about the investigative work of the police?

If we value constitutional protections of property and individual lives and liberty, such a cop-out won't do. If police don't know who is inside a home when they raid it, they probably shouldn't go in with guns drawn ready to shoot at the first thing that moves. That's worse than looking for trouble; that's provoking it.

Wrong House

Three cousins—Salvador Huerta, Marcos Huerta, and Vicente Huerta, all young men who worked at a San Antonio restaurant—were sitting around their apartment after work watching TV the evening of November 20, 2002. Around 8 P.M. a dozen SWAT officers invaded the home, firing tear gas, allegedly shouting profanities, and violently beating two of the men. "We were kicked and punched at least 20 times," said Salvador, who suffered a broken front tooth and a swollen face. Marcos's face was cut and his head bruised. Vicente didn't stick around for his. He lit off instead of taking the boot. After a vain search for drugs and guns, the police realized they were at the wrong apartment. According to the *San Antonio Express-News*, "police apologized several times and went five apartments down and arrested two people. . . ."[39]

Jesus and Wendy Olveda of Dalton, Wisconsin, found themselves on the floor after four armed men decked head-to-toe in black burst through the door and cuffed the couple, their three-year-old girl watching in horror. Unfortunately, as reported in the *Beaver Dam Daily Citizen*, the Green Lake County Drug Task Force was barking up the wrong tree in its October 2000 raid. The Olvedas' next-door neighbor was the actual target.[40]

Wendy, five months pregnant, tried to inform the officers that they were in the wrong house. "I could hear my wife saying, 'You're at the wrong address,'" said Jesus, "but they didn't listen." When Wendy told the officers she was pregnant, "they responded by pushing her head down on the ground in front of her daughter." Jesus also tried to tell them they had the wrong house: "When I lifted my head to say they got the wrong address, one of them put a knee on my head and ground it into the floor." Officers proceeded to tear through the house in a vain search for drugs.

According to Jesus, "once members of the task force realized they had searched the wrong home and were holding innocent people, several of the officers rushed through the garage door and ran across the property to the Griffin residence." Todd Griffin, the real suspect, was later busted on various marijuana charges. Afterward, Jesus said that one of the bumbling raiders had to return to retrieve the search warrant so they could properly bust Griffin.

Ironically, Wendy, a fifth-grade teacher, is a founding member of the local drug-prevention program. "This is a very traumatic experience for my whole family," she said. "I don't know how I'm going to be able to sleep. How can such a thing happen to an innocent family?" It's a question rattling around in many other people's minds.

Mary and Cornelius Jefferson were not expecting visitors the night of June 24, 1997; they were getting ready for bed. Suddenly a thunderous banging began on the front door of their Bronx apartment. When the door finally splintered, police poured in, packing heat and a search warrant. "The warrant—based on the word of a paid confidential informer with a criminal record—told of a young Hispanic man who was selling cocaine from the apartment," reported the *New York Times*. "Instead the police found a terrified couple in their 60s, living in a meticulous apartment where plastic slipcovers protect the sofas and diplomas and awards line the walls."[41] "I thought they were coming to rob us, coming to kill us," said Mary.

In Brooklyn, an informant told police they'd find a heroin and illegal gun dealer named Lucky behind "a grey metal door clearly marked with the letter and number '2M.'" When police found no such door at the address, they simply moved over and raided an address marked "2L" with a red door. Surprise, surprise: Lucky wasn't there. Neither was the dope. Just a stunned woman and her two kids.[42]

While watching TV in their southeast Washington DC home, George and Katrina Stokes had visitors. The local SWAT team crashed through the front door unannounced. At gunpoint, George was ordered to the ground, cutting his head in the process. Meanwhile, his wife fell down the basement stairs, unsuccessfully evading the invaders. Making it one of those more memorable moments, an accompanying camera crew from a local TV station had video rolling. Needless to say, they captured some prime footage—especially the part where the team realized they had stormed the wrong house. With cameras still rolling, the Keystone SWATs ran back to the cars and drove off in search of the right address.[43]

A similar case happened in King County, Washington, when a police team, *Cops* cameras in tow, burst into a house, rousting both parents and children from bed. It wasn't until officers handcuffed half-naked Theresa Glover that they realized they were in the wrong home. "They pulled me out of bed and put a gun on me," said Glover. "Here I am with my butt showing, and I see the camera." Police mistakenly raided the wrong side of a duplex, something that Major Larry Mayes found as embarrassing as the prospect of the footage running on national television (then again, it's not his butt). "Just the fact that you go in the wrong door is embarrassing in itself," he said, when faced with the possibility that *Cops* would broadcast Glover's gluteus maximus—additional humiliation for the police (not to mention Glover). "How much more embarrassing can it get?" Mayes asked. Sadly, the answer is *a lot*. This same force had recently fumbled two similar raids, improbably raiding the same wrong house *twice* in a year's time. Officers fouled up the addresses on the search warrants in both cases.[44] Perhaps it should have been Mayes's butt on TV.

During a 1992 raid in Venice, Missouri, the Grim Reaper almost bagged a mayor. According to the *St. Louis Post-Dispatch*, police got the wrong address and accidentally raided the home of Mayor Tyrone Echols. Naturally, they didn't find the crack they were looking for, and they're lucky they didn't find the mayor either. Had he been home, "I probably would've taken my pistol and shot through the door," he said. Had that happened, he probably would have been shot and killed. They were looking for a dealer who lived a block and a half away.[45]

Sloppy Police Work

While all of these accounts point to frustrating foul-ups on the part of the police, some stories of drug-raid miscalculation are criminally tragic.

It was 10:00 P.M. on October 4, 2000, and about the only thing sixty-two-year-old John Adams was interested in doing was relaxing in his easy chair and catching a bit of TV. Little did he know that a handful of Lebanon, Tennessee's finest were standing outside his door getting ready to cancel his show.

After hearing knocking at the door, John's wife, Loraine, went to answer. There was no reply when she asked for identification. As she stood there, the door was kicked in and five officers stormed the house, immediately cuffing her. John wasn't so fortunate. "I thought it was a home invasion," said Loraine. "I said 'Baby, get your gun!'" While there is some dispute as to whether John actually fired at police, family members say he believed the raid to be a home-invasion robbery and police claim that, as officers rounded the corner into the room where he sat, John discharged a shotgun. Officers Kyle Shedran and Greg Day, both in their mid-twenties, were forced to fire back, according to police. John took at least three bullets. He didn't live through the night, dying in surgery at Vanderbilt University Medical Center.[46]

"It was a severe, costly mistake," said Lebanon police chief Billy Weeks after the incident. "They were not the target of our investigation." Although Adams's address appeared on the search warrant, the description of the targeted home did not match his. The jig should have been up for a female suspect living next door—at the only other house on the street. According to Weeks, the intended house was under surveillance and, as the *Tennessean* reported, "a drug purchase had been made from one of the residents. . . . That was the basis for the warrant."[47]

Later testifying in a resulting criminal case, one detective, Tommy Maggart, said he suspected they had the wrong address. After a final drive-by shortly before the raid he told his superior he thought a mix-up had occurred—to no effect.[48] They went forward with the raid. Detective Steve Nokes, the head of the narcotics unit, surveilled the actual house where the drug purchase occurred and *also* participated in the raid at the wrong house as the lead officer.[49] How did he miss the mistake? Curiously, he testified that, like Maggart, he tried to stop the raid beforehand. Nokes was fired shortly afterward and was later indicted in the shooting but acquitted. For our purposes, which officer was actually responsible is irrelevant. The fact that one or both raised the red flag should have been enough to call off or delay the raid, to pause to assess the situation and validate the police info.

All of these cases point to a puzzling fact: What fewer and fewer people seem to expect from police is actual *police work*. It's more important to make the bust than build the case. One would think that police, knowing lethal force might have to be used, endangering both officers and suspects, would carefully check things out before hitting the start gate. A threat assessment is routine, but haste and inadequate intelligence sometimes seem just as common a characteristic of tactical police raids.

Adams's friend Natchel Palmer, a former county commissioner, said it best: "Why do you have to die because somebody doesn't know what they are doing? . . . They got the wrong damn house and killed my friend."[50]

War Zone

Killings like these will continue for one basic reason: With the ever-increasing militarization of police, law enforcement officers are becoming shock troops in the war on drugs and crime. Confrontation is replacing investigation.

Officers in SWAT and similar special-response units dress more like soldiers than police. They come decked in ballistic helmets, in all-black fatigues or cammies, sometimes schlepping ballistic shields.

Police are also armed more like soldiers, using surplus military equipment and sporting military or military-like weaponry, including Colt-made M-16s and AR-15s, Ruger Mini 14s, Steyr AUGs, Ingram MAC 10s, and, most popular, Heckler and Koch MP-5s. These automatic-fire assault rifles and submachine guns, explains Snow, "are favored because they are compact, reliable, and very accurate. SWAT teams also like them because they can be set to fire a single shot, set to fire two or three shot bursts, or set on automatic fire."[51]

Much of this equipment comes from the US government, starting in 1981 with the Military Cooperation with Law Enforcement Officials Act. That act, explains *Washington Times* reporter Rowan Scarborough, "injected the Pentagon directly into the drug war, authorizing the transfer of equipment and expertise."[52] The new law "encouraged the military to (a) make available equipment, military bases, and research facilities to federal, state, and local police; (b) train and advise civilian police on the use of the equipment; and (c) assist law enforcement personnel in keeping drugs from entering the country," writes Diane Cecelia Weber in a Cato Institute briefing paper, "Warrior Cops."[53] Previously, the Posse Comitatus Act of 1878 proscribed such transfers. The idea behind the law was to codify a longstanding tradition in America of separating the police from the military; it forbade the cooperation increasingly seen today. But as the 1980s waxed, Posse Comitatus waned, and the federal government began chipping away at those longstanding protections to expand the military's role in antidrug police efforts.

In 1987 Congress worked to make it easier for local police departments to score military hardware with a more streamlined process. Six years later, in 1993, Congress ordered the Department of Defense to get the lead out on such transfers, ordering the sale of surplus equipment for anti-narcotics purposes.

The results have been profound. "Between 1995 and 1997 the Department of Defense gave police departments 1.2 million pieces of military hardware, including 73 grenade launchers and 112 armored personnel carriers. The Los Angeles Police Department has acquired 600 Army surplus M-16s," writes Weber. Given that SWAT was born in the City of Angels, maybe that last bit isn't too surprising, but the militarism trend is national. "Even small-town police departments are getting into the act. The seven-officer department in Jasper, Florida, is now equipped with fully automatic M-16s."[54]

The H&K MP-5 machine pistol, notes David B. Kopel of the Denver–based Independence Institute, is usually purchased by police rather than donated. "These weapons are sold almost exclusively to the military and police. The advertising to civilian law enforcement conveys the message that by owning the weapon, the civilian officer will be the equivalent of a member of an élite military strike force, such as the Navy SEALs." One example of H&K ad copy Kopel provides: "From the Gulf War to the Drug War."[55]

Trained to Kill

Kopel points out that while these weapons may be fine functionally, issues beyond bare mechanics are more important. "[W]hen law enforcement agencies are procuring weapons, they need to consider not only their mechanical characteristics, but also how officers in the field will use them. When a weapon's advertising and styling deliberately blur the line between warfare and law enforcement, it is not unreasonable to expect that some officers—especially when under stress—will start behaving as if they were in the military."[56]

Defenders may quickly shoot back with the defense, "That's what training is for." But increasingly, the training is problematic as well. To begin with, SWAT teams are replete with ex-military men. Usually because, out of the service, they are eminently qualified to work such a job—the two are startlingly close. Also, SWAT teams rely heavily on military training to teach them how to cope in operations. According to a survey by Peter Kraska, of police departments with tactical police units, 46 percent have received training from active-duty armed forces.[57]

The problem goes back to the metaphor itself. War and policing are vastly different. In common parlance the military's job is to kill people and break things. As Reagan administration assistant secretary of defense Lawrence Korb puts it, soldiers are supposed to "vaporize, not 'Mirandize.'" On the other hand, police are trained to solve problems with scrupulous attention to suspects' civil rights and with a multitude of solutions, lethal violence being the last rung on the escalating ladder of force. No-knock raids race up the ladder, going straight to the threat of lethal force.

Some police chiefs recognize the contradiction in roles and the danger of mixing them. "I was offered tanks, bazookas, anything I wanted," said Nick Pastore, former police chief in New Haven, Connecticut. Pastore said he "turned it all down because it feeds a mind-set that you're not a police officer serving a community, you're a soldier at war."[58]

In a war, there's no such thing as due process before depriving a man of life, liberty, or property—as required by the Fifth Amendment to the Constitution. Which is more than understandable. The goal of war is to win, and recalling the wisdom of General George S. Patton, you don't win a war by dying for your country; you make the other "poor dumb bastard" die for his. Most any tactic in war is excused and commended provided it results in victory. Hence enemies have little in the way of rights, and if they are the aggressor nation, they've forfeited whatever rights they might have had. The bully who starts a fight should not be surprised if his cry of "uncle" is met with a few more fists to the teeth and boots to the kidneys.

But the drug war is not a war. It's a policy. A policy crafted in a nation whose overarching legal doctrines are contained in the Constitution and Bill of Rights and to which the policy must conform.

Police State, USA

When Don Santarelli started pushing the idea of no-knock raids in 1967 and later under Nixon, he knew he was dealing with something volatile in terms of the Fourth Amendment. Nixon aide Egil "Bud" Krogh would later admit as much as well. Mentioning programs that "got too close to breaching the wall of what is not acceptable under the Fourth Amendment" and specifically highlighting no-knock raids, Krogh told PBS's *Frontline* in 2000, "I think those kinds of programs can lead to abuses—and I think they have."[59]

As many innocent victims suffer because of unannounced, dynamic entries, none suffer quite so badly as the Fourth Amendment, which clearly defends "the right of the people to be secure in their persons, houses, papers, and effects, against unreasonable searches and seizures." It's a little hard to be secure in anything when a dozen unannounced police officers bust in, force your face into the carpet, and drill a pistol barrel into your ear—or so one would think.

In the salad days of the drug war, no-knock provisions passed only because they were packed with safety valves; police, for instance, had to provide piles of evidence before getting a warrant to kick in the doors of a man's castle. More than thirty years later, no-knock, high-risk raids are almost casual. Across the nation, the results have been deadly.

In *Ker v. California* (1963), Supreme Court Justice William Brennan opined that "[r]igid restrictions upon unannounced entries are essential if the Fourth Amendment's prohibition against invasion of the security and privacy of the home is to have any meaning." In our mad rush to catch every drug dealer in America, we are ensuring that the Fourth Amendment and constitutionally guaranteed privacy mean less every day.

As dopers figure out new and creative ways to flout prohibition, law enforcement is forced to crack down with renewed vigor and creativity—usually and increasingly at the expense of our liberties. The Fourth Amendment has already suffered greatly because of drug-courier profiling and police playing fast and loose with search and seizure restrictions. The way things are going, we'll continue this ridiculous obsession to control what our neighbors' stick in their bodies until both they *and we* are all very sober residents of the gulag.

8

LOCKDOWN, USA

Prohibition packs the prisons, needlessly and expensively.

FOR MILLIONS OF AMERICANS, THE END RESULT OF DRUG-WAR crackdowns is prison—or rather *prisons*, plural. The country needs an ever-increasing number of them to house the drug war's multitudinous victims.

By 2002, America's inmate population tallied more than 2.1 million adults sitting in federal prisons, state pens, or local jails, making for a mind-boggling incarceration rate of 701 inmates per every one hundred thousand residents. Need a comparison for perspective? Such striking models of modern democracy as Belarus and Turkmenistan jail fewer of their citizens per capita than the US.[1] Numbers released by the Justice Department toward the end of summer 2003 paint a more encompassing picture, showing more than 5.6 million living Americans either formerly incarcerated or currently imprisoned.[2]

"We have the wealthiest society in human history, and we maintain the highest level of imprisonment," says Marc Mauer, assistant director of the Washington DC–based Sentencing Project. "It's striking what that says about our approach to social problems and inequality."[3] "Social problems" in Mauer's usage is almost shorthand for drugs. Counting both federal and state prison populations, nearly 25 percent of all inmates are jailed because of drug-related crimes. At just the federal level, it's over half of the inmate population, 55 percent.[4]

Jailing the Multitude

The biggest cause for this incredible upsurge in prison populations are mandatory minimum sentences. House Speaker Tip O'Neill pushed for their passage in the summer of 1986 after the death of basketball player Len Bias. A star player, drafted from the University of Maryland to shoot hoops with the Boston Celtics, Bias's death came as a shock to the nation, not the least reason for which was the drug on which he overdosed—crack cocaine. Here was innocence. Here was hope. Here was youth. All ruined by this new and blood-curdling mutation of cocaine. His death would lead to the biggest drug scare of the 1980s. It would also lead O'Neill to a terrible decision.

The Democrats had long been seen as velvety soft when it came to drug policy, and O'Neill saw Bias's death as a tool to shake that perception. Reagan swallowed the Democrats whole in 1984, and O'Neill considered new Democrat-sponsored antidrug legislation vital to stemming the tide of the Reagan Revolution in the upcoming midterm elections. Eric E. Sterling of the Criminal Justice Policy Foundation was there in the thick of it; at the time, he was counsel to the US House Committee on the Judiciary.

"O'Neill knew that for Democrats to take credit for an antidrug program in November elections, the bill had to get out of both Houses of Congress by early October," Sterling recounts. "That required action on the House floor by early September, which meant that committees had to finish their work before the August recess."[5]

This created a time crunch for the speaker. To overcome it, the legislation had to be crafted and drafted in less than a month—just days, in fact. Sterling should know; the House version of the bill came right out of his word processor.

Contained in the legislation was language creating mandatory minimum sentences for various drug offenses. Mandatory minimums were sold as part of the get-tough approach to drugs and crime that O'Neill desperately needed to out-cop Reagan. The idea was straight-forward enough: If a person was busted on a federal drug charge, he was looking at serious, hard time. No pinko judge was going to lighten the load. The sentence was the sentence. And the sentence was severe. A thousand marijuana plants (or a thousand kilos—the law counted each plant as a kilo, no matter its actual weight) could land a person in jail for a minimum of ten years. Just five grams of crack was worth half that.

"It was a type of penalty that had been removed from federal law in 1970 after extensive and careful consideration," recalls Sterling. "But in 1986, no hearings were held on this idea. No experts on the relevant issues, no judges, no one from the Bureau of Prisons, or from any other office in the government, provided advice on the idea before it was rushed through the committee and into law. Only a few comments were received on an informal basis."[6]

The electioneering possibilities of the bill hit Congress faster than a toke from a crack pipe zings its psychoactive substance to the brain. It was pandemonium. One *Washington Post* report called the eruption of activity "the legislative equivalent of a cattle stampede" with the House "rushing pell mell to approve a sweeping antidrug bill." And the tougher, the better. "Right now you could put through an amendment to hang, draw, and quarter," said one congressman.[7] All that mattered was lowering the boom on dopers. After a brief, intense flurry between House and Senate, the Anti-Drug Abuse Act of 1986 was passed and signed by Reagan—just in time for *both* parties to claim credit and parlay the tough stance into votes.

"Why, I've never seen such solidarity and love," said Republican Congressman Bob Dornan, who posed for photos with Democrat colleague Charles Rangel. "I think it comes down to one young man not dying in vain," he said.[8]

If dying for a purpose meant serving as the pretext to lock up an ever-increasing number of Americans, then Bias's death was definitely not in vain. In the twenty-two years between 1970 and 2002, the number of drug offenders in the federal poke jacked upwards roughly 2,000 percent.[9] And if a person scans a chart tracking the hike, after 1986 the climb gets steep indeed.

Finking for Freedom

This was all well and good for politicians, but what about the people stuck in the jaws of this new system? After O'Neill got his legislation, there was only one way of dodging the full force of a mandatory minimum: snitching about others in the trade or setting them up for a bust.

By providing "substantial assistance" in the apprehension of other offenders, a suspect could squeeze out of an indictment or have time knocked off an otherwise straitjacketed sentence. Coupled with drug conspiracy laws, this became a powerful tool for prosecutors to round up dozens of defendants. The intention was not to try each and every one but to put the squeeze on them all and see who would squeal on the others and, hopefully, offenders involved further up the chain. The conspiracy laws, passed as another electioneering boost in 1988, basically made anyone connected to the activity of a narcotics organization responsible for all the activity of that organization. In the eyes of the law, this made a mule the same as a kingpin.

Thanks to the conspiracy provision, a one-time drug courier hauling twenty-five kilos of cocaine in his trunk, if busted, can be threatened with a much bigger sentence than fitting for the amount in his trunk. Suddenly, he's responsible not for transporting twenty-five kilos of powder but, say, five hundred kilos. Staring down the business end of that sentence makes a man think very seriously about his future—or rather, lack thereof. The only way to mitigate the severity of the sentence is to sing as prettily as possible about his associates. If a defendant hits all the right notes, he might mitigate his sentence or get off entirely.

"In a pool of defendants, a few are guaranteed to testify, whether it's the underlings or the bosses who roll over," writes Cynthia Cotts. "The downside comes when a minor defendant doesn't know enough to be useful and is left open a harsh sentence."[10] Minor defendants like twenty-three-year-old Clarence Aaron, who was paid fifteen hundred dollars to drive some high-school buddies and a cousin to meet with acquaintances who dealt drugs. When his friends were later busted, they all faced life sentences and ducked the full time by ratting on Aaron. The kingpin of the outfit got twelve years. Two of Aaron's friends got less than half that, and his cousin got no time at all. Aaron? He got three concurrent life sentences, no parole.[11]

Aaron's plight is common. According to the US Sentencing Commission's survey of cocaine convictions between 1995 and 2000:

Contrary to the general objective of the 1986 legislation to target "serious" and "major" traffickers, two-thirds of federal crack cocaine offenders were street-level dealers. Only 5.9 percent of federal crack cocaine offenders performed trafficking functions most consistent with the functions described in the legislative history of the Anti-Drug Abuse Act of 1986 as warranting a five-year penalty, and 15.2 percent performed trafficking functions most consistent with the functions described as warranting a ten-year penalty. . . .[12]

Instead of striking at the head of drug organizations, what the mandatory minimums and conspiracy laws have done is dispatch thousands of small-fries in a scurry to fink on everyone they know, no matter how loose their connection to the trade, in order to nick some time off their otherwise weighty sentences. Since many do not know enough people of any stature in the trade, they rat on fellows like themselves— hence the tremendous number of street-level dealers overfilling the federal pens.

This distortion is the direct result of a legislative overstep. Sentences are left with judges precisely because they are independent and impartial. This goes back to the entire purpose of a constitutional division of powers. Congress passes a broad-scope law. Judges apply it to individual cases. Nothing one-size-fits-all ever really fits all. Rather than solely taking the broad view, judges focus on the details and nuances of a particular case and adjudicate the matter accordingly, to make sure justice is truly done. Thanks to the drug war, instead we have legislatures dictating justice over the heads of the judiciary. No surprise, this has left judges with a bad taste in their mouth.[13] "I thought this was a good job before I got it," says a district court judge for southern Iowa. "I didn't come here to put away poor people for low-level, nonviolent drug crimes, but that's what the job amounts to." Because of the mandatories, "[a]ll you can do is bitch about it."[14] The complaining goes up to the top. Both Supreme Court Chief Justice William H. Rehnquist and Justice Anthony Kennedy have mouthed their disapproval. Says the latter, "In too many cases, mandatory minimum sentences are unwise or unjust."[15] And from Rehnquist: "Our resources are misspent, our punishments too severe, our sentences too long."[16]

But justice aside, as with so many other drug war tactics, a large number of states have aped the federal government's drug war tactics and compounded the problem. More than thirty states have now passed mandatory minimums of their own. New York has the most notorious mandatory minimums, the Rockefeller laws, so severe and misdirected that even law-and-order Republicans like Governor George Pataki and former state senator John Dunne are against them. "They have not stemmed the drug trade," says Dunne. "The only thing they've done is fill the prisons."[17]

Mostly Harmless

Because such a whopping tally trapped in this inmate inflation are only marginally involved in the business, they are often what are called drug-only offenders—in the words of criminologist John J. DiIulio Jr., "felons whose only crimes, detected or undetected, have been low-level, nonviolent drug offenses." An increasingly common shibboleth in drug-reform debates, they are also known shorthand as "nonviolent offenders."

The onetime director of President Bush's faith-based initiative, DiIulio had always been a hardnose on crime, an outspoken proponent of prisons and get-tough policies. But after surveying incoming male inmates in New York, Arizona, and New Mexico, he noticed something that upset his apple cart: A sizeable chunk was composed of nonviolent, drug-only offenders. Since the key reason for prisons is to keep violent, predatory people away from the rest of us, DiIulio found the results of the study troubling.[18] After all, here were scads of people who probably shouldn't be behind bars. It changed the way he thought about prisons and who we're putting away.

"Current laws put too many nonviolent drug offenders in prison," DiIulio explains. "A 1997 study by Harvard economist Anne Morrison Piehl found that in Massachusetts, about half of recently incarcerated drug offenders had previously been charged, and a third had previously been convicted, of a violent offense. But most of the state's drug offenders had no known record of violence, while half its probation population consisted of violent felons."[19] In other words, some offenders ought to be in the clink, but many who were coming in shouldn't. Worse, violent offenders were being released to make room for people who were mostly harmless.

What kind of total numbers are we talking about here? It's hard to say. While Bill Clinton occupied the Oval Office, the number of federal prisoners jumped from 73,000 to more than 146,000. Based on extrapolations from 1994 Justice Department numbers, Eric Sterling estimates that some 24,000 of this population qualify as nonviolent drug offenders. "It could be a little more, could be less," he says. "Even if we're off by a few thousand, it's still more than at any time in history."[20]

Considering that we have fifty different states, a far bigger number of counties, and a federal system to boot, pegging the figure of nonviolent offenders with any accuracy is probably not possible—estimates are all over the map—but when DiIulio advanced several sentence reforms in 1999, he claimed, "Such changes would undoubtedly reduce the number of drug-only offenders in federal prisons by tens of thousands."[21]

Apply his conclusions to states with even the most conservative estimation and the number of beds cleared for muggers, burglars, rapists, robbers, and killers would be astounding.

Drug warriors are very touchy about the idea that they may be unjustly locking up large slices of the citizenry.

"Some 24% of state prison drug offenders are violent recidivists, while 83% have prior criminal histories," federal drug czar John P. Walters wrote for the *Wall Street Journal*. "Only 17% are in prison for 'first time offenses,' while nominal 'low-level' offenders are often criminals who plea-bargain to escape more serious charges."[22] These numbers are intriguing. The first thing to note is that a huge percentage of state drug offenders are *not* "violent recidivists." The fact that they have prior convictions might mean very little—two convictions for pot only means someone is a slow learner, not that he's a threat to society. Recall from Chapter One that the majority of recidivist drug offenders are in jail for further drug offenses, not property or violent crime.[23] Also, Walters's plea bargaining statement is too simplistic. Prosecutors accept pleas on lesser charges sometimes because they don't have enough to make the more serious charges stick, the same way they might go after a civil forfeiture case if they don't have enough goods to prevail in a criminal case.

Elsewhere, Walters takes a crack at the "myth" that "we are imprisoning too many people for merely possessing illegal drugs," saying, "in 1997 only 8.8 percent of the 1,046,705 individuals in state prisons were there for drug possession. . . . Throughout the 1980s and 1990s, violent crimes vastly outpaced drug offenses as the cause of the prison population's rapid growth." He feels even more confident at the federal level. "In fiscal year 1999, just 2.2 percent of federal drug convictions were for simple possession."[24]

First, violent crimes outpacing drug offenses at the state level for prison growth is a red herring. Of course they outpace drug offenses. States are concerned with enforcing many more laws than possession and trafficking. The feds, on the other hand, are swinging at far fewer pitches, and border security and dope are two of the leading concerns. According to Federal Bureau of Prisons data, drugs and illegal immigration are the biggest growth factors in federal prisons.

Next, the federal prison population in 1999 was approximately 136,000. Using Walters's stats, that works out to nearly 3,000 people in federal prison for simply possessing illegal drugs—not harming or defrauding the neighbors, just owning drugs. That's bad enough, but far more ominous is his 8.8 percent figure among state prisons. That's over 92,000 people jailed for simple possession. It'd take a bureaucrat like Walters to miss the fact that 95,000 people is a significant sum to incarcerate for doing nothing more harmful than possessing contraband. (Note, however, that the "possession" criterion here is somewhat meaningless. The key issue is whether or not an offender is violent, whether he's a danger to his community, not whether he pays his rent with money from peddling dime bags. But by keeping the numbers in abstract statistics and not talking in absolute figures, Walters and others can downplay the real flesh-and-blood tally of people stuck in jail and why they are there.)

Some may argue that, regardless of whether someone is violent or nonviolent, an offender needs to be punished for breaking the law, period. The law is, after all, the law. While common, this sentiment is hardly sensible and presumes far too much legitimacy in the current system. Think of it in terms of restorative justice: The whole idea is to make something right by paying back what was lost, damaged, taken, etc. But take a nonviolent drug dealer out of jail and what is there to restore? He hasn't robbed anyone; his customers volunteer their cash. He hasn't physically hurt anyone; that's what we mean when we call him nonviolent. So there's nothing to restore. And if there is nothing to restore, can we honestly say anyone's been wronged? And if no one has been wronged, then what cause do we have to jail him? The justice system should only deal with those who have harmed or defrauded their neighbors; without harm or fraud, by definition things are already just.

Going for Broke

Florida Governor Jeb Bush doesn't see it that way. Even though the state's serious crime rate was the lowest it's been since Nixon was trying to wheedle his way out of his own crimes, in August 2003, Bush pushed for a budget-busting bevy of new prisons—even arguing the prudence of pulling $66 million from the state's emergency fund to pay for them.[25]

It's not just Florida. North Carolina is also facing an inmate glut. To respond to the problem, the state is building three additional prisons. But if estimates are correct, they won't be nearly enough. "Even when the third of the three prisons approved this year [2003] opens in 2008, the state will be nearly 2,000 beds short," according to the Associated Press. "That's the size of two typical 1,000-bed maximum-security prisons, which costs the state about $80 million to build and $17 million a year to operate."[26] The state legislature is hardly being smart about it. In 2004 lawmakers are expected to toughen meth penalties—a move sure to boost the prison population even more.

Overcrowding is a huge problem among many states. Indiana's prisons are designed to hold about sixteen thousand. Right now seven thousand over that are sardined into the limited space, and there's no more money in the budget to open new facilities.[27] In Montana, meth convictions are driving prison populations past capacity. "The inn is full," said the state prison warden.[28] Hawaii, well known for its illicit pot growers, has also been straining in the influx of meth offenders. Mandatory minimums to deter the trade have worsened an already hard-pressed prison system.[29] In all, Justice Department statistics show half the states operating either at or above full capacity.[30]

None of this is cheap. "[H]ousing, feeding, and caring for a prison inmate is roughly $20,000 per year, or about $40 billion nationwide using 2002 figures," explains reporter Curt Anderson, using Sentencing Project stats. "Construction costs are about $100,000 per cell."[31]

"States can't continue to support the current population growth given the budget crisis they're facing," notes Department of Justice statistician Paige Harrison.[32]

The feds can't afford it either. Federal spending has been soaring in the last few years, and politicians refuse to take the responsibility to tighten belts.[33] The end result has been quick-growing deficits. Spending more to bulk up prisons is hardly a sensible option. And overcrowding is just as big a problem in federal facilities as it is among the states. The federal prison system started the year 2003 already operating 33 percent over capacity.[34]

In late 2003, Okalahoma prosecutors were busy looking for ways to trim the rate of prison growth to save money. They ignored the most obvious: Quit prosecuting nonviolent drug offenders.[35]

Counting the Human Costs

There are other reasons beside the economic costs to the State to stave off prosecutions and imprisonment. The most obvious costs here are those incurred by individual inmates and their families. When thinking about how many thousands of Americans are jailed for nonviolent drug offenses, compare their relatively harmless offenses with their penalties.

Prisoners suffer many losses when the cell doors close: loss of liberty, autonomy, and security; loss of personal property, goods, and services; loss of family, community, and heterosexual relationships.[36] These are the things that make life what it is; if a man is married, for instance, his wife is part of him. Take her away for years at a whack, and the symmetry of his life will be thrown radically off balance. Almost everything that grounds a man is taken from him in prison: familiar routines, friends, home. They're all gone. About the only thing not taken from a man in prison are his thoughts and spiritual life, and even those are put under tremendous strain. It turns his entire world upside down.

Predators and thugs deserve such treatment. But for nonviolent people—whether dealers or simple users—the sentence is grossly disproportionate to their crime.

If the rationale for imprisoning people who use drugs is to keep them from hurting themselves, I'm not sure how inflicting a more comprehensive and profound harm makes their lives any better. "Sixty years ago nearly every small town had its village idiots, its 'peculiar' citizens, its town drunks, and those people who needed more drugs than others," writes Wesley C. Westman in his 1970 book, *The Drug Epidemic*. "Somehow we were able to exist during those years, and people made allowances for such citizens. But with our progress and sophistication . . . we now pass laws against these people, place them in institutions, and feel that we have done them a beneficial service."[37] We haven't. Violent, hurtful people belong where they cannot hurt others, but we defeat the purpose of prison if we jail nonviolent people with these predators.

Some go in for relatively minor offenses and end up brutalized in prison. Charles Colson and Daniel Van Ness recount the story of a shy young man who tried scoring favor among his peers by giving them five-dollar bags of marijuana. To cover his expenses, Tim Starnes stole checks from his mother, forged, and cashed them. Before she knew the identity of the forger, a warrant was issued and her son was quickly fingered as the thief. She wanted the charges dropped, but the State wanted to make an example of him. "I knew they would abuse him," she said. "He was one day over eighteen years old. He was a pretty boy. I knew what would happen to him in prison." It did. "Tim was raped," write Colson and Van Ness. "He tried to resist the assault, and suffered all the more. His attackers, all of them older and stronger, beat him with metal pipes. He still bears the scars—physical and emotional—from the attack. . . ."[38]

Jailhouse buggery is all too common—the "unwritten part" of a person's sentence, notes Christian Parenti, who explores the topic in some depth in his book, *Lockdown America*.[39] The jailhouse ethos is not live and let live. Consider many of the people housed there. It's the strong take the weak. Suffice it to say, the most likely victims of prison rape are nonviolent people, like many drug war victims. So a relatively harmless, productive person can go to prison on a marijuana or minor cocaine conviction and come out abused and possibly an abuser, psychologically damaged goods, with a hard time adjusting to life on the outside. "They took something from me that I can never replace," said one prison-rape victim, quoted by Parenti. "I've tried so many nights to forget about it, but the feeling just doesn't go away. Every time I'm with my wife, it comes back what he did to me. I want to close the story. I want some salvation. But it keeps going on and on."[40]

Even if a person leaves prison unviolated and still has his mental joists in place, he can have a hard time making the transition out of jail.

Many in the pen pick up a slew of new antisocial skills and coping tactics that are utilized to stay afloat in the brutal prison environment but are crippling on the outside. "Jail is whacked, man. Whacked," says one young man shortly after his release. "I picked up some violent s— in there. You're with people locked up for murder, gun charges. Eventually that s—'s going to wear on you."[41] It does. Prisoners quickly learn to adopt a tough attitude and act aggressively—character traits that take a person really far in, say, customer service.

Quick tempers and violent reactions make finding work a chore, though that's not the biggest hurdle. A sunny disposition hardly improves a job resume with the entry: "Tended laundry at San Quentin." Try impressing a potential boss with that one. Try not being escorted out by security with that one. Granted, it's hard to feel sorry for someone in this predicament who preyed upon his neighbors—further fruit of his misdeeds. But what about the guy who's crime was simple possession of cocaine? Growing pot for personal use? Selling pot to some college buddies? We not only jail him for crimes in which he's neither harmed nor defrauded anyone but then release him into a society that makes it hard now to make a living *without* harming or defrauding others. If legitimate work is hard to find, what are his options?

Well, he can always sell drugs.

Learning the Trade

Given high recidivism rates, it's plain that "correction" and "correctional facilities" are nearly contradictions in terms. As Carnegie-Mellon criminologist Alfred Blumstein explains, "Incarceration can move the prisoner to a more serious level of criminal activity . . . as a result of association with other more serious offenders."[42] It's the old bad-company-corrupts-good-morals problem. While the focus of Blumstein's observation was violent crime, it's just as true of drugs.

Drug warriors frequently underplay the entrepreneurial angle of the drug trade. Traffickers and dealers are ruthless thugs, they say. Sometimes yes, but don't forget what many of them are in addition: inventive, smart, crafty, and always looking for a way to get their product to the consumer without landing in jail. Now, imagine a place where thousands of "narco-preneurs" all across the country are conspiring to sell drugs, talking about the dos and don'ts of successful trafficking, and explaining the tricks of the trade. Welcome to prison—otherwise known as crime school—where inmates with varying levels of skills and smarts come together and teach each other how to sling dope.

George Jung, one of the key players in the exploding cocaine markets of the late 1970s and early 1980s, met his partner Carlos Lehder at Danbury federal prison. Busted for pot, Jung came out the king of coke. Lehder was also busy in prison. He kept files on what he learned about boats, planes, and real estate. After meeting a former bank president who embezzled more than eight billion dollars, Bruce Porter writes, "Carlos taught him Spanish in return for lectures on how the banking system worked, what transactions had to be reported to the government, how to set up accounts in offshore institutions and move money around in ways no one could follow, which banks had the numbered accounts. . . ."[43] All of this would come into play in Jung and Lehder's smuggling operations.

It may not take the form of lectures and note-taking, but these guys are learning the business and have a financial incentive to listen up for any piece of information that gets floated.

Funny enough, sometimes it does take the form of lectures and note-taking. For his part, Jung got time knocked off his sentence by helping a class of poorly educated cons pass their GEDs, which would theoretically help them get jobs after prison. The only hitch was that they didn't want to sit still in class and learn. Jung had to spice it up. He taught them all the basics: history, math, English, geography, how to smuggle pot from Mexico without getting caught—the basics. Says Jung, "Danbury was a regular mind factory."[44]

This sort of thing goes on in every prison across the fruited plain. So here's the absurdity: Guys go to jail on a drug charge and come out knowing how to do the same thing better. But perhaps the biggest slap at the effectiveness of using prisons as a tool in the drug war is the fact that authorities can't even keep the stuff out of prison.

Jailhouse Rock

Insight magazine reported in 2002 about the number of drug overdoses in US prisons. The numbers are slippery because recordkeeping is spotty, but with tenacity and some Freedom of Information requests, reporter Timothy W. Maier was able to find that between 1998 and 2001, California had thirty-one lethal ODs, Maryland sixteen, and Texas twelve.

It could be worse than that. Some states are less than thorough in their death records. Alabama, for instance, reported sixty-nine deaths in 1999 but tagged fifty-two as unexplained. As with the general populace, lethal overdoses are going to be few in number compared to the total body of inmates—but *any* such ODs point to drug use behind bars that are supposed to keep out such things.[45]

Drug testing is also a window into the failure of prison security. In Nebraska—which, according to Maier's findings, keeps no records of prison overdoses—some 7 percent of inmates flagged positive in random drug tests in 2000.[46] Federal prisons, in which more than half the population are there on drug charges, are notoriously flush with dope. Drug testing flags more than 2,800 cases of use among inmates each year, according to a 2003 Justice Department study. Since 2000, more than 1,100 drug finds have been made and logged in federal corrections facilities. And since 1997, some 500 inmates have died from overdoses.[47]

How do the drugs get in? One con quoted by Maier claimed that outsiders would pack dope into tennis balls and chuck them into the yard. After speaking with George Brosan, deputy secretary for the Maryland Department of Public Safety and Correctional Services, Maier notes that "drugs enter prisons when visitors exchange watches or shoes. Women hide drugs in their bras or stuff them in a baby's diaper. The most common method? Mouth-to-mouth by passing a balloon full of heroin with a passionate kiss. . . . The inmate swallows the balloon to avoid detection during routine strip searches after visitation ends, and then attempts to regurgitate the balloon after drinking warm water."[48]

Besides smuggling drugs in fuzzy green spheres or behind luscious visiting lips, corrupt guards and vendors are also known to secret narcotics into prisons. Even the mail carrier gets some blame. One prison guard highlighted the US mail as the biggest source of incoming dope. "Drug smugglers are ingenious," said the unnamed guard, who fingered care packages sent from dealers, not dad. "We've had them go so far as to crush Trix cereal and coat small balls of heroin in the crumbs to make them look like the rest of the cereal." The guard noted that tar heroin can be pasted between two sheets of countless court papers or the flap of an envelope. "There are a million ways to get it into prison."[49]

Insight editor Paul Rodriguez asks the obvious question: "If authorities couldn't prevent drug trafficking and heroin overdose in prison, what hope could there be for the war on drugs?"[50]

CONCLUSION

DRUG-WAR DETOX

When the Eighteenth Amendment was passed I earnestly hoped . . .
that it would be generally supported by public opinion and thus the
day be hastened when the value to society of men with minds and
bodies free from the undermining effects of alcohol would be generally realized. That this has not been the result, but rather that drinking has generally increased; that the speakeasy has replaced the
saloon . . . that a vast army of lawbreakers has been recruited and
financed on a colossal scale; that many of our best citizens . . . have
openly and unabashedly disregarded the Eighteenth Amendment;
that . . . respect for all law has been greatly lessened; that crime has
increased to an unprecedented degree—I have slowly and reluctantly
come to believe. . . .

—JOHN D. ROCKEFELLER JR.,
writing in support of a national referendum to repeal Prohibition[1]

WHEN I ORIGINALLY PITCHED THE IDEA FOR THIS BOOK, THE
publisher was greatly interested in my conclusion: Would I advocate
legalization?

There are few lightning-rod issues as jarring. Many people are scandalized by the very word. I've never understood exactly why.

If I were to be scandalized by anything, it'd be a policy that exacerbates crime, especially in communities often the least able to bear it;
that produces so much corruption in the ranks of those charged with

enforcing it; that empowers terrorists and insurgents with easy money; that squanders immense resources trying to interdict drug shipments; that requires the erosion of property and privacy rights to sufficiently enforce it; that encourages the outright looting of the American people to pad drug-war budgets; that militarizes police and threatens innocent citizens' lives; and that unjustly imprisons so many people for either a preference of their own taste or a crime problem created by the government in the first place.

How could it possibly be scandalous to say we should stop all of this?

In the same way, how could it possibly be scandalous to say we should keep the federal government true to its charter? The Constitution clearly delineates the role of the central government. Article 1, Section 8, spells out specifically what Congress has the authority to do. It says exactly nothing about banning drugs or launching a bellicose policy against them. Amendments Nine and Ten are doubly damning to the drug war, saying in so many words that whatever the Constitution does not allow Congress to do, it must leave for the states and the people to deal with on their own. Even so centralist a founder as Alexander Hamilton was quick to admit, "There is one transcendent advantage belonging to the province of the State governments. . . . I mean the ordinary administration of criminal and civil justice."[2] If there is to be any regulation of drugs at all, it should be at the state level.

So which is actually scandalous: Saying we should act as if the Constitution mattered, or giving a middle finger to the founders' original intent because it suits our particular agenda?

"Modern Federalism reaffirms the ideal of the US Constitution that the powers of the government should always be applied at the right place and the right time, in just the amount needed to achieve legitimate goals," explains Barry Goldwater in *Where I Stand*. "Alongside these goals, however desirable they may seem, we must balance the possible costs of lessened personal freedom. In the rush to cure all the ills to which humans are heir, liberty is too often an innocent bystander—and an accidental casualty."[3] In the case of drug prohibition, liberty is *far* too often an innocent bystander thanks to the heavy involvement of the federal government.

Undoing the Disaster

Some policy of legalization must be followed if we are to pull ourselves out of this mess. Reticence is understandable, but consider the fundamental issue. As drug prohibition is the direct cause of so many ills, scrapping it is the surest way of treating them.

Doubters should trace back the problems catalogued in this book to their root. Why is drug crime a problem? It has very little to do with the pharmacological effect of a particular substance on the mind of an individual. Rather, it is because prohibition creates an environment in which thugs prosper and traditional legal structures that peacefully govern markets are traded for guns and turf battles.

What about police corruption? Prohibition places police in a unique position to prosper from the drug trade, and, flush with cash, dealers seek out those whose price tag is lower than their level of compunction. Some take advantage, others are taken advantage of. Either way, all of law enforcement is undermined, and good cops are stuck dealing with the mess.

Terrorism? Nothing else could generate the kind of money terrorists have access to because of prohibition-inflated drug prices. Like the common criminals that benefit from the drug war, terrorists also have the comparative advantage in violence needed to leverage the market. And they do so at every opportunity.

As for smuggling (and all the money wasted trying to stop it), it is the direct result of prohibition and restrictive regulation, plain and simple. No one smuggles cucumbers.

What about the erosion of the Fourth Amendment? Prohibition means drug users and sellers must avoid detection while conducting business. Voluntarily violating the law together, it is not likely that either party will rat the other out. As such, police insist on broad, invasive investigative powers to generate the leads necessary to enforce the law.

The Fifth suffers likewise. When drug entrepreneurs make such vast sums of money—thanks to prohibition inflating drug prices—enforcing the law requires that government undermine constitutional protections for property so it can more easily seize and forfeit what it suspects is ill gotten gain.

And militarized police? As the drug war has escalated over the decades, police and dopers have entered a Cold War-like arms race in which one side is forever trying to outgun the other. Indianapolis police captain Robert L. Snow says the problem is that "drug dealers have . . . increased their affinity for violence."[4] To whatever extent this is true, it fails to explain the real issue. Some drug dealers might get their jollies from violence, but most get their jollies from succeeding in their trade—no different than a stockbroker or Sears manager. Prohibition-created cash, not cruelty, is the great motivator. Police are an obstacle to the pay-off, so drug dealers must rely on bigger, better guns to overcome the obstacle. Police don't take this lying down and, in fact, walk up the ladder of lethality. Hello, SWAT teams and no-knock raids.

Prisons are swelling and straining at the seams nationwide because all manner of offenders, from thug to petty dealer to user, are jailed at a rate unheard of in the free world. Besides the sheer cost of housing two million offenders, prisons manifest another distinct drawback: They serve as crime schools for the recidivists that recycle through like DVD rentals at a Blockbuster store.

As prohibition is the root of all these problems, the fix lies in repeal.

Sending a Message?

Before we get there, however, we have to blow past the most common rejoinder to repeal: Legalizing drugs will *not* send a message that drug abuse is okay. Coming out against Prohibition didn't make John D. Rockefeller Jr. an evangelist for booze. By itself, negating one thing is not affirming another. To wit: I'm against stringent environmental controls, but I don't approve of pollution. I'm against gun control, but I don't support shooting up liquor stores.

A husband not demonstrating proper love for his wife is probably the most socially destructive, immoral action around. It's the most common cause of divorce and family breakdown, precursors to societal breakdown. Yet take a hint from St. Paul. He leans on husbands to love their wives in his epistles, but he never recommends people start lobbying for legislation to enforce it. Lacking legislation that requires husbands to love their wives does not mean that society approves of spousal disharmony and neglect. It only means it's not something the law should be concerned with. Same thing with environmental laws. Same thing with gun control. Same thing with lots more.

"Here's one of the hard truths that offends the modern age," says William J. Bennett, "not only are there some tasks that government cannot do, in a nation of free and sovereign people, there are some tasks that government should not do."[5] And just as government shouldn't prevent people from gambling, it shouldn't prevent people from using drugs. It doesn't mean that drugs are good, any more than shooting craps or playing slots is good. It only means that there are things of indifference to the State.

What if those "free and sovereign people" wish to use drugs? Doubtless if we legalize drugs, many more will do so. With the threat of punishment gone and the prices down, certainly more people will be free to use and even abuse drugs. People behaving in ways one might not like is always a possibility with freedom, a lesson most of us should have learned before leaving grade school. But losing sleep over this prospect is not worth the Nyquil bill.

Discussing the ups and downs of legalizing drugs, Raphael Perl, international narcoterrorism expert for the Congressional Research Service, forthrightly admits that legalization cuts crime. But the downside is that there is more drug use. Ergo, the question: Do we want to make a trade-off in our society, where we have more drug use and less crime? No question about where Perl stands: Drug use "scares me," he says, explaining in the words of one account that his concern is "based on the technological advances which will make it possible to create even more addictive drugs."[6]

While more drug use will likely arise from legalization, this is something of a red herring. When folks imagine legalized drugs, they typically picture crazed dope fiends murdering the neighbors and looting the cities. Either that or they're imagined doped out of their gourds—useless human beings chemically induced into semi-vegetative states. One prominent critic of legalization points to a million heroin addicts on welfare, "totally zonked," costing taxpayers untold billions of dollars.[7]

In reality, it is prohibition that spurs use of more dangerous drugs. It happened with the Eighteenth Amendment. Bootleggers could get more bang for their buck moving hard alcohol than they could for beer. Likewise, opium importation fell off after passage of the first US antidrug law in 1914, replaced by greater amounts of heroin. The story is similar with marijuana and cocaine in the late seventies and cocaine and crack in middle eighties. Writes Walter E. Williams,

> There is no mystery why people use mind-altering drugs. It makes them feel good, at least temporarily. That's not only true about cocaine, heroin, and marijuana use; it's also true about mind-altering products like cigarettes, cigars, coffee, tea, wine, and whiskey. There's considerable evidence that people prefer their vices in diluted form, hence the popularity of filtered cigarettes, light beer, wine coolers, and mixed drinks. The same seems to be true, at least to some extent, about illicit drugs.
>
> When vices are legally prohibited, some supply responses change people's behavior. Imagine there's a supplier of illegal marijuana. Government steps up its effort to stop his supply by increasing interdiction efforts, along with stiffer fines and prison sentences. Which is easier to conceal or transport—a million dollars' worth of marijuana or a million dollars' worth of cocaine? Obviously, it's cocaine because there is far less bulk per dollar of value. Thus one effect of prohibition is the tendency toward increased sales and use of

more concentrated forms of vice such as crack cocaine and ice [metham-phetamine].[8]

When the legal squeeze is on, traffickers and pushers opt to move more potent, profitable drugs. It helps better justify their risks. When Prohibition was finally corked, beer and wine made a comeback. Most likely, so will softer, less harmful drugs if legalized. In short, what scares Perl is a bogeyman.

Depending on how drugs are legalized such fears are even less founded. If pot is legalized first and we move incrementally toward legalizing stronger drugs, people will gravitate toward what's legally available first. There's little point going to prison for smack when you can score pot for the cost of a cup of coffee and won't get dropped in a holding tank after the purchase. This supply-supported shift toward pot will begin shaping patterns of use that start acclimating the society toward controlled, moderated drug consumption. The road will be a bit bumpy at first, but soon there will be various accepted rituals and cultural controls for cannabis the same way there are for alcohol and tobacco. Of course there will be abuses, but most can be hemmed in with social sanctions—exactly as they are with alcohol today. A massive slice of America imbibes, but the percentage that can't (or refuses to) hold its liquor is pretty small.

The question for many will be: How do we establish these cultural controls?

Keeping Things in Check

Despite the incredible disaster of drug prohibition, people bristle at the concept of legalization. If they're even remotely interested, they're very rigorous about details. They want to know exactly how it will work. I find this quite puzzling because after ninety years of drug laws, no one seems to know exactly how prohibition is supposed to work. If proposals for prohibition were held to the same exacting standards today as is legalization, they'd get laughed out of legislatures, off podiums, out of pulpits, off streets, and into gutters.

"Yeah, well, better the devil you know," some might rebut.

But we *do* know about controlling drugs without the State's interference. At least, we used to. Our society is steeped in prohibitionist solutions to nearly everything. Consequently, it downplays the importance of non-legal cultural controls and social sanctions. These mores and rituals are vital to a society's controlling the use and abuse of intoxicants.[9]

This is the other great, often unrecognized crime of the drug war: With prohibition serving as a crutch, many of the preexisting social controls have been abandoned or have withered away like rarely-used muscles. It all goes back to the complaint by Albert Jay Nock during the New Deal days that government kept growing while other institutions in society kept shrinking. "If we look beneath the surface of our public affairs," he wrote, "we can discern one fundamental fact, namely: a great redistribution of power between the society and the State," which he both saw and lamented was "an increase of State power and a corresponding decrease of social power."[10]

Discussing this power switch, Nock mainly focused on how the State, in removing money from the people, via taxes, limits their wherewithal to deal with circumstances in society without turning to government. But it goes beyond money. Certain cultural institutions serve when they are needed and wither when deemed unnecessary.

As a general rule, what the State does, the society quits doing. This is true for the poor (compare today's stifling welfare to the boisterous pre–New Deal and Great Society charity industry), the elderly (think Social Security, which, pre–New Deal, somehow the elderly got along without thanks to family-care structures), even substance abusers (who were, before prohibition, mainly dealt with by physicians, church, and family).[11] But who needs the myriad private institutions, social conventions, and cultural mores that previously dealt with problems when the government is ready, willing, and—optimists blush—able to take care of business?

Seeing the resounding failure of the State's tactics, it's time we get back to cultural controls.

Ditching prohibition is the first step to getting them back, maybe not at once, but certainly eventually. As already mentioned, there will likely be an upsurge in drug use—nothing catastrophic, especially if prohibition is dismantled gradually—but we have to be realistic and admit that effective societal controls will not root overnight. They need time to develop, as people model responsible drug use before those who are thinking of using drugs, thus teaching from the outset responsible use, and people see the negative consequences of irresponsible use.

The great policy fumble will be falling into old habits and thinking this development needs some sort of direction or intervention from the State. The growth of social controls is spontaneous. It's not like people have to plan for culture. It just happens as history unfolds, based on the values of everyday people going about their lives. When those values are destructive, they fall out of favor. When they are positive, they stay in use. History bears this out time and again.

Historian David Musto, studying the early twentieth century "cocaine epidemic," noticed the decline in use that happened in the mid-1900s. He saw it as a generational learning pattern. David T. Courtwright summarizes Musto's findings: "A new drug generates enthusiasm. Use rises. Then problems—overdose, compulsion, paranoia—begin to appear among significant minority of users. Would-be recruits think twice. Use declines."[12] A whole generation learns a lesson.

Likewise, in addressing need for cultural revival to stymie the progress of the sexual revolution, popular Christian writer Frederica Mathewes-Green points to drugs as a marker of hope in the struggle. During the sixties, mind-altering drugs were seen as healthy, their use beneficial. But, she says, use waned as people increasingly became burned by their experiences. Given these bad trips, the popularity of such drugs diminished. "Mind-altering drugs did not lose their status because of a clever anti-drug campaign, or hard-hitting public service announcements, or improved anti-drug legislation. They lost their cachet because they were found to be damaging. Drugs turned out to be not as advertised." Mathewes-Green notes that drug use didn't cease in toto, neither did the disillusionment of the time translate into total abstinence today. But things certainly did improve, and it wasn't the law that did it. It was simply the realization that drugs failed to deliver and were sometimes extremely dangerous. The upshot from this lesson is clear: "it is possible for cultures to change for the better, once given a dose of truth. Like a body, a culture has an innate impulse to health. Though this can be subverted in a million ways, it can be nurtured as well. That should give us hope."[13]

When the gin craze wracked London, it wasn't the continuous legislation pouring out of Parliament that curbed the guzzlers; neither was it the rat-fink informants and abysmal jails. It was simply the fact that folks learned better. When the drink was new, folks knocked back mugs of the stuff as they did with beer. It was too new for anyone to know any better. But as time wore on, people's experience with the more powerful potation increased and consumption mellowed.[14]

Heroin was much like this. The jazz world in the fifties was awash in "horse" as it was called. Many folks were tickled into using by their admiration, in particular, of bebop master Charlie Parker. Perhaps, they thought, it was the drugs that made his playing so unique, made him so cool. Then again, perhaps not. Over time, people realized that shooting smack wasn't so cool. It hurt careers, damaged relationships. Parker died, and the fad began petering out. People learned. One sax player said of his quitting, "I guess you could say I diminuendoed out of it."[15]

Crack, the drug that supposedly was going to hasten Armageddon, hardly makes the headlines any longer. The very fact that people saw the drug's effects were often so destructive was a substantial put-off for many. People observed what the drug was doing to their siblings, friends, and parents and decided against using it. Says retired DEA special agent Robert Stutman,

In my opinion, law enforcement, although it had something to do with . . . the lessening of crack—not the demise—it had far less to do with it than the fact that the people who crack affected have simply said, "Enough." I think that it is the indigenous population that was integrated into the crack users who have said, "We've had enough of this crap. We've had enough of kids getting shot, beaten. We have enough spousal abuse." I think the biggest war against crack was won by the people that were affected by crack, not by law enforcement.[16]

Obviously, people still use crack, just as they still use heroin, but the near-epidemic levels widely and loudly reported in the 1980s are gone.

Basic self-interest and risk aversion dictates that the more dangerous a drug's perception with the public, the better the society's ability to control it. There's a reason very few people use PCP compared to those that use marijuana. While it does have something to do with availability, PCP is perceived by the public as wildly dangerous. Pot is not. As such, more people smoke weed than use PCP. Pretty simple.

Faith and Family

There are two social institutions in particular that can help encourage these sorts of social controls: the Church and family. When people mount soapboxes and go frothy in advocating some social policy or other, very often the family is not factored as a vital piece of the puzzle. This is because, since the Progressive era and the New Deal, people have increasingly turned to the State to solve their problems, to the neglect of more foundational and instrumental institutions. What could be more fundamental to social policy than the most basic social structure—mom, pop, and two screaming kids?

It is into families that children are born and in families where morals and virtue are inculcated. It's no mystery why kids with absentee parents tend to have a bigger problem with drugs than others.[17] Same story for kids raised without mothers.[18] Even drug smugglers are wise to this fact. "We don't have a drug problem in this country. We have a problem of parental guidance," says infamous narcotrafficker George Jung. "People concentrate more on the guy who repairs their car than on the teacher who teaches their kids. [Until] they wake up to that fact, the tragedy will continue. . . . If people can't grasp it, then they don't want to."[19]

It's not just the parents' fault, of course. A large part of parental abdication is simply the result of societal controls being ceded to the State almost a century ago.

With our prohibitionist, just-say-no solution, we've effectively ruled out any real parental instruction on intoxicants. It's simply an either-or question. Don't use drugs, you'll be fine. Use 'em and you're in deep trouble. Given that peoples from every moment in history have used some sort of intoxicant, a one-sized-fits-all rule, no exceptions, is irrational, unhistorical, and just begging to be broken.

If we want to take full advantage of Musto's findings, generations that learn the lesson must pass it down. A more effective approach to drug control and prohibition would be to allow the drugs legal status and simply encourage parents to do as parents are supposed to do—train up a child in the way that he should go. In some cases this will involve religious reasons for abstention. In others, it will involve teaching regarding moderation. Still in others, it will involve a mixture of the two. This is what Europe has done with alcohol, and it works.

Similarly, I grew up in a family where wine was served at meals, even made in the backyard. I vividly remember a wine press at my grandfather's house, squeezing out juice. I remember the carboys in which the juice fermented. Later, I used some of those same carboys to make beer. While some of my friends who grew up in more abstemious households hit the bottle shortly after hitting their late teens, my sister and I had ingrained habits and carefully modeled examples of consumption that helped prevent excesses. Will all parents take the time to train up their children? No, but neither are those parents doing it now. Worse for the kids, instead of seeing healthier consumption of intoxicants modeled around them even if denied at home, because of prohibition, the only modeling they see occurs in an illicit subculture known for criminality, recklessness, and rebelliousness—hardly a good place to learn anything, let alone how to deal with drugs.

Another important social institution is the Church. For a variety of reasons, over the last hundred years, the potency of the American pulpit has diminished. But the Church can and should be a powerful force against drug abuse in the culture.

From their pulpits, pastors should inveigh against inebriation and encourage moderation. Churches can also help in counseling and addiction recovery efforts. Drug abuse is a soul problem, not a substance problem. Legislation can't fix that. In fact, it can only muddle the real issues.

Tying substance abuse to violence, for instance, results in a skewed perspective of the violence and its real causes—a helpful lie in many cases. Nicolette Bautista, executive director of Women Escaping A Violent Environment, notes that many WEAVE clients report abusers' use of alcohol and admits boozing can make a bad situation worse. But she also notes, "Substance abuse is *not* the cause of domestic violence." Instead it's often a ready fig leaf for the rotten behavior people exhibit. "The cause of it is a controlling personality. It's about power and control."[20]

And this is only the beginning. Substance abuse goes beyond a few foul character traits and gets swallowed up in a twisted matrix of self- and society-justifying behavior.

"Drinking (or claiming to be drunk) provides the perfect excuse for instances of domestic violence," write sociology professors Richard Gelles and Murray Straus. All violent people must do is feign ignorance of their actions and suddenly they are absolved from thumping their wife or children. Thus, "violent parents and partners learn that if they do not want to be held responsible for their violence, they should drink and hit, or at least say they were drunk." Substance abuse becomes a cover for fouler things. "The statistical connection between drunkenness and wife beating exists principally because households predisposed to violence are also predisposed to abuse of alcohol, as well as the abuse of drugs and many other social problems."[21]

And so drug and alcohol abuse become a scapegoat for family breakdown, eroded cultural mores, individual slumps, and just good old-fashioned sin. In the overwhelming number of cases, people don't beat their wives because they're drunk, anymore than people commit crimes because they're stoned; they do these things because they're twisted inside.

A society loath to chalk things up to the depravity of man is ever in need of things outside of man to pin for his misdeeds. Drugs just happen to be a handy donkey on which to pin the tail. By blaming a substance, the individual doesn't have to face his own depravity; neither does the society have to face the reality that its conception of humanity is skewed. Believing in the basic goodness of people is a cinch if you can find fault for the obvious badness of people in something other than the people. Hypocritically enough, while drug warriors decry the escapist nature of drug abuse, our nation's drug policies serve as a construct to allow people to avoid an honest glimpse of life.

Nobody's Fault but Mine

In the end, all of this comes back to the individual. Says conservative writer Frank Meyer, "The form of [social] institutions has no power to make bad men good or good men bad. They can, under the circumstances of the kind we have seen too much of in this unhappy century, restrict freedom and undermine the responsibility of the individual so that they become a serious impediment to the growth of virtue; but they cannot, of their own power, make men good. At their best, they can create favorable conditions—and that is all."[22]

Considering the apparent moral slide America is in, many people are not happy with leaving a man's virtue up to himself. The truth is, they never are. Thomas Jefferson already addressed the issue in his first inaugural: "Sometimes it is said that man cannot be trusted with the government of himself. Can he, then, be trusted with the government of others? Or have we found angels in the form of kings to govern him? Let history answer this question."

Having recently dealt with such angelic kings, the founders weren't keen to cede much power to the State at all—power can be abused and usually is. This is why the austere Austrian economist Ludwig von Mises—hardly the stereotypical picture of the druggie—inveighed so strongly against prohibition. He knew where it would lead. In *Human Action*, Mises warned about the expansionist threat inherent to prohibition schemes. "Opium and morphine are certainly dangerous, habit-forming drugs," he conceded. "But once the principle is admitted that it is the duty of government to protect the individual against his own foolishness, no serious objections can be advanced against further encroachments. A good case could be made . . . in favor of the prohibition of alcohol and nicotine."[23]

Unfortunately, compromise on this point produces compromise elsewhere, and we're already seeing the encroachers on individual liberty making hard advances. Not only is nicotine being heavily assaulted by health Nazis, but social drinking has recently come under attack as well.[24] Obesity is fast on its way to becoming the next national health scare; to stem the tide and lighten the load, Yale Professor Kelly Brownell has even recommended taxing what he considers unhealthy foods.[25] Because of concessions over time, there's nothing to stop the prohibitionist mindset from coming over for dinner and making sure that you don't get any.

What we have to remember is that not every thing is under our control. If people are free in any meaningful sense of the word, that means they are at liberty to foul up their lives as much as make something grand of them. That's the gamble we all take. That's the risk of liberty. Nobody wants others to screw up their lives, but each must be free to do so for themselves.

What about those who will not curb their appetites? Thankfully, they will always be a minority. Yes, the problems they cause will be chronic, but chronic problems are the easiest to deal with. You can plan for them because you know they're coming. Not so with the expansion of the State under a prohibitionist regime. The best we can know is that it's going to get worse, that the grip of the leviathan will tighten. But as long as we are addicted to the drug-war mentality, we'll be powerless to stop the liberty-squelching growth of government.

Get Yourself Free

What about specific legalization plans? There is little space to deal in details, but a few broad strokes might help paint a useful picture.

Some people recommend outright legalization, that the government just grab the big eraser and strike the prohibition laws. This is well and good (ideally I'm all for it), except it requires politicians act with resolve. If more comment is needed to cast doubts on the outcome of such an endeavor, note simply the strange anatomy of politicians—huge jaws, no spine. I doubt very seriously the ability to get such an across-the-board reform accomplished. Privatizing Social Security seems a picnic by comparison. Instead, we may be stuck with partial repeals, one-cheek reforms, and the incremental dismantling of the drug-war juggernaut. Sadly, Mick Jagger's verdict is true: "You can't always get what you want."

I'm not wild about the success of any national sort of treatment or monitoring program either. Not only is the federal government well practiced in high spending and bureaucratic wastefulness, the idea that Uncle Sam is supposed to compassionately pull all junkies into his warm, hairy bosom is frighteningly out of alignment with the proper role of government. Recalling the wisdom of William Bennett, "there are some tasks that government cannot do . . . there are some tasks that government should not do." This is one. Regarding drug treatment, it presupposes government knows what to do, how to do it, and to whom to do it. I don't think politicians are wise and insightful enough to know this. Though many of the more ambitious and power-hungry types will be willing to grab the opportunity to try, it is asking far too much. They are not counselors, friends, siblings, parents, priests, rabbis, pastors, psychologists, psychiatrists, doctors, or even bartenders. Some may be any one or two or even three of those things. But they are not all of those things to all of us. As such, turning to the State to provide these services is folly. We must turn to those people in our own communities and families, in our own congregations and social circles.

Dealing with drugs is just more than the government can handle.

But not being able to cut the umbilical cord in one fell swoop means we're stuck with the maternal State, at least for now.

If we can't get outright repeal, at the very least we should push to de-federalize the war and let the states sort matters out for themselves.

This won't solve every problem, of course. Federal-brand tyranny is already widely cribbed by local governments, and so many of the current abuses will continue in a decentralized system. But ultimately, the beauty is that instead of one top-down, ham-fisted regimen, drug policy will be set in fifty different state-houses, allowing for fifty different experiments in what works and what doesn't. Some of the Western states like California, Nevada, and Alaska might well decriminalize marijuana possession, possibly other drugs. The merits of decriminalization will become apparent to many, and other states will follow.[26]

Under federalism, "States and localities would be free to sculpt themselves into whatever kind of place the denizens prefer," explains Ann Coulter. "If an individual feels unduly oppressed by those laws, he can move. And it's a lot easier to move to the town next door, or even the state next door, than to move to Canada. That's how federalism creates the maximum freedom possible."[27]

We're already seeing some headway being made at the state level with medical marijuana in defiance of the federal drug warriors and asset forfeiture reform. While conservatives may buck at it, they must at least appreciate the basic issue of local control and the Constitution—the feds have no authority here.[28]

When alcohol Prohibition was dismantled, regulation of booze didn't evaporate the moment the celebratory corks were popped. It simply devolved to the state, county, and city governments. While ridding the nation entirely of drug prohibition seems like a straightforward and efficient idea, it won't happen any time soon. And perhaps it's fitting and even humbling that we are restrained in reforming prohibition by the very document that guarantees liberty to all within the confines of the fifty states, the Constitution. We are a nation of diverse people with diverse needs, tastes, and ways of living. The founders knew this and created a system of government that by its very *inflexibility* (Article 1, Section 8) provides the *flexibility* needed for different sectors of society to govern themselves as they best see fit (Amendments Nine and Ten).

The theme has always been freedom, and sometimes that freedom is used in ways we don't like or approve of. Such is life in a nation of free and sovereign individuals.

"What do people get out of using drugs?" asks Thomas Sowell. "I don't know. I haven't even tried marijuana. But there is all the difference in the world between deciding that you don't want to do something and trying to force other people to live your way."[29]

Sadly, the drug warriors haven't yet learned the difference, and the rest of the nation suffers for it.

ACKNOWLEDGMENTS

WITHOUT JOSEPH FARAH AND WORLDNETDAILY.COM, THIS BOOK wouldn't exist. As my interest in the drug war kicked into gear in late 1999 and early 2000, Joseph gave me free rein to explore the topic at WND. As commentary editor, I was provided an immediate outlet for my thoughts on the topic and immediate feedback from WND's large readership. All of this was invaluable. Just as important, as my flirtation with the issue morphed into a book project, Joseph continued to back my work. For his mentorship and support I remain indebted and deeply grateful.

David Dunham and Michael Hyatt, my bosses at WND Books, really looked out for this project and walked it through the minefield that is the approval process. Without their courage, support, and trust, "Bad Trip" would better describe the path the project took through the publisher's board.

Wes Driver applied his deft and careful editing to the manuscript, reminding me when attempts at novelty failed and metaphors were stretched too far. He helped keep me from going overboard more than a few times. As a co-laborer, I've come to greatly respect Wes's insight, sense of humor, and willingness to offer genuine assistance.

Many people knocked time out of their busy schedules to provide criticisms both big and small regarding the manuscript: Andrew P. Napolitano, Jacob Sullum, Lew Rockwell, Timothy Roloff, Jack Cole, Jon Dougherty, Dave Kopel, Mark Thornton, Tom Ambrose, and Abby and Will Locket. Thanks to Eric Sterling for returning the last-minute phone call and Ron Strom for the last-minute critique. Thanks to Matthew Saxelby for the Lindhurst High articles and Harry Browne for the digitally condensed pile of research. Early on, Jeremy Lott reminded me that my prose isn't really worth too much. Cut, cut, cut. Which I did, did, did. Jeremy, like so many others, has now endured years of my rants and ramblings on this subject. I'm indebted to you all.

Particular resources and organizations of indispensable help in researching the topic: The Media Awareness Project (MAPinc.org), the Drug Reform Coordination Network (DRCNet.org), *Reason*, the Cato Institute, Independent Institute, NORML, the Drug Policy Foundation, and CannabisNews.com.

My parents deserve special honor. They got me started thinking about these issues and spent many years encouraging me. My father also had a library packed with Rothbard, Mises, Hayek, and many others, plus a sizeable heap of *Reason* and *Freeman* back issues—what every growing boy needs.

Most important, my wife: Lydia was longsuffering and patient during the whole researching and writing process, especially toward the end when I spent hours of each evening and most of the weekends cluttering the house with countless articles and books, ignoring the family while I pounded away on the keyboard, trying to tie all my loose ends and not desecrate my deadline too badly. She should have poisoned my coffee and been done with it. Instead, she stood by me and offered more help than I deserved. I couldn't have done it without her prayers, encouragement, and support.

This book is for her.

BIBLIOGRAPHY

For readers interested in reading more on the topic of illicit drugs, prohibition, and related subjects, I recommend the following:

Andrew Barr, *Drink: A Social History of America* (New York: Carroll & Graf, 1999). There is no better introduction to the issue of intoxicants and their use in American culture. Barr is also an enjoyable writer.

Dan Baum, *Smoke and Mirrors: The War on Drugs and the Politics of Failure* (New York: Bay Back, 1997). Incredibly valuable history of the drug war from the Nixon years through the middle 1990s.

Daniel K. Benjamin and Roger LeRoy Miller, *Undoing Drugs: Beyond Legalization* (New York: BasicBooks, 1991). The first book I know of that recommends a decentralized, states-rights approach. Benjamin and Miller's analysis of the drug-war problem was very helpful to me early in my research. And the book stands up well more than ten years after first publication.

Alan Bock, *Waiting to Inhale: The Politics of Medical Marijuana* (Santa Ana: Seven Locks, 2000). Single best source to explain the ins and outs of medical marijuana—history, science, politics, everything—from a very thoughtful writer.

Martin Booth, *Opium: A History* (New York: Thomas Dunn, 1996). Like all of the authors in the this bibliography, I don't agree with everything Booth writes, but he provides here a peerless history of a substance that has changed the world.

James Bovard, *Lost Rights: The Destruction of American Liberty* (New York: St. Martin's Griffin, 1995). Bovard's scope is well beyond the drug war, but like *Undoing Drugs*, it's very helpful in explaining key issues, namely Fourth and Fifth Amendment abuses. Bovard is also good at providing the theoretical and philosophical underpinnings that help ground his subject.

Ted Galen Carpenter, *Bad Neighbor Policy: Washington's Futile War on Drugs in Latin America* (New York: Palgrave, 2003). The subtitle pretty much says it all. Our "pharmaceutical colonialism" in the Southern Hemisphere has reaped a bumper crop of failure, disaster, frustration, and ill will. Carpenter deftly navigates the issues and events to explain why.

David T. Courtwright, *Forces of Habit: Drugs and the Making of the Modern World* (Cambridge: Harvard University, 2001). An concise history of the rise of our polydrug culture. New insight into how trade and culture affect the traffic in psychoactive substances: cannabis, alcohol, tea, cocaine, heroin, coffee, the usual.

Richard Davenport-Hines, *The Pursuit of Oblivion: A Global History of Narcotics* (New York: W.W. Norton, 2002). A sweeping, huge history of dope. Few books can match Davenport-Hines's scope.

Steven B. Duke and Albert C. Gross, *America's Longest War: Rethinking our Tragic Crusade Against Drugs* (New York: Tarcher/Putnam, 1993). An exhaustive case against the drug war and a careful presentation/analysis of various legalization schemes.

Judge James P. Gray, *Why our Drug Laws have Failed and What we can do About It: A Judicial Indictment of the War on Drugs* (Philadelphia: Temple University Press, 2001). The view from the bench. Judge Gray confirms that many of those responsible for jailing drug offenders are not convinced the effort is a good idea—and he provides a heavy load of reasons why doubt and outright dissent on the drug war exists.

Mike Gray, *Drug Crazy: How We Got Into This Mess And How We Can Get Out* (New York: Routledge, 2000). An enjoyable read, hypercritical, and fast-paced. Gray races readers through the ins and outs of the policy and history of drug prohibition in an energetic style.

Ronald Hamowy, ed., *Dealing With Drugs: Consequences of Government Control* (San Francisco: Pacific Research Institute, 1987). Features thoughtful, academic essays on many angles of drug policy: history, morals, economics, foreign policy, medicine, addiction, and more. Many of the essays are still invaluable after all these years.

Douglas Husak, *Legalize This! The Case for Decriminalizing Drugs* (New York: Verso, 2002). Compelling, non-libertarian argument for ending the drug war. Laid out very logically and philosophically, the book makes its case on the merits of the argument almost exclusively.

John Kobler, *Ardent Spirits: The Rise and Fall of Prohibition* (New York: Putnam, 1973). One the most enjoyable histories of those dreadful 13 years—Alcohol Prohibition. Kobler takes readers through the early temperance days into the mire of crime, corruption, and failure that so perfectly defined the Ignoble Experiment.

Cynthia Kuhn et al, *Buzzed: The Straight Facts About the Most Used and Abused Drugs from Alcohol to Ecstasy* (New York: W.W. Norton, 1998). If you want to know the effects of drugs and what they mean for the individuals taking them, this is a good place to start.

Timothy Lynch, ed., *After Prohibition: An Adult Approach to Drug Policies in the 21st Century* (Washington DC: Cato, 2000). Lynch brings together some of the best minds and most colorful experiences together in this collection of essays.

David Musto, *The American Disease: Origins of Narcotics Control*, expanded edition (New York: Oxford University Press, 1987). Foundational history of drug policy in American from the Civil War to the Reagan years.

Bruce Porter, *Blow: How a Small-Town Boy Made $100 Million with the Medellín Cocaine Cartel and Lost it All* (New York: St. Martin's, 1993). Fascinating biography of narcotrafficker George Jung. The tragic arc is less dramatized than in the movie *Blow*, but Jung's story is a real eye-opener into the nature of the drug trade. An important piece of criminal history.

Paul Craig Roberts and Lawrence M. Stratton, *The Tyranny of Good Intentions: How Prosecutors and Bureaucrats are Trampling the Constitution in the Name of Justice* (Roseville: Forum, 2000). No other recently published book explains the loss of traditional rights and liberties across the entire judicial system as poignantly as Roberts and Stratton's.

Robert Sabbag, *Smokescreen: A True Adventure* (Edinburgh: Canongate, 2003). Sabbag is a wonderful storyweaver—gritty, funny, captivating. Tells the gripping tale of pot smuggler Allen Long.

Robert Sabbag, *Snowblind: A Brief Career in the Cocaine Trade* (New York: Grove, 1990). See above, except this volume is about coke smuggler Zachary Swan.

Dominic Streatfeild, *Cocaine: An Unauthorized Autobiography* (New York: Thomas Dunn, 2002). From the Incas to crack, from patent cures to Pablo Escobar, from Freud to FARC, Streatfeild does an incredible job of firsthand and investigative reporting covering the length and breadth cocaine. Cutting, humorous, insightful—gonzo journalism at its best.

Jacob Sullum, *Saying Yes: In Defense of Drug Use* (New York: Tarcher/Putnam, 2003). While some readers may object to any book defending drug use, they will not find a smarter, more in-depth look into what drug use is really like. Sullum cuts through so much bull, readers will be shocked how many myths they're all but forced to discard after finishing his book.

Thomas Szasz, *Our Right to Drugs: The Case for a Free Market* (Westport: Praeger, 1992). Straight libertarianism, no chaser from one of America's most consistently iconoclastic thinkers. Szasz starts with the premise that drugs are a property-rights issue and demolishes the artifices of prohibition from there.

Mark Thornton, *The Economics of Prohibition* (Salt Lake City: University of Utah, 1991). Probably the best book on the topic. Importantly, Thornton looks at the history behind the arguments in favor of prohibition. The prohibitionist connection to progressive and socialist thinkers is well documented.

Jessica Warner, *Craze: Gin and Debauchery in an Age of Reason* (New York: Four Walls Eight Windows, 2002). An entertaining, biting history that serves as a compelling parable about modern day drug use.

Edward T. Welch, *Addictions: A Banquet in the Grave: Finding Hope in the Power of the Gospel* (Phillipsburg: P&R, 2001). A solid, Christian exploration into the nature of addictions.

Lynn Zimmer and John P. Morgan, *Marijuana Myths, Marijuana Facts: A Review of the Scientific Evidence* (New York: Lindesmith Center, 1997). No other book presents such straightforward myth-busting about pot. And with more than seventy pages of notes and citations, it's incredibly well researched.

NOTES

INTRODUCTION

1. John Dillenberger, ed., *Martin Luther: Selections from his Writings* (Garden City: Anchor, 1961), 397.

2. Marc Santora, "Stray bullet increases unease on 'Death Lane'," *New York Times*, 30 December 2002.

3. Santora, "Stray bullet increases unease on 'Death Lane'."

1. CRACK VIALS AND VIOLENCE

1. John Kobler, *Ardent Spirits* (New York: Putnam, 1973), 187.

2. Andrew Barr, *Drink: A Social History of America* (New York: Carroll & Graf, 1999), 328-329. The League's data is worse than dubious in many respects. League propaganda even borders on comical when looking at other vices supposedly created by bars and booze: "The saloon is responsible for most of the 60,000 girls who go astray into immoral lives every year. . . ."

3. William H. Rusher, "Dealing with the crime problem," *Conservative Chronicle*, 29 December 1993.

4. Don Feder, "Drug legalizers have pot party at Harvard," *Conservative Chronicle*, 1 June 1994.

5. Gary L. Bauer, *Our Hopes, Our Dreams* (Colorado Springs: Focus on the Family Publishing, 1996), 46.

6. Gary L. Bauer, "Washington update," *Family Research Council Memo*, 6 April 1995.

7. David Downie, "Going Dutch," Salon.com, 13 March 2000.

8. Downie, "Going Dutch."

9. Portugal, with its laissez faire approach is not suffering for its decision. More than a year after drug use was decriminalized, "the drugs free-for-all that some people feared" failed to materialize. (Alasdair Sanford, "Portugal muses relaxed drugs policy," BBC News, news.bbc.co.uk, 26 November 2002.)

10. J.A. Getzlaff, "Germany OKs drug-injection rooms," Salon.com, 13 March 2000.

11. Christine Lucassen, "Dutch rebuke US drug adviser," Reuters, 14 July 1998.

12. Lucassen, "Dutch rebuke US drug adviser."

13. Admittedly, along with other nations, such as Australia, Sweden, and Canada, Holland does sport high marks in violent crime. But there is something else to consider besides availability of drugs. These nations score very low in private gun ownership, and as research conducted by John Lott and presented in his landmark book *More Guns, Less Crime* makes clear, private gun ownership is key to lower crime rates. For instance, while the US did not even rank in the top 10 of industrialized nations victimized per capita by crime, a study by Holland's Leiden University found that England and Wales, where draconian firearms restriction is the norm, ranked second overall in violent crime. The fact that England is much less permissive of drugs than Holland matters little for drug warriors. When they see high crime stats, ignoring other factors to narrow in on dope is the *modus operandi*.

14. Harry J. Anslinger and Courtney Ryley Cooper, "Marihuana: Assassin of youth," *The American Magazine*, July 1937.

15. Richard Davenport-Hines, *The Pursuit of Oblivion* (New York: W.W. Norton, 2002), 347-348.

16. Ronald Hamowy, ed., "Introduction: Illicit drugs and government control," *Dealing With Drugs* (San Francisco: Pacific Research Institute, 1987), 20.

17. Dominic Streatfeild, *Cocaine: An Unauthorized Biography* (New York: St. Martin's, 2002), 144.

18. Lynn Zimmer and John P. Morgan, *Marijuana Myths, Marijuana Facts* (New York: Lindesmith Center, 1997), 88.

19. Donna E. Shalala, "Say 'no' to legalization of marijuana," *Wall Street Journal*, 18 August 1995; Zimmer and Morgan, 88. Interestingly, Shalala has admitted to smoking pot (*Baltimore Sun*, 25 August 1996). Given her strong faith in the dubious correlation

between crime and weed, we must consider it miraculous that she survived her drug experience without going to prison for a hatchet murder. Instead, like many millions of others who have used the drug, she ended up a fairly successful person. Go figure.

20. Streatfeild, 60-61.

21. Paul Eddy et al, *Cocaine Wars* (New York: Bantam, 1989), 20.

22. David Musto, *The American Disease* (New York: Oxford University Press, 1987), 282.

23. Musto, 282.

24. Streatfeild, 142.

25. Musto, 7; Streatfeild, 143.

26. Streatfeild, 296.

27. Dan Baum, *Smoke and Mirrors* (New York: Bay Back, 1997), 220-221. Observers could tell that the story got old when Armageddon failed to explode out the end of a crack pipe. As use waned by the middle 1990s, so did the rhetoric—if not the quantity of it, certainly the quality. "Crack cocaine is. . . most likely to be associated with violent crimes, burglaries, car jackings, drive-by shootings, *whatever*," warned Republican Congressman Ed Bryant in support of tough federal penalties on crack (David G. Savage and Paul Richter, "Clinton to sign bill preserving stiff penalties for crack," *Los Angeles Times*, 27 October 1995, emphasis added).

28. Andrew Buncombe, "Friendly fire deaths linked to US pilots 'on speed,'" *London Independent*, 3 August 2002.

29. Jeff Franks, "US Air Force defends 'speed' use by pilots," Reuters, 16 January 2003.

30. Jonathan Stevenson, "Krazy khat," *New Republic*, 23 November 1992. Qat is also sometimes spelled "khat."

31. "US importing greater amounts of khat," Agence France-Presse, 30 May 2000.

32. Peter Kalix, "Chewing khat," *World Health*, June 1986.

33. Jacob Sullum, "Khat calls," *Reason*, March 1993.

34. Stephanie V. Siek, "Use of drug khat up in some cities," Associated Press, 10 September 2002.

35. "Marihuana: A Signal of Misunderstanding," National Commission on Marihuana and Drug Abuse, 22 March 1972, chapter 3. Interestingly, the Shafer report was thoroughly unnecessary. In 1938 New York Mayor Fiorello H. LaGuardia commissioned the New York Academy of Medicine to study the use of marijuana in the city. The Mayor's Committee, as the investigative team was known, was composed of dozens of leading pharmacologists, physicians, psychologists, sociologists, and others, including six police officers working in investigative and supportive roles. The team filed their report some six years later

in 1944. Among other conclusions, the Committee found that "Marihuana is not the determining factor in the commission of major crimes." The Committee also pooh-poohed the theory that pot smoking would lead to harder drugs: "The use of marihuana does not lead to morphine or heroin or cocaine addiction and no effort is made to create a market for these narcotics by stimulating the practice of marihuana smoking." (For further details, the entire report, "The Marihuana Problem in The City of New York: Mayor LaGuardia's Committee on Marihuana," is published in David Solomon, ed., *The Marihuana Papers* [New York: Signet, 1966), 277-410.)

36. Sam Staley, *Drug Policy and the Decline of American Cities* (New Brunswick: Transaction, 1992), 109.

37. Hamowy, "Introduction," 22.

38. Hamowy, "Introduction," 21.

39. James Ostrowski, "Thinking about drug legalization," Cato Institute Policy Analysis, 25 May 1989.

40. Patrick J. Buchanan, "Why not provide addicts their heroin for free?" *Sacramento Union*, 24 December 1976.

41. Baum, 256-257.

42. Streatfield, 143.

43. Davenport-Hines, 477.

44. Rachel Ehrenfeld, *Narco-Terrorism* (New York: BasicBooks, 1990), 146-147.

45. Jim Kearny, "Ramsey links PCP to rise in homicides," *Washington Times*, 11 December 2002.

46. Jacob Sullum, "Killer drugs: Is PCP guilty of homicide?" TownHall.com, 3 January 2003.

47. Norman E. Zinberg, "The use and misuse of intoxicants," *Dealing With Drugs*, ed. Ronald Hamowy (San Francisco: Pacific Research Institute, 1987), 255.

48. Sullum, "Killer drugs."

49. Bruce L. Benson and David W. Rasmussen, "Illicit drugs and crime," *Independent Policy Report*, Independent Institute, 1996.

50. Nancy Weaver Teichert, "Study disputes drug link to violence," *Sacramento Bee*, 9 December 2002.

51. Carlos Sadovi and Frank Main, "Chasing dirty money," *Chicago Sun-Times*, 8 April 2002.

52. Faustino Ballvé, *The Essentials of Economics* (Irvington-on-Hudson: Foundation for Economic Education, 1963), 76, 18.

53. Davenport-Hines, 235.

54. Mike Gray, *Drug Crazy* (New York: Routledge, 2000), 53.

55. Michael Massing, *The Fix* (New York: Simon & Schuster, 1998), 66, 71.

56. Daniel K. Benjamin, "Federal Policy Pushes Heroin," Independent Institute, 21 October 1992.

57. Bruce Porter, *Blow* (New York: St. Martin's Griffin, 1993), 17-18.

58. Porter, 173.

59. Porter, 173-174. Porter and journalist Robert Sabbag both note that this kind of money became a real irritation for traffickers. Just its bulk made storing or transporting it a hassle. Money became big-time cargo, *even more than the drugs.* "[T]he volume of cash exceeding the volume of cocaine, every kilo of cocaine generat[ed] about three kilos of currency in singles, fives, tens, and twenties," writes Sabbag. Jung even said that dealing with the money began taking the fun out of his work: "It was tedious as hell." (Robert Sabbag, *Smokescreen* [Edinburgh, Scotland: Canongate, 2003], 329; "Drug Wars," *Frontline*, PBS, 9-10 October 2000.)

60. Sabbag, 329.

61. Sadovi and Main, "Chasing dirty money."

62. Robert Patton, "Drug legislation—mainline to disaster," *The Freeman*, January 1973.

63. Thomas Sowell, *Basic Economics* (New York: BasicBooks, 2000), 19-20.

64. Milton and Rose Friedman, *Free to Choose* (New York: Avon, 1981), 215-216.

65. Thomas Szasz, "The morality of drug controls," *Dealing With Drugs*, ed. Ronald Hamowy (San Francisco: Pacific Research Institute, 1987), 330.

66. George F. Will, *The Leveling Wind* (New York: Penguin, 1994), 97.

67. Sarah Bolen, "Drug war causes more crime," *Western Herald*, 27 November 2002.

68. Steven Elbow, "A special report: Hooked on SWAT," *Capitol Times*, 18 August 2001.

69. Will, 97.

70. Walter Williams, *More Liberty Means Less Government* (Stanford: Hoover Press, 1999), 262.

71. "Gun study packs a surprise," *Sacramento Bee*, 8 October 1995.

72. David W. Rasmussen and Bruce L. Benson, *The Economic Anatomy of a Drug War* (Lanham: Rowman and Littlefield, 1994), 102.

73. Kobler, 320.

74. Mark Thornton, *The Economics of Prohibition* (Salt Lake City: University of Utah Press, 1991), 122-124.

75. Kirby R. Cundiff, "Homicide rates and substance control policy," Independent Institute Working Paper, No. 34, May 2001.

76. David A. Fahrenthold, "Homicide count up 12% this year," *Washington Post*, 29 December 2002.

77. Fahrenthold, "Homicide count up 12% this year."

78. Baum, 256-257.

79. Fox Butterfield, "Rise in killings spurs new steps to fight gangs," *New York Times*, 17 January 2004.

80. Rasmussen and Benson, 102-106.

2. DIRTY BLUE

1. Todd Lightly, "Former cop crossed line, destroyed it," *Chicago Tribune*, 19 January 2003; "Rogue cop's ally gets 5 years," *Chicago Tribune*, 1 February 2003.

2. Mike Robinson, "Feds indict second narcotics officer," *Chicago Sun-Times*, 22 September 2000.

3. Gregory A. Hall, "Ex-detective Watson testifies against partner," *Louisville Courier-Journal*, 30 January 2003; Hall, "Ex-detective says partner fully to blame," *Louisville Courier-Journal*, 1 February 2003; Hall, "Ex-detective found guilty on 21 counts," *Louisville Courier-Journal*, 7 February 2003.

4. Steven R. Donziger, ed., *The Real War on Crime* (New York: Harper,1996), 164.

5. Donziger, 164.

6. Jack Nelson and Ronald J. Ostrow, "Illegal drug scene spurs rise in police corruption," *Los Angeles Times*, 13 June 1998.

7. "Economic consequences of the war on drugs," Drug Policy Alliance, 2002.

8. Ludwig von Mises, *Human Action*, 3rd rev. ed. (Chicago: Regnery, 1966), 735-736.

9. Bill Estep and Tom Lasseter, "Eastern Kentucky's recent past supports conclusion," *Lexington Herald-Leader*, 29 January 2003.

10. Mark Gillispie, "Cleveland police officer indicted in cocaine ring," *Cleveland Plain Dealer*, 19 January 2000.

11. "Ex-Caswell deputy nabbed in drug bust," *Durham Herald-Sun*, 3 February 2003.

12. Jack Warner, "Coffee County sheriff faces marijuana charges," *Atlanta Journal-Constitution*, 3 October 2000; "Indicted Ga. Sheriff found dead," *Washington Post*, October 3, 2000.

13. Mary Bennett Peterson, "Thou shalt not drink," *The Freeman*, April 1971.

14. David W. Rasmussen and Bruce L. Benson, *The Economic Anatomy of a Drug War* (Lanham: Rowman and Littlefield, 1994), 116.

15. "Hard lessons in Davidson," *Salisbury Post*, 24 July 2002.

16. Bartholomew Sullivan, "Jury convicts ex-cop in drug money plot," *Memphis Commercial Appeal*, 25 January 2003.

17. Tim Wells and William Triplet, "The drug wars: Voices from the street," *Busted*, ed. Mike Gray (New York: Thunder's Mouth/Nation Books, 2002), 140.

18. Nelson and Ostrow, "Illegal drug scene."

19. Mark Thornton, *The Economics of Prohibition* (Salt Lake City: University of Utah Press, 1991), 132.

20. Thornton, 132.

21. Arthur Niederhoffer, *Behind the Shield* (Garden City: Doubleday, 1967), 65.

22. Rasmussen and Benson, 117.

23. Angela Simoneaux, "Jury convicts former police chief," *Lafayette Advocate*, 17 February 2000.

24. Ruben Castandeda, "Former D.C. officer gets 15 years," *Washington Post*, 28 September 2000.

25. Debra Baryuga, "Bad Maui cop had potential, chief says," *Honolulu Star-Bulletin*, 17 February 2003.

26. Interestingly, she didn't get any jail time for this either. Instead, she was sentenced to two years of rehab with five years of parole following. "Judge charged with drug use," *Sacramento Bee*, 24 October 1999; Jeffrey Bair, "No jail for ex-district justice who told drug dealer of raid," *Philadelphia Daily News*, 21 February 2001; "Judge won't reconsider district justice's term," *Philadelphia Daily News*, 10 March 2001.

27. Nelson and Ostrow, "Illegal drug scene."

28. "Corruption: Police conviction is reassuring," *Clarion-Ledger*, 3 October 2000.

29. Estep and Lasseter, "Eastern Kentucky's recent past."

30. Murray Rothbard, *For a New Liberty* (New York: Collier, 1978), 113.

31. Joseph McNamara, "Gangster cops," *ReconsiDer Quarterly*, Winter 2000-2001, Vol. 1, No. 3.

32. Kristen Johnson, "Drug sentences over 54 years," *Thomasville Times*, 25 July 2002. Kepley makes poor victim material. This twenty-six-year-old son of a county commissioner was the officers' source for their steroids and was described as "a major steroids dealer and distributor. . . ."

33. Michael Beebe and Dan Herbeck, "Buffalo's tarnished badges," *Buffalo News*, 31 January 2003.

34. "Chicago police officer arrested on extortion charge," *Munster Times*, 16 September 2001.

35. Donziger, 164-165.

36. Nelson and Ostrow, "Illegal drug scene."

37. "Corruption: Police conviction is reassuring."

38. "Chatham sheriff says more than ton of pot stolen from department," Associated Press, 17 February 2001.

39. Kristen Moczynski, "$456,000 in drugs gone from evidence compound," *Daytona Beach News-Journal*, 27 January 2004.

40. Frank Main, "Retired cop charged with stealing cocaine," *Chicago Sun-Times*, 7 February 2003.

41. "Former drug agent sentenced to life," *New York Times*, 19 January 2000.

42. Nelson and Ostrow, "Illegal drug scene."

43. Joseph McNamara, "When cops become gangsters," *Los Angeles Times*, 21 September 1999.

44. J.A. Getzlaff, "Nipple-ring blues," Salon.com, 3 April 2000.

45. "Suspected drug dealer caught with drugs in court," Associated Press, 7 May 2002.

46. McNamara, "Gangster cops."

47. Randy E. Barnett, "Curing the drug-law addiction," *Dealing With Drugs*, ed. Ronald Hamowy (San Francisco: Pacific Research Institute, 1987), 94.

48. James Bovard, *Lost Rights* (New York: St. Martin's Griffin, 1995), 229.

49. Mike Gray, *Drug Crazy* (New York: Routledge, 2000), 37.

50. McNamara, "Gangster cops."

51. Phoebe Zerwick, "A detour: Sometimes justice takes a curvy road," *Winston-Salem Journal*, 24 March 2002.

52. Zerwick, "A detour: Sometimes justice takes a curvy road."

53. "Woodall admits drug plant," *Thomasville Times*, 27 November 2002.

54. "Sarasota woman framed by corrupt deputies files federal lawsuit," *Naples Daily News*, 17 November 2001.

55. Steve Mills and Maurice Possley, "City probes cop's role in drug arrest," *Chicago Tribune*, 3 February 2003.

56. Richard Miniter, "Ill-gotten gains," *Reason*, August/September 1993.

57. Hall, "Ex-detective Watson testifies against partner."

58. Steven B. Duke and Albert C. Gross, *America's Longest War* (New York: Putnam, 1994), 135.

59. Barnett, 94.

60. Os Guinness, *Time for Truth* (Grand Rapids: Baker, 2000), 118.

61. Tom Lasseter and Bill Estep, "A climate of fear, mistrust," *Lexington Herald-Leader*, 3 February 2003.

62. Lasseter and Estep, "A climate of fear, mistrust."

3. JUNK FOR JIHAD

1. Ira Teinowitz, "White House brings back ads linking drugs to terror," AdAge.com, 17 September 2002.

2. Ira Teinowitz, "White House to end drugs and terror ads," AdAge.com, 1 April 2003.

3. A little Saudi oil money is a big help as well.

4. David T. Courtwright, *Forces of Habit* (Cambridge: Harvard University Press, 2001), 184.

5. Lee Davidson, "Hatch links drugs, terror," *Utah Daily Herald*, 21 May 2003.

6. Robert D. Novak, "Ignoring narco-terrorism," TownHall.com, 10 December 2001.

7. Rachel Ehrenfeld, *Narco-Terrorism* (New York: BasicBooks, 1990), 24.

8. Stanley Penn and Edward T. Pound, "Havana haven," *Wall Street Journal*, 30 April 1984; Ehrenfeld, 31-51.

9. Dominic Streatfeild, *Cocaine: An Unauthorized Biography* (New York: St. Martin's, 2002), 324-344.

10. Ehrenfeld, 56-66.

11. Martin Booth, *Opium* (New York: St. Martin's, 1996), 313.

12. Ehrenfeld, 5, 69.

13. Ehrenfeld, 69.

14. James Meek, "Time running out in the opium war," *London Guardian*, 26 November 2001.

15. Ahmed Rashid, *Taliban* (New Haven: Yale Nota Bene, 2001), 119.

16. Rashid, 118.

17. Yossef Bodansky, *Bin Laden: The Man Who Declared War on America* (Roseville: Prima Forum, 2001), 315.

18. While the total sums do seem high at first glance, consider: "Estimates of the total money laundered around the world range from $500 billion to $1.5 trillion,

most of it from the illegal drugs trade—and around 70 percent of the world's opium comes from Afghanistan," notes Jermyn Brooks ("Terrorism, organized crime, money laundering," *International Herald Tribune*, 30 October 2001).

19. Bodansky, 322.

20. Rashid, 124.

21. Bodansky, 315.

22. Rashid, viii.

23. Greg Krikorian, "Blood money: Drug cases eyed for ties to Mideast terrorists," *Union Leader*, 26 December 2002.

24. Dan Eggen, "US foils swap of drugs for weapons," *Washington Post*, 7 November 2002.

25. "DEA traces drug money to Hezbollah," *San Francisco Chronicle*, May 11, 2002; "DEA: Drug money funds terror group," ABCNews.com, 1 September 2002.

26. Krikorian, "Blood money."

27. "Afghanistan, drugs and terrorism," *Drugs and Conflict*, Transnational Institute, December 2001.

28. Ted Galen Carpenter, *Bad Neighbor Policy* (New York: Palgrave Macmillan, 2003), 60.

29. Scott Wilson, "rampage by Colombian rebels marks new level of brutality," *Washington Post*, 3 June 2001; "Revolutionary Armed Forces of Colombia (FARC)," *Patterns of Global Terrorism, 2002*, United States Department of State, April 2003.

30. Michael Catanzaro, "South America's drug-terror link," *American Enterprise*, June 2002.

31. Robin Kirk, *More Terrible Than Death* (New York: Public Affairs, 2003), 100-101.

32. Mark Bowden, *Killing Pablo* (New York: Atlantic Monthly Press, 2001), 43.

33. Kirk, 235.

34. Carpenter, 68.

35. Kirk, 236.

36. Timothy Pratt, "The drug war's southern front," *Reason*, April 2000.

37. Carpenter, 68.

38. Catanzaro, "South America's drug-terror link."

39. Scott Wilson, "Colombian fighters' drug trade is detailed," *Washington Post*, 27 June 2003.

40. Wilson, "Colombian fighters' drug trade is detailed."

41. "Colombian terrorists arrested in cocaine-for-weapons deal," DEA press release, 6 November 2002; Eggen, "US foils swap of drugs for weapons."

42. Pratt, "The drug war's southern front."

43. "'Plan Colombia' not shifting US cocaine prices, US says," CNN.com, 23 May 2001.

44. Carpenter, 107.

45. Carpenter, 108.

46. Monique Stauder, "Colombian cocaine runs through it," *Christian Science Monitor*, 13 June 2001.

47. Carpenter, 111.

48. Laurie Goering, "Coca crop survives 1st wave," *Chicago Tribune*, 20 May 2001.

49. "The balloon goes up," *The Economist*, 6 March 2003.

50. "Specters stir in Peru," *The Economist*, 14 February 2002.

51. James Meek, "Time running out in the opium war," *Guardian*, 26 November 2001.

52. Marc Perelman, "US taking heat for an Afghan drug boom," *The Forward*, 6 June 2003.

53. Art Harris, "Bumper Afghan opium crop, UN warns," CNN.com, 30 October 2003.

54. Pamela Constable, "Afghan poppies sprout again," WashingtonPost.com, 9 November 2003.

55. "Turkey makes record heroin bust worth millions of euros," Agence France-Press, 29 January 2004.

56. "Pakistan seizes huge haul of Afghan heroin," Reuters, 29 January 2004.

57. Scott Baldauf, "Poppies bloom in Afghan fields, again," *Christian Science Monitor*, 21 August 2002.

58. The "20 times" figure comes from Constable, "Afghan poppies sprout again."

59. Baldauf, "Poppies bloom in Afghan fields, again."

60. April Witt, "Afghan poppies proliferate," *Washington Post*, 10 July 2003.

61. Eggen, "US foils swap of drugs."

62. Eggen, "US foils swap of drugs."

63. Catanzaro, "South America's drug-terror link." Ballenger's exclusion of marijuana here points to a lie in some of the ONDCP ads, like the "Dan" one—namely, the fact that plenty of pot smoked in the US is homegrown and has nothing to do with terrorist financing. The joint that Dan bought probably is helping some lower income farmer in Kentucky send is daughter to college.

64. Isambard Wilkinson, "Cannabis profits 'funding terrorism,'" *London Telegraph*, 9 August 2003.

65. David R. Henderson, "Supporting the drug war supports terrorists," Hoover Institution, 20 May 2002.

66. Patricial Wilson, "Bush to Americans: Quit drugs, join war effort," Reuters, 14 December 2001.

67. Steven W. Casteel, remarks made at DEA's National Symposium on Narcoterrorism, "Target America: Traffickers, Terrorists, and Your Kids," hosted by the DEA Museum, 4 December 2001.

4. SMUGGLERS' PARADISE

1. Robert Sabbag, *Snowblind* (New York: Grove, 1990), 16.

2. Mark Thornton, *The Economics of Prohibition* (Salt Lake City: University of Utah Press, 1991), 82. The discussion 79-83 is useful; also see Ludwig von Mises, *Bureaucracy* (New Rochelle: Arlington House, 1969). Says Mises, "The plain citizen compares the operation of the bureaus with the working of the profit system. . . . Then he discovers that bureaucratic management is wasteful, inefficient, slow, and rolled up in red tape. He simply cannot understand how reasonable people allow such a mischievous system to endure" (48).

3. Matthew Brzezinski, "Heroin's now the ultimate global product," *Sacramento Bee*, 30 June 2002.

4. Kirk Semple, "The submarine next door," *New York Times*, 3 December 2000.

5. Ruth Morris, "High-Tech Cartel," *San Jose Mercury News*, 8 September 2000.

6. Juanita Darling, "Colombian cocaine sub linked to Russian Mafia," *Medford Mail-Tribune*, 12 November 2000.

7. Paul Kaihla, "The technology secrets of Cocaine Inc., *Business 2.0*, July 2002.

8. Mark Hodgson, "Super-speedboats piloting Colombia's cocaine trade," *Christian Science Monitor*, 18 September 2002.

9. Mary Jordan, "Terrorism fight hurts drug war," *Washington Post*, 13 December 2001.

10. Hodgson, "Super-speedboats"; Jordan, "Terrorism fight hurts drug war."

11. Paul Eddy, et al, *The Cocaine Wars* (New York: Bantam, 1989), 83.

12. Hodgson, "Super-speedboats."

13. Kaihla, "The technology secrets of Cocaine Inc."

14. "Customs reveals bizarre drug hauls," Ananova.com, 1 January 2001.

15. "Cocaine found hidden inside fruit," Ananova.com, 10 July 2000.

16. Patty Machelor, "False business logos on smugglers' vehicles," *Arizona Daily Star*, 6 July 2002.

17. "Customs stop 'James Bond-style' smuggler's lorry," Ananova.com, 8 August 2001. Cig smuggling into England is serious biz with jail time and asset forfeiture featuring as punishments, just as with America's drug war.

18. "SUVs not what they seem," *Arizona Daily Star*, 20 February 2003.

19. Chuck Ashman and Pamela Trescott, *Diplomatic Crimes* (New York: PaperJacks, 1988), 165.

20. Martin Booth, *Opium* (New York: St. Martin's, 1996), 237.

21. Catherine Wilson, "US indicts Saudi prince on drug-smuggling charges," Associated Press, 18 July 2002. It's a good thing the prince's plane didn't swing by a home for a visit. Saudi Arabia executes drug traffickers. And two thousand kilos is a mind-boggling amount of cocaine. Given the heft, the prince, Nayef bin Sultan bin Fawwaz Al-Shaalan, would have a hard time convincing his pops it was for personal use.

22. Booth, 235.

23. Booth, 236. While the average is seventy to eighty, "British customs have found 260 in one person: it may yet prove to be the world record."

24. "Smuggler had clothes starched with heroin say police," Ananova.com, 15 February 2002.

25. "Opium-soaked tablecloths seized at US airport," Anaova.com, 27 April 2002.

26. Booth, 352.

27. "Cocaine found in fiberglass doghouse," *Los Angeles Times*, 27 October 1992, cited in Duke and Gross, 206.

28. Duke and Gross, 204.; the Canadian border figure counts Alaska's stretch along with that of the lower forty-eight.

29. Shannon McCaffrey, "Marijuana invades US—from North," *St. Paul Pioneer Press*, 2 June 2003.

30. McCaffrey, "Marijuana invades US."

31. George Will, *The Woven Figure* (New York: Scribner, 1997), 136.

32. Brzezinski, "Heroin's now."

33. Mike Gray, *Drug Crazy* (New York: Routledge, 2000), 146; Will, 137.

34. Brzezinski, "Heroin's now."

35. Gray, 146.

36. Brzezinski, "Heroin's now."

37. Jon E. Dougherty, *Illegals* (Nashville: WND Books, 2004), 106.

38. "Mexican trucks get full access," *Washington Post*, 28 November 2002.

39. Will, 137.

40. Dominic Streatfeild, *Cocaine* (New York: St. Martin's, 2002), 365.

41. John Stossel, "War on drugs, a war on ourselves," ABC News, 30 July 2002.

42. James Bovard, *Terrorism and Tyranny* (New York: Palgrave Macmillan, 2003), 254.

43. Rebecca Hagelin, "Train trouble," *Whistleblower*, February 2002.

44. Hagelin, "Train trouble."

45. David Hendee and Shannon Henson, "Railcar became a tomb," *Omaha World-Herald*, 15 October 2002.

46. Gray, 151.

47. Gray, 152.

48. Streatfeild, 367.

49. Duke and Gross, 206-207.

50. Shaikh Azizur Rahman, "Birds courier heroin," *The Australian*, 20 May 2003; "Drug-smuggling pigeon grounded by police," Ananova.com, 14 August 2001.

51. J. Zane Walley, "Life in the war zone," *Whistleblower*, February 2002.

52. Walley, "Life in the war zone."

53. Susan Carroll, "Civilians patrol border," *Tucson Citizen*, 28 October 2002.

54. Carroll, "Civilians patrol borders."

55. Diana Washington Valdez, "Shots fired at border agents," *El Paso Times*, 7 December 2001.

56. Jon Dougherty, "Gun for the border," WorldNetDaily.com, 4 June 2000.

57. Jerry Seper, "Border War: Mexican police join drug lords," *Washington Times*, 25 September 2002; Kevin Johnson, "Drugs invade via Indian land," *USA Today*, 7 August 2003. The Itak Gate was installed by Indians living on the reservation who wearied of having to repair the border fence, constantly mowed down and pushed over by drug runners. "The hope was that the smugglers would use the gate and close it when they passed," according to Cray. "The tribal members got tired of having to chase their cattle wandering into Mexico."

58. Joseph Farah, "The shooting war on the Mexican border," WorldNetDaily.com, 27 June 1997.

59. Seper, "Border war"; "Mexico police tided to traffic of immigrants," *Arizona Republic*, 6 July 2001.

60. Jon Dougherty, "Border accident or bounty hunting?" WorldNetDaily.com, 28 March 2000; Jon Dougherty, "Mexicans shoot at Border Patrol," WorldNetDaily.com, 1 November 2000.

61. Seper, "Border war."

62. Seper, "Border war."

63. Julie Watson, "Mexico drug smugglers tunnel under border," *Newsday*, 12 May 2002.

64. Kevin Sullivan, "Billions in drugs moved via tunnel," *Washington Post*, 1 March 2002.

65. Matea Gold, "Tunnel under border may be 20 years old," *Los Angeles Times*, 19 May 2002.

66. Sebastian Rotella, "Food company owners charged in drug tunnel case," *Los Angeles Times*, 29 September 1995.

67. Arthur H. Rotstein, "Authorities find Arizona drug tunnel," Associated Press, 12 December 2001.

68. Diana Vallejo, "Cops discover sealed drug tunnel is back in business," *Nogales International*, 16 March 2002.

69. Rotstein, "Authorities find Arizona drug tunnel."

70. Streatfeild, 370.

71. Streatfeild, 369-370.

72. Watson, "Mexico drug smugglers."

73. Vallejo, "Cops discover sealed drug tunnel."

74. Vallejo, "Cops discover sealed drug tunnel."

75. Fox Butterfield, "Security brings more drug seizures," *New York Times*, 16 December 2001.

76. *Global Illicit Drug Trends 2001* (Vienna: United Nations International Drug Control Programme, 2001).

77. *Global Illicit Drug Trends 2001*, 107, 207.

78. John Kobler, *Ardent Spirits* (New York: Putnam, 1973), 239.

79. The plan was dashed when the "priest" tried to fix a punctured tire he got while pulling out of the checkpoint. Declining help from the agent at hand, he decided to take care of it himself, failed, and bellowed, "G— d— this son of a bitch!" The "unpriestly exasperation" blew the disguise, and the agent found booze aplenty in the car. I heard of a man who smuggled marijuana in the 1960s using a similar scheme, trading Levis jeans for pot in Mexico and reentering the States dressed as a monk. He supposedly got away with it a number of times before being discovered.

80. Kobler, 239.

81. Christopher Ketcham, "The new bootleggers," *Maxim*, October 2002.

82. Ketcham, "The new bootleggers."

83. Brad Smith, "Marijuana planted on public property growing problem," *Ventura County Star*, 12 January 2004.

84. Margot Roosevelt, "Busted!" *Time*, 4 August 2003.

85. Charles McCarthy and Louis Galvan, "Officers discover opium poppies," *Fresno Bee*, 20 June 2003. Stacy Finz, "Opium plantation in Sierra," *San Francisco Chronicle*, 21 June 2003.

86. "County targets meth trade," *Josephine County Newsletter*, Winter 2000.

87. Roosevelt, "Busted!"

88. Patrik Jonsson, "Appalachia's new cottage industry: meth," *Christian Science Monitor*, 21 March 2003.

89. J.J. Stambaugh, "Roots of destruction," Knoxville News Sentinel, 16 November 2003.

90. Diana Aitchison, "Rural drug makers vex authorities," *Boston Globe*, 21 December 2002.

91. Remarks made at DEA's National Symposium on Narcoterrorism, "Target America: Traffickers, Terrorists, and Your Kids," hosted by the DEA Museum, December 4, 2001.

92. Bovard, 254.

93. "Round and round the coca bush," *The Economist*, 28 June 1997; see also "U.N. estimates drug business equal to 8 percent of world trade," Associated Press, 26 June 1997.

5. BUTTING IN

1. Robin Fitzgerald, "Chief gets tough on drugs," *Sun Herald*, 15 December 2003.

2. William J. Bennett, "Drugs: Should their sale and use be legalized?" *Current Issues and Enduring Questions* 3rd ed., eds. Sylvan Barnet, Hugo Bedau (Boston: Bedford, 1993), 352. This is a reprint of a speech given by Bennett at Harvard in 1989, during his drug czar tenure.

3. Stephen Wisotsky, "A society of suspects: The war on drugs and civil liberties," Cato Institute Policy Analysis, 2 October 1992.

4. Adam Smith, *The Wealth of Nations*, book 5, chapter 2, article 4. The Adam Smith Institute in Britain has the full text of the classic work available online at AdamSmith.org.

5. John C. Miller, *Origins of the American Revolution* (Boston: Atlantic Monthly Press, 1943), 288; Andrew Barr, *Drink: A Social History of America* (New York: Carroll & Graf, 1999), 311. The Crown later backed off from its prosecution of Hancock, but it kept his ship.

6. Esther Forbes, *Paul Revere and the World He Lived In* (Boston: Houghton and Mifflin, 1942), 61.

7. James Bovard, *Lost Rights* (New York: St. Martin's Griffin, 1995), 227-228.

8. John Clark, *James Otis: The Pre-Revolutionist* (Chicago: Union School Furnishing Company, 1903), 144-149.

9. Eric Blumenson and Eva Nilsen, "The drug war's hidden economic agenda," *The Nation*, 9 March 1998.

10. Richard Glenn Boire, *Marijuana Law*, 2nd ed. (Berkeley: Ronin, 1996), 53.

11. Martin Schwartz, "Police investigatory stops," *New York Law Journal*, 19 February 2002.

12. David Cole, *No Equal Justice* (New York: New Press, 1999), 47.

13. Steven B. Duke and Albert C. Gross, *America's Longest War* (New York: Tarcher/Putnam, 1994), 125.

14. David Cole, 48-49.

15. Duke and Gross, 125-126.

16. Guillermo Contreras, "Immigrant wants DEA to give his $148,000 back," *Albuquerque Journal*, 11 April 2001; Jeff Jones, "Amtrak helps DEA hunt drug couriers," *Albuquerque Journal*, 11 April 2001.

17. "Court: Police wrongly searched bus," *Las Vegas Sun*, 28 June 2001.

18. Bovard, *Lost Rights*, 230.

19. David Cole, 49.

20. Bovard, *Lost Rights*, 229.

21. "No constitutional violation when police officer has probable cause to stop vehicle," *New York Law Journal*, 19 December 2001.

22. Mark R. Miller, *Police Patrol Operations* (Incline Village: Copperhouse Publishing Company, 1995), 250-254.

23. David Cole, 49.

24. David Cole, 49.

25. "No constitutional violation when police officer has probable cause to stop vehicle," *New York Law Journal*.

26. "Justices give police leeway in car searchers," Associated Press, 18 November 1996.

27. Tracy Thompson, "Fourth Amendment is trampled in drug offensive, critics say," *Washington Post*, 7 May 1990, cited in Bovard, *Lost Rights*, 232.

28. Bovard, *Lost Rights* 232.

29. Duke and Gross, 126.

30. James P. Gray, *Why Our Drug Laws have Failed and What We Can Do About It* (Philadelphia: Temple University Press, 2001), 103.

31. Jacob Sullum, "Stopping points," Reason.com, 5 December 2000; Joan Biskupic "Court to hear Indianapolis case on drug roadblocks," *Washington Post*, 23 February 2000.

32. Robyn Blumner, "Resist insidious searches," *St. Petersburg Times*, 1 October 2000.

33. James Vicini, "Supreme Court strikes down drug roadblocks," Reuters, 28 November 2000; Sullum, "Stopping points."

34. Sullum, "Stopping points."

35. "Missouri sheriff overrules Supreme Court on roadblocks," *Drug War Chronicle*, DRCNet.org, 8 December 2000.

36. "Fake checkpoints to discover drugs OK'd by court," *The Oklahoman*, 16 August 2003; "Fake checkpoints OK'd in sniffing out criminals," *The Daily Camera*, 17 August 2003.

37. Charles Lane, "Justices' ruling sets broad 'probable Cause' standard in drug arrests," *Washington Post*, 16 December 2003.

38. Eric Peters, "Your paper's please! A victory for motorists," National Motorists Association, 22 December 2000.

39. David Kocieniewski, "Civil rights groups plan boycott over antidrug effort," *New York Times*, 30 April 1999; David Kocieniewski, "New Jersey troopers use hotel staffs in drug war," *New York Times*, 29 April 1999.

40. Kocieniewski, "New Jersey troopers use hotel staffs in drug war."

41. Joe Rodriguez, "Police to extend anti-crime program to hotels, motels," *Wichita Eagle*, 13 June 2002; Celeste Williams, "City taking aim at 4 more motels," Indianapolis Star, 12 February 2002.

42. Solveig Singleton, Testimony before the US House of Representatives Committee on Banking and Financial Services, Oversight hearing regarding the Bank Secrecy Act and reporting requirements, 20 April 1999.

43. John Berlau, "Show us your money," *Reason*, November 2003.

44. Singleton, Testimony.

45. "Making 'dirty' cash clean," *Edmonton Sun*, 2 January 2004; "Traffickers laundering money through casinos: US," *Toronto Star*, 19 November 2003. One novel method of money laundering was recently discovered. "The owner of a long-established Manhattan gold refining business pleaded guilty . . . to a scheme in which he molded gold into tools and screws for Colombian drug lords. . . ." The idea was to take drug proceeds in exchange for precious metal disguised as items that could clear customs. "Among items recovered by federal authorities . . . was a working

solid gold wrench . . . worth about $10,000" (NY refiner made gold tools for drug lords," Reuters, 22 January 2004).

46. Berlau, "Show us your money."

47. This tremendous database plays into another danger Berlau points to—there's far too much info. While federal agencies are being deluged with information they cannot possibly manage or even use, they still yap for powers to suck more into the intelligence maw of government in an effort to not only bust drug dealers but also terrorists. The problem is that the investigative scope is too broad and shallow. Innocent people are being wronged, while terrorists evade detection. "I'm pro-law-enforcement, but I've seen the same problem throughout my FBI career: Punish everyone to send a message to one," says former FBI agent Gary Aldrich. "I think it dilutes the government's ability to actually catch suspicious people because the flow of information into some central authority becomes so huge it cannot be analyzed fast enough to make any sense of it" (John Berlau, "Banks and suspicion," *Insight*, 26 October 2001).

48. Ross E. Milloy, "D.E.A. direct," *New York Times*, 15 April 2001.

49. Jeff Jones, "Amtrak helps DEA hunt drug couriers," *Albuquerque Journal*, 11 April 2001.

50. Jones, "Amtrak helps DEA hunt drug couriers."

51. Jeff Jones, "Amtrak pulls DEA computer," *Albuquerque Journal*, 25 April 2001.

52. Paul Craig Roberts and Lawrence M. Stratton, *The Tyranny of Good Intentions* (Roseville: Forum, 2000), 3.

53. Diane Barnes, "Does anti-drug education program work? DARE indoctrination fails to work and ends up endangering families," *Detroit News*, 2 April 2000.

54. James Bovard, *Shakedown: How the Government Screws You From A to Z* (New York: Viking, 1995), 28.

55. "High schoolers can get $1,000 bounty under new drug 'snitch' program," Libertarian Party news release, 11 February 1999.

56. Iain Gately, *Tobacco: A Cultural History of How an Exotic Plant Seduced Civilization* (New York: Grove Atlantic, 2001), 86.

57. Raghuram Vadarevu, "Radical drug message is LEAP of faith," *Hackensack Record*, 6 February 2004; Nina Shapiro, "Cops against the drug war," *Seattle Weekly*, 13 August 2003.

58. Sheila McLaughlin, "Major drugs trove seized," *Cincinnati Enquirer*, 31 January 2004.

59. Glenn Maffei, "Battle against drugs a frustrating task," *Beaufort Gazette*, 3 February 2004.

60. Nate Blakeslee, "Drug warriors," *Austin Chronicle*, 5 November 1999.

61. The gun was later shown to be unloaded, with the safety on. The clip was not even in the weapon. Nate Blakeslee, "Drug warriors."

62. Tom Lasseter and David Stephenson, "Turning informant," *Lexington Herald-Leader*, 7 December 2003.

63. Cynthia Cotts, "Year of the rat," *Reason*, May 1992.

64. Nate Blakeslee, "Drug warriors."

65. Ta-Nehisi Coates, "A dirty sweep," *Village Voice*, 18 December 2002.

66. "Snitch," *Frontline*, PBS, 12 January 1999.

67. Bill Archer, "Police, courts struggle to put drug dealers in prison," *Bluefield Daily Telegraph*, 15 September 2003.

68. David Bruser, "Wearing the wire: The life of a C.I.," *The Enterprise-Journal*, 9 December 2002.

69. Michael Lynch, "Battlefield conversions: *Reason* talks with three ex-warriors who now fight against the War on Drugs," *Reason*, January 2002.

70. Sheriff Bill Masters, *Drug War Addiction* (Lonedell: Accurate Press, 2001), 31.

71. George F. Cole, *The American System of Criminal Justice* (New York: Wadsworth, 1995) 197.

72. *Appeal-Democrat*, 25 April 2001.

73. James Bovard, "DARE scare: Turning children into informants?" *Washington Post*, 29 January 1994.

74. *Appeal-Democrat*, 17 October 2001.

75. "Students talk about undercover officers," *Burlington Times-News*, 7 February 2004; for more background on the story, Mark Tosczak, "Students arrested in drug sting," *Greensboro News and Record*, 5 February 2004. One student quoted in the *Burlington Times-News* story, had some interesting news. After all that trickery and throwing sexual stumbling blocks in the paths of teenage boys, they didn't get everyone involved. "There's a lot of people left," said the boy. "They didn't catch hardly anybody."

76. Shapiro, "Cops against the drug war."

77. David B. Caruso, "Prosecutors increasingly turn to Patriot Act," *The Oklahoman*, 15 September 2003; Eric Lichtblau, "US uses terror law to pursue crimes from drugs to swindling," *New York Times*, 27 September 2003.

78. Jason Reagan, "DA uses new law in meth lab bust," *Watauga Democrat*, 16 July 2003; "DAs try antiterror laws for drug cases," *Charlotte Observer*, 21 July 2003; Kathy Helms-Hughes, "DA ups ante on meth producers under anti-terrorism

law," *Elizabethton Star*, 4 August 2003; Bronwyn Lance Chester, "Note to prosecutors: Drugs and Drano aren't WMDs," *Virginian-Pilot*, 30 July 2003.

79. "Snitch," *Frontline*, PBS, 12 January 1999.

6. RENDER UNTO SEIZURE

1. Deborah Alexander, "2nd airport cash seizure raises more racial-profiling questions," *Omaha World Herald*, 6 July 2001.

2. Chris Di Edoardo, "Drug link common in forfeiture cases," *Las Vegas Review-Journal*, 1 April 2001.

3. Guillermo Contreras, "Immigrant wants DEA to give his $148,000 back," *Albuquerque Journal*, 11 April 2001; Jeff Jones, "Amtrak helps DEA hunt drug couriers," *Albuquerque Journal*, 11 April 2001.

4. Chris Osher, "Most cash bears traces of cocaine, FBI expert says," *Arkansas Democrat-Gazette*, 27 June 1999. "Cash seized from drug dealers isn't destroyed but goes back into circulation," reports Osher. "The cocaine from those bills falls into the mechanical currency counters banks use . . . and those counters then spread the cocaine to the other bills they sort, essentially 'homogenizing' the monetary supply." As a result of this homogenization, "In 1997, the 7th US Circuit Court of Appeals in Chicago ordered the return of about $500,000 police confiscated from a pizzeria. In that ruling, the judicial panel stated, 'recent cases have verified our belief that the probative value of dog sniffs is, at most, minimal.'"

5. Caroline J. Keough, "Drug-stained cash widespread in South Florida," *Miami Herald*, 9 September 2000.

6. Keough, "Drug-stained cash widespread in South Florida."

7. Michael G. Wagner, "Why there's cocaine on your money," *Sacramento Bee*, 16 November 1994.

8. Alexander, "2nd airport cash seizure raises more racial-profiling questions."

9. Brant Hadaway, "Executive privateers," *University of Miami Law Review*, vol. 55, no. 1.

10. Eric Blumenson and Eva Nilsen, "The drug war's hidden economic agenda," *The Nation*, 9 March 1998. A lengthier version of this article ran in the *University of Chicago Law Review*, under the title "Policing for Profit." All references in this chapter are to the *Nation* version.

11. H.J. Storing, *The Complete Anti-Federalist*, Vol. 3 (Chicago: University of Chicago Press, 1981), cited in Donald J. Boudreaux and A.C. Pritchard, "Book Reviews: License to Steal," *Cato Journal*, vol., 16, no. 1.

12. Dan Baum, *Smoke and Mirrors* (New York: Bay Back, 1997), 11.

13. Muriel Dobbin, "How to stop pot growers: Seize land," *Sacramento Union*, 3 August 1982; Baum, 173.

14. Baum, 173.

15. Dobbin, "How to stop pot growers."

16. Dobbin, "How to stop pot growers."

17. David Doege, "Seizure of house protested," *Milwaukee Journal Sentinel*, 23 August 2003.

18. Paul Craig Roberts and Lawrence M. Stratton, *The Tyranny of Good Intentions* (Roseville: Prima, 2000), 124. Lungren was hardly a conservative heartthrob. Though Catholic and prolife, he was steadfastly antigun and bollixed his shot at governor in part because he refused to publicly back a plan to return a $12+ billion budget surplus to taxpayers. Taking their guns and their money is no way to endear oneself to California Republicans. Strangely, GOP loyalists rarely see the statist similarities between Lungren's support of forfeiture and his lack of support for the rights of gun owners and taxpayers.

19. Roberts and Stratton, 124-125.

20. Stefan B. Herpel, "United States v. One Assortment of 89 Firearms," *Reason*, May 1990.

21. The fact that these are legal actions against property can be no better shown than by looking at the case titles, e.g., *State of New Jersey v. One 1990 Ford Thunderbird* or *United States v. $405,089.23 in United States Currency*.

22. Creators Syndicate, 14 September 2000.

23. Roberts and Stratton, 127-128.

24. Kyla Dunn, "Reining in forfeiture: Common sense reform in the war on drugs," online companion article to "Drug Wars," *Frontline*, PBS, 9-10 October 2000, available at PBS.org.

25. Jeff Gould, "Drug money: What comes around goes around," *Metrowest Daily News*, 17 February 2003.

26. Kelly Patricia O'Meara, "When feds say seize and desist," *Insight*, 7 August 2000.

27. Deborah Tedford, "No vacancy for drug dealers: Feds seize hotel," *Huston Chronicle*, 17 February 1998.

28. For further discussion, see iconoclastic psychiatrist Thomas Szasz's *Our Right to Drugs* (Westport: Praeger, 1992). "The right to chew or smoke a plant that grows wild in nature, such as hemp (marijuana), is anterior to and more basic than the right to vote," he writes. "I want to show that—because both our bodies and drugs

are types of property [in this, he is saying nothing different than Locke]—producing, trading in, and using drugs are property rights, and drug prohibitions constitute a deprivation of basic constitutional rights."

29. Remarks by Hyde at Cato Institute Conference, "Forfeiture reform: Now or never?" held in Washington DC, 18 June 1999.

30. Michael W. Lynch, "Police beat," *Reason*, July 1999.

31. Denise A. Raymo, "DA targets drugs, truants," *Plattsburgh Press-Republican*, 27 December 2001.

32. Chris Osher, "Arkansas' legal theft? Police reap profit of forfeited cash," *Arkansas Democrat-Gazette*, 27 June 1999.

33. Di Edoardo, "Drug link common in forfeiture cases."

34. "Asset forfeiture: Florida task force so out of control even the feds are embarrassed" *Drug War Chronicle*, DRCNet.org., 14 July 2000.

35. Michelle Malkin, "Seizure disorder," *Reason*, March 1999.

36. Di Edoardo, "Drug link common in forfeiture cases."

37. Millard K. Ives, "Cased dropped, money kept," *Wilmington Morning Star*, 19 November 2002.

38. Press release, 1 June 2000.

39. Karen Dillon, "Forfeiture package offers minimal reform, some say," *Kansas City Star*, 20 May 2000.

40. Carlos Sadovi and Frank Main, "Chasing dirty money," *Chicago Sun-Times*, 8 April 2002.

41. "Alabama benefits form millions in drug forfeitures," *Sun Herald*, 28 November 2003.

42. Mike Wowk, "Police save by using cash from forfeitures," *Detroit News*, 19 November 2003.

43. Gould, "Drug money: What comes around goes around."

44. Karen Dillon, "Committee proposes changes to Kansas forfeiture law," *Kansas City Star*, 18 September 2000.

45. "Missouri sheriff overrules Supreme Court on roadblocks," *Drug War Chronicle*, DRCNet.org, 8 December 2000.

46. Karen Dillon, "Forfeiture law could be altered: Kansas legislators seek tighter restrictions," *Kansas City Star*, 19 September 2000.

47. Gould, "Drug money: What comes around goes around."

48. Scott Bullock, "Asset forfeiture victory," *Liberty and Law*, Institute for Justice, March 2001.

49. Blumenson and Nilsen, "The drug war's hidden economic agenda."

50. Blumenson and Nilsen, "The drug war's hidden economic agenda."

51. Paul Craig Roberts, "The state as a lawful bandito?" *Washington Times*, 1 November 1993.

52. Richard Miniter, "Ill-gotten gains," *Reason*, August/September 1993.

53. Mike Saewitz, "The Sarasota connection: Drug stings bring in big dealers while raising cash and questions," *Sarasota Herald-Tribune*, 7 October 2003.

54. Tom Zoellner, "S.F. to consider seizing cars of drug, sex clients," *San Francisco Chronicle*, 18 September 2000.

55. Zoellner, "S.F. to consider seizing cars of drug, sex clients."

56. *San Francisco Examiner*, 26 September 2000.

57. *San Francisco Examiner*, 20 September 2000.

58. "Asset forfeiture: Florida task force so out of control even the feds are embarrassed," *Drug War Chronicle*.

59. "Asset forfeiture: Florida task force so out of control even the feds are embarrassed," *Drug War Chronicle*.

60. Scott Bullock, "Don't take my car: Ex sheriff wages fight against forfeiture abuses," *Liberty and Law*, Institute for Justice, June 2000.

61. Scott Bullock, "Asset forfeiture victory," *Liberty and Law*, Institute for Justice, March 2001.

62. John Curran, "New Jersey judge rules forfeiture law unconstitutional," *Salina Journal*, 13 December 2002; Scott Bullock, "Court seizes the day," *Liberty and Law*, Institute for Justice, February 2003.

63. Ari Armstrong, "Reforming asset forfeiture," *Liberty*, August 2002.

64. Armstrong, "Reforming asset forfeiture."

65. Karen Dillon, "Police, federal agencies resist change," *Kansas City Star*, 20 May 2000.

7. BIG GUNS

1. Information on Maricopa Sheriff Arpaio's tank and other community services can be found online at MCSO.org.

2. Sean Gardiner and Daryl Kahn, "Cops 'saddened' by botched raid," *New York Newsday*, 16 May 2003; "Woman has fatal heart attack in bungled police raid," CNN.com, May 16, 2003; Donald E. Wilkes Jr., "Explosive dynamic entry," *Flagpole*, 30 July 2003.

3. Cathy Mong, "Tip lead to deadly raid in Preble," *Dayton Daily News*, 5 October 2002.

4. "The NORML state guide to marijuana laws," available online at NORML.org

5. Lawrence Budd, "Fatal drug raid shooting to be investigated," *Dayton Daily News*, 28 September 2002.

6. Rebecca Nolan, "Neighbors call tactics in drug raid militaristic," *Register-Guard*, 5 December 2002; Rebecca Nolan, "Whiteaker drug raid spurs lawsuit from residents," *Register-Guard*, 29 April 2003.

7. Nolan, "Neighbors call tactics."

8. Nolan, "Whiteaker drug raid spurs lawsuit from residents."

9. The team claimed to find evidence of cannabis cultivation but nothing that was not explained away by other factors, including Monroe's landscaping business along with the equipment and materials from renovation work being done on two of the houses. The contractor doing the renovation, in fact, said she saw no evidence of drug growing or distribution.

10. Jim Dwyer, "Police raid gone awry," *New York Times*, 29 June 2003.

11. Dwyer, "Police raid gone awry."

12. Nolan, "Neighbors call tactics."

13. Capt. Robert P. Snow, *SWAT Teams: Explosive Face-offs With America's Deadliest Criminals* (Cambridge: Perseus, 1996), 230.

14. Snow, 230.

15. Christian Parenti, *Lockdown America* (New York: Verso, 2000), 23, 112.

16. Immediately hit by fierce criticism, Gates stood by his statement. "I'm glad I said it," he said a few days later. When asked about his son, who had a history of drug problems, Gates' dodged the hypocrisy and waxed surprisingly cold. "He is an addict," he deflected. "He's not a casual user. He was a casual user, and that's what leads to addiction. And I think everybody ought to recognize that all the poor addicts shot themselves already. . . . He shot himself." Had Gates got his wish, by the way, the death toll would have been monstrous. At the time, the most recent National Household Survey on Drug Abuse tagged the number of Americans who admitted to using drugs in the past thirty days at 14.5 million. (Ronald J. Ostrow, "Casual drug users should be shot, Gates says," *Los Angeles Times*, 6 September 1990; Richard A. Serrano and Jane Fritsch, "'Yeah, I mean it!' Gates says of idea to shoot drug users," *Los Angeles Times*, 8 September 1990; Jeff Wilson, "Police chief's shoot-drug-users remark has rights groups seething," Associated Press, 6 September 1990.)

17. Parenti, 112.

18. Dan Baum, *Smoke and Mirrors* (New York: Bay Back, 1997), 41.

19. Parenti, 11.

20. United States Code, Title 18, Section 3109. Emphasis added.

21. Actually, the cliché is the legal doctrine, a product of seventeenth century legal reforms in England ensuring equality before the law for both the high and mighty and the lowly and bedraggled. Ruled an English court in 1603, "In all cases where the King is party, the sheriff ... ought first to signify the cause of his coming, and make request to open the doors" (James Bovard, *Shakedown* [New York: Viking, 1995], 82).

22. Parenti, 10.

23. Snow, 223.

24. James Bovard, *Shakedown* (New York: Viking, 1995), 88.

25. Cassandra Stern, "FBI probes fatal drug raid in California," *Washington Post*, 6 September 1999.

26. Given the date of the raid and the hype around the time, the Paz's explanation that the money was their life-savings and was taken out of the bank for fear of a Y2K disaster is entirely plausible.

27. Stern, "FBI probes fatal drug raid in California."

28. Stern, "FBI probes fatal drug raid in California."

29. Anne-Marie O'Connor, "Bereft family disputes police shooting report," *Los Angeles Times*, 26 August 1999.

30. Connie Piloto, "Family says man didn't understand police orders," *Dallas Morning News*, 30 September 2000.

31. Parenti, 128.

32. T.J. Wilham, "Woman thought cop was a burglar," *The Star Press*, 4 February 2003.

33. "6 shot to death in home invasion," CNN.com, 6 January 2003.

34. Rebecca Trounson, "Deaths raises questions about SWAT teams," *Los Angeles Times*, 1 November 2000.

35. Kevin Taylor, "Raid hits suspected drug house," *Spokane Spokesman-Review*, 14 January 2003.

36. Wilkes, "Explosive dynamic entry."

37. Trounson, "Deaths raises questions about SWAT teams."

38. Anne-Marie O'Connor, "No drug link to family in fatal raid, police say," *Los Angeles Times*, 28 August 1999.

39. Jesse Bogan, "SWAT raid roughs up wrong guys," *San Antonio Express-News*, 21 November 2002.

40. Ken Pritchard, "Dalton bust goes awry," *Beaver Dam Daily Citizen*, 11 October 2002.

41. Michael Cooper, "As number of police raids increase, so do questions," *New York Times*, 26 May 1998.

42. Michael Cooper, "As number of police raids increase, so do questions."

43. Daniel K. Benjamin and Roger LeRoy Miller, *Undoing Drugs* (New York: BasicBooks, 1993), 136-137.

44. Christy Scattarella, "Wrong raid captured for 'Cops' show," *Seattle Times*, 24 May 1992.

45. Patrick E. Gauen, "Drug raid angers mayor," *St. Louis Post-Dispatch*, 5 June 1992.

46. Warren Duzak, "Innocent man dies in police blunder," *Tennessean*, 6 October 2000; "Cops under investigation after killing man during raid on wrong house," NewsChannel5.com, 5 October 2000; Vicki Brown, "Cops kill man, raid wrong house," *Washington Post*, 6 October 2000.

47. Duzak, "Innocent man dies in police blunder."

48. Warren Duzak, "Officer testified to doubts before botched raid on home," *Tennessean*, 7 June 2001.

49. Kathy Carlson, "Deadly raid's leader indicted," *Tennessean*, 4 November 2000.

50. Duzak, "Innocent man dies in police blunder."

51. Snow, 106.

52. Rowan Scarborough, "Military training of civilian police steadily expands," *Washington Times*, 9 September 1999.

53. Diane Cecilia Weber, "Warrior cops: The ominous growth of paramilitarism in American police departments," Cato Institute Briefing Papers, 26 August 1999.

54. Weber, "Warrior cops."

55. David B. Kopel, "Militarized law enforcement," *After Prohibition*, ed. Timothy Lynch (Washington DC: Cato, 2000), 76.

56. Kopel, 76.

57. Peter Kraska and Victor Kappeler, "Militarizing American police," *Social Problems*, February 1997; Kopel, 80.

58. Weber, "Warrior cops."

59. "Drug Wars," *Frontline*, PBS, 9-10 October 2000.

8. LOCKDOWN, USA

1. Maxim Kniazkov, "US prison population grows to 2m," *Herald Sun*, 28 July 2003.

2. "US notches world's highest incarceration rate," *Christian Science Monitor*, 18 August 2003.

3. "US notches world's highest," *Christian Science Monitor*.

4. Paige M. Harrison and Allen J. Beck, Ph.D., "Prisoners in 2002," US Department of Justice, Bureau of Justice Statistics, July 2003 (rev. 27 August 2003); Curt Anderson, "Growing prison population is growing problem for cash-strapped states," Associated Press, 27 July 2003; "US notches world's highest," *Christian Science Monitor*.

5. Eric E. Sterling, Esq., "Drug laws and snitching—a primer," online companion feature to "Snitch," *Frontline*, PBS, 12 January 1999, available online at PBS.org.

6. Sterling, "Drug laws and snitching—a primer."

7. Edward Walsh, "Bias' death fueled antidrug fervor," *Washington Post*, 14 September 1986.

8. Walsh, "Bias' death fueled antidrug fervor."

9. Bill Freehling, "Drugs war filling Virginia's prisons," *Lynchburg News & Advance*, 31 December 2003.

10. Cynthia Cotts, "Year of the rat," *Reason*, May 1992.

11. "Snitch," *Frontline*, PBS, 12 January 1999; also see: Debra Saunders, "With little chance of pardon, Aaron sentence is barbaric, *Pasadena Star-News*, 26 December 2003.

12. US Sentencing Commission, press release, 22 May 2002.

13. Linda Satter, "Judges in a stew on federal sentences," *Arkansas Democrat-Gazette*, 1 September 2003.

14. Steve France, "The anguish of the drug-war judges," Salon.com, 19 June 2001.

15. Cokie Roberts and Steven Roberts, "Sentencing modifications gains some unlikely allies," *The City Paper*, 29 August 2003.

16. Satter, "Judges in a stew on federal sentences."

17. Ellen Perlman, "Terms of imprisonment," *Governing Magazine*, April 2000.

18. Jacob Sullum, "Prison conversion," *Reason*, August/September 1999.

19. John J. DiIulio Jr., "Two million prisoners are enough," *Wall Street Journal*, 12 March 1999.

20. Anthony York, "Clergy asks Clinton for a final act: Religious leaders call for clemency for thousands of imprisoned nonviolent drug offenders," Salon.com, 22 December 2000.

21. DiIulio, "Two million prisoners are enough."

22. John P. Walters, "Don't legalize drugs," *Wall Street Journal*, 19 July 2002.

23. Bruce L. Benson and David W. Rasmussen, "Illicit drugs and crime," *Independent Policy Report*, Independent Institute, 1996.

24. John P. Walters, "Drug wars: Just say no . . . to treatment without law enforcement," *Weekly Standard*, 6 March 2001.

25. Myriam Marquez, "Not fiscally sound or morally justified," *Orlando Sentinel*, 26 August 2003.

26. "Building more prisons, but not nearly fast enough," Associated Press, 28 December 2003.

27. Lesley Stedman Weidenbener, "Overcrowding of prisons is growing," *Courier-Journal*, 6 November 2003.

28. "Meth pushing state's prisons past capacity," *Billings Gazette*, 22 January 2004.

29. Johnny Brannon, "Mandatory prison terms fail to fully deter ice users," *Honolulu Advertiser*, 20 January 2004.

30. Harrison and Beck, "Prisoners in 2002."

31. Anderson, "Growing prison population is growing problem for cash-strapped states."

32. Mike Clements, "Prison population boom means added costs for states," Stateline.org, 1 August 2003.

33. Brian M. Riedl, "$20,000 per household: The highest level of federal spending since World War II," Heritage Foundation Backgrounder, 3 December 2003.

34. Harrison and Beck, "Prisoners in 2002."

35. Jack Money, "Prosecutors look for ways to stunt prison growth," *Oklahoman*, 12 December 2003.

36. Daniel W. Van Ness, *Crime and its Victims* (Downers Grove: InterVarsity, 1986), 47-59.

37. Wesley C. Westman, *The Drug Epidemic* (New York: Dial, 1970), 79.

38. Charles Colson and Daniel Van Ness, *Convicted* (Westchester: Crossway, 1989), 21-22.

39. Christian Parenti, *Lockdown America* (New York: Verso, 2000), 182-193.

40. Parenti, 183.

41. Sasha Abramsky, "Breeding violence," MotherJones.com, 10 July 2001. Article is part of the MotherJones.com special report, "Debt to Society," available at http://www.motherjones.com/news/special_reports/prisons/.

42. Abramsky, "Breeding violence."

43. Bruce Porter, *Blow* (New York: St. Martin's, 1993), 111.

44. Porter, 109-111.

45. Timothy W. Maier, "On dope row," *Insight*, 25 February 2002.

46. Robynn Tysver, "Nebraska battling drugs behind bars," *Omaha World-Herald*, 18 February 2001.

47. Deborah Charles, "Prisoners have easy drug access, report says," *Detroit News*, 23 January 2003.

48. Maier, "On dope row."

49. "Guard details how drugs get into prisons," *Insight*, 11 March 2002.

50. Paul Rodriguez, "Behind this investigative report," *Insight*, 25 February 2002.

CONCLUSION

1. John Kobler, *Ardent Spirits* (New York: Putnam, 1973), 336-337.

2. Federalist, 17.

3. Barry Goldwater, *Where I Stand* (New York: McGraw-Hill, 1964), 37-38.

4. Robert L. Snow, *SWAT Teams* (Cambridge: Perseus, 1996), 223.

5. From the foreword by Bennett to Don E. Eberly, *Restoring the Good Society: A New Vision for Politics and Culture* (Grand Rapids: Baker, 1994), 12.

6. Interestingly, Perl made these remarks in Jamaica. "I don't like legalization," he admitted but, recognizing the validity of the option, also said, "I think that this is a decision that each society has to make for itself." Apparently, it's okay for Jamaicans to discuss legalization; just don't utter those sentiments here in the US. (*Jamaica Daily Gleaner*, 30 April 2002)

7. James Q. Wilson, "Legalizing drugs makes matters worse," Slate.com, 1 September 2000.

8. Walter E. Williams, *More Liberty Means Less Government* (Stanford: Hoover Institution Press, 1999), 261.

9. Norman E. Zinberg, "The use and misuse of intoxicants: Factors in the development of controlled use," *Dealing With Drugs*, ed. Ronald Hamowy (San Francisco: Pacific Research Institute, 1990), 247. This entire essay is well worth reading to see the vital importance of nonlegal social controls in regulating drugs.

10. Albert Jay Nock, *Our Enemy the State* (New York: Libertarian Review Foundation, 1989 [originally published by William Morrow, 1935]), 3.

11. For a general discussion of this, see Marvin Olaksy, *The Tragedy of American Compassion* (Washington DC: Regnery, 1995).

12. David T. Courtwright, *Forces of Habit* (Cambridge: Harvard University Press, 2001), 51.

13. Frederica Mathewes-Green, "The Oneida experiment," *Touchstone*, November 2002. An example of this self-regulation in action: Civil rights attorney and author John W. Whitehead recounts his young fling with LSD. The first experience was euphoric, others also, but he could see the stuff could get you killed if you were driving and began to also have unwanted flashbacks. "From then on, I decided I would stick with the lighter stuff like marijuana and alcohol" (John W. Whitehead, *Slaying Dragons: The Truth Behind the Man Who Defended Paula Jones* [Nashville: Thomas Nelson, 1999], 81).

14. Jessica Warner, *Craze: Gin and Debauchery in an Age of Reason* (New York: Four Walls Eight Windows, 2002), 181-219.

15. Davenport-Hines, 354. Other jazz icons used heroin, e.g., Billy Holliday. But to blame her early death, along with those of others, solely on heroin abuse misses an important fact: Life in the jazz scene was hard, especially when touring. Drinking was rife as a way of coping. For many in that scene, taking care of oneself was secondary to the music. Trumpet man Clifford Brown was an oddity precisely because he was so abundantly talented *and* didn't live such a life.

16. Supplemental interviews for "Drug Wars," *Frontline*, PBS, 9-10 October 2000, available online at http://www.pbs.org/wgbh/pages/frontline/shows/drugs/interviews/stutman.html.

17. Lou Marano, "Affluent kids: Both pressured and ignored," UPI, 17 September 2002.

18. "Kids in single-dad homes use more drugs," *Register-Guard*, 20 July 2001.

19. Interview with filmmaker Ted Demme, contained in the bonus material on DVD release of *Blow* (New Line Home Entertainment, 2001).

20. Nancy Weaver Teichert, "Study disputes drug link to violence," *Sacramento Bee*, 9 December 2002.

21. Andrew Barr, *Drink: A Social History of America* (New York: Carroll & Graf, 1999), 25.

22. Frank S. Meyer, *In Defense of Freedom: A Conservative Credo* (Chicago: Regnery, 1962), 149.

23. Ludwig von Mises, *Human Action*, 3rd rev. ed. (Chicago: Regnery, 1963), 733.

24. Radley Balko, "Back door to prohibition: The new war on social drinking," Cato Institute, 5 December 2003.

25. Kelly D. Brownell and Katherine Battle Horgen, *Food Fight* (New York: Contemporary Books, 2004), 217-229. For a more helpful analysis of why Americans are straining the scales and what to do about it, see Michael Fumento, *The Fat of the Land: The Obesity Epidemic and How Overweight Americans can Help Themselves* (New York: Viking, 1997).

26. Anybody looking to explore this idea further, must procure a copy of Daniel K. Benjamin and Roger LeRoy Miller, *Undoing Drugs: Beyond Legalization* (New York: BasicBooks, 1991).

27. Ann Coulter, "Must Christian conservatives be fascists?" JewishWorldReview.com, 17 October 2000.

28. Some may complain that this will create too many different legal standards across the nation, but that is exactly the situation we live in now. Regulations on any number of things vary state to state: taxes, incorporation laws, environmental codes, you name it. I've lived in only three states. Each has had a different way of handling booze. In California, it's available seven days a week, most hours of the day. Wine, beer, and liquor are all available in the same place, even grocery stores. With plenty of outlets, the pricing can be very competitive and advantageous to the buyer. In Oregon, wine and beer can be had at the grocery store, but the harder stuff is only available at a state-licensed liquor store—of which there are few. Prices tend to be high. In Tennessee, a person can get beer at the corner grocer's but nothing harder. On Sunday, beer can only be purchased after noon. Nothing else can be purchased on Sunday (ironically, not even Communion wine), and the rest of the week anything stronger than beer must be purchased through liquor stores. Unlike Oregon, there are many of these. Prices are fair. That's how true federalism works. Every state finds its own balance.

29. Thomas Sowell, *Is Reality Optional?* (Stanford: Hoover Institution Press, 1993), 96.

INDEX